RUGBY LEAGUE REVIEW
1982-1983

Paul Fitzpatrick

RUGBY LEAGUE REVIEW 1982-1983

Sponsored by Shopacheck

faber and faber
LONDON · BOSTON

*First published in 1983
by Faber and Faber Limited
3 Queen Square London WC1N 3AU
Printed in Great Britain by
Redwood Burn Ltd, Trowbridge
All rights reserved*

© *Paul Fitzpatrick, 1983*

For Anne and Kate with love

CONDITIONS OF SALE

This book is sold subject to the condition that it shall not, by way of trade or otherwise, be lent, resold, hired out or otherwise circulated without the publisher's prior consent in any form of binding or cover other than that in which it is published and without a similar condition including this condition being imposed on the subsequent purchaser

British Library Cataloguing in Publication Data

Fitzpatrick, Paul
Rugby league review 1982–83.
1. Rugby football—History
I. Title
796.33′3′09   GV 944.85
ISBN 0–571–13144–1
ISBN 0–571–13186–7 Pbk

Contents

	Preface *by David Oxley*	*page* 6
	Foreword *by Brian Snape*	7
	Acknowledgements	9
1	The Australian Tour	11
2	The International Season	91
3	The John Player Trophy, the Webster's Yorkshire Cup and the Forshaws Lancashire Cup	109
4	The State Express Challenge Cup	127
5	The Slalom Lager Championship and Premiership Trophy	149
6	Reflections	172
	Afterword *by Phil Larder*	186
	Appendixes	188

Preface

Travelling together from Paris to Avignon to watch the first Test between France and Australia in December 1982, I remember Paul Fitzpatrick expressing his regret that he had never seen in action many of the great players of the past. However, lacking preconceptions about what the game once was, Paul is admirably placed to assess modern Rugby League at its true worth—and he loves it! Indeed, regular readers of Paul's extended features and match accounts in the *Guardian* cannot fail to find there a deep commitment to the game and a rapidly maturing understanding of its characters, its personalities and its heritage. And he must be the only RL sports writer who, coming fresh to the game, has sent himself on a coaching course at Lilleshall the better to understand its special skills!

The Rugby League season of 1982–83, captured in the pages which follow, was a season packed with incident and drama. Inevitably, much of the book is devoted to the Australians' all-conquering tour and the lessons we must learn if we are seriously to challenge them for supremacy. Balance, perspective, and good sense are the qualities that Paul Fitzpatrick so ably brings to this section of the book, while the domestic season, culminating in Featherstone's dramatic victory at Wembley and a superb Premiership final at Headingley, is recalled with a vividness to excite the reader's enthusiasm in the first months of a new season.

This book will greatly enhance the literature of our game and will confirm Paul Fitzpatrick's reputation as one of Rugby League's outstanding writers. My sincere thanks to him and to our good friends at Shopacheck, whose continued support for ventures of this kind is a major encouragement to us all.

David Oxley
Secretary-General of the Rugby Football League

Foreword

I was agreeably surprised to be asked to write a foreword to this most entertaining survey of the 1982–83 season and to give my support to Paul Fitzpatrick, whose Rugby League commentaries in the *Guardian* are so perceptive.

The highlights of the season are duly recorded in the pages that follow: the Hull club are to be congratulated on their successes in the Yorkshire Cup and in the championship, while the resurgence at Wigan has been rewarded by their winning the John Player Trophy. The Wembley final produced the most unexpected result of the season: Featherstone Rovers provided the football and the fitness to gain their success, and their preparation in all cup matches reflected great credit on their coach, Allan Agar. Once again, the Premiership final produced the showpiece of the season, and Widnes gave a display of Rugby League magic, with the half-backs surprisingly being allowed to develop the kind of flowing game that is such a delight to watch. The Harry Sunderland award winner, Tony Myler, established himself as the outstanding young player of the season; he has so much natural talent that his selection as Great Britain skipper cannot long be delayed.

The most important event of the season was certainly the visit of the Australian tourists. It is difficult to find anything new to say of their breathtaking performances. In scoring ninety-seven tries against seven in this country and sixty-nine tries against two in France, their complete superiority was indisputable. It was generally assumed before their arrival that the Australians would win most of their matches, but no one could possibly have imagined to what extent we were to be humiliated. Much has been written and many discussions held about the ineptitude of our players and the shortcomings of our selectors, but undoubtedly the contrast between the sides is due to the intelligence of the Australian coaches in producing a much more aggressive and entertaining style of football. The simple basics of tackling, ball-handling and support play were superbly executed by a new breed of

Foreword

super-fit and dedicated athletes. Superior fitness enabled players to be in support and in the right place both in defence and in attack. Our players, by contrast, coached to play one-man rugby for so long, were unable to compete with these high-speed tactics.

In an effort to improve fitness, stamina and playing skills throughout the country the panel of the National Coaching Scheme did well to appoint Phil Larder, a graduate of Loughborough College and a former professional player, as the new National Director of Coaching. With Les Bettinson, formerly a student of Carnegie College and now senior education adviser to the Metropolitan Borough of Stockport, as the chairman of the Rugby League's coaching committee, these two specialists are capable of raising standards throughout the game despite signs of dissent from some club coaches.

The success of the British Amateur Rugby League Association, with more clubs and teams involved practically every week, has enabled the Sports Council truthfully to describe Rugby League as Britain's fastest growing sport. Now the gap between school and club football has been filled by the formation of the British Upper Schools and Sixth Form Amateur Rugby League Association (BUSCARLA), generously supported by the Rugby Football League and encouraged by Peter Deakin and Harry Edgar of *Open Rugby* Magazine.

A motion in the House of Commons following the Hull v. Featherstone final congratulated the players and spectators of both clubs and went on to say that the House encouraged schools throughout the UK to introduce 'this splendid game of Rugby League' into their curricula. There is no doubt that the rules of Rugby League make it a safer game for youngsters at an early age and we would do well to follow the example of Rugby Union in fostering more mini-rugby in schools. Indeed, amateur and professional clubs should do more to encourage youngsters to play the game on their grounds at week-ends and during school holidays.

I hope these random reflections on a season ended will make us pause for further self-examination as the winter begins. In the past, complacency has often proved the League's Achilles heel, and the times are now too difficult for us to be thus handicapped again. That is why I give such a warm welcome to this *Review*. So long as there are articulate critics of the game like Paul Fitzpatrick and imaginative sponsors like Shopacheck determined to give the game its literature, we need not fear that British Rugby League will lack informed and constructive comment or energetic spokesmen for necessary change and innovation in the years ahead.

Brian Snape
Formerly Chairman of the Rugby League Council, 1974–76, and of Salford RLFC

Acknowledgements

I would like to thank everyone who has helped me, directly or indirectly, with this book. I am grateful to Brian Snape, Roy Waudby, David Oxley, David Howes, Renee Grant, Raymond Fletcher, Harry Edgar, Jack MacNamara, Trevor Watson, Richard Tingle, and John Sexton. Mrs Anne Wallis gave me invaluable—and flawless—help with the typing. I owe an especially large debt of gratitude to Phil Larder.

P.F.
June 1983

For permission to include photographs the publisher's thanks are due to the following agencies: John Leatherbarrow (3–5, 12–14, 23–24), North West Counties Press (30–32), *Open Rugby* magazine (7, 17, 36), *Rugby Leaguer* (11, 35) and the Andrew Varley Picture Agency (1–2, 6, 8–10, 15–16, 18–22, 25–29, 33–34, 37–38).

1

THE AUSTRALIAN TOUR

INTRODUCTION

The origins of Rugby League in Australia are not dissimilar to the beginnings of the game in this country. When the first Australian Rugby Union players turned professional some twelve years after the formation of the Northern Rugby Union in England in 1895, it was an attempt not so much to win financial reward as to seek compensation for time lost at work and financial protection against injury. There were similarities in the way the game developed as well. In Britain it was and is a sport largely restricted to the north of England. In Australia too—on a somewhat grander scale, admittedly—it is confined chiefly to New South Wales and Queensland.

Rugby League in Britain must stand accused of underestimating, even ignoring, the progress made in the sport in Australia during the last twenty years. When the Australian game came of age is a matter for speculation, though many critics would claim that it arrived with the establishment of Australia's National Coaching Scheme in the late 1960s. This scheme, ambitious, demanding and comprehensive, guaranteed the game's health at all levels and ensured a steady supply of talented youngsters to the professional clubs. The rewards for success were considerable ... and so were the demands made on a player's devotion and fitness. Standards rose; the game received even more devoted attention from television and written media; adulation equivalent to that of England's leading soccer players was heaped upon the Cronins, the Eadies and the Prices; searches were made elsewhere (into the American grid-iron game, notably) for fresh tactics, training methods and ways of motivation. The sport was bursting with energy and ideas, and there was no shortage of qualified coaches to tap the rich seams.

In Britain, meanwhile, the game plodded on, stoically as always, but

The Australian Tour

changing little. Australia's victories in 1978 and 1979 sent out ripples on the pond, but they quickly settled. Most British Rugby League players would have been deeply envious if they could have tasted the lifestyle, enjoyed the financial rewards and had access to the training facilities of their Australian counterparts. No matter, the living in Britain could be generous too. Sponsorship money, thanks to the enterprise shown at Rugby League headquarters, had continued to flow into the game; a lengthy run in any of the major competitions could be financially lucrative; and was there much wrong with a sport whose showpiece competition, the Challenge Cup, could provide a match as entertaining as the 1982 final between Widnes and Hull at Wembley and a replay at the packed Leeds United ground that will be remembered as one of the sport's greatest occasions?

Matches such as those tended to harden that dangerous but long-cherished belief that while Australia might have many advantages—the fitness and the power, the glamour, wealth and prestige—Britain still monopolized the skills ... and wasn't that what the game was all about? Even such a luminary as Brian Snape, now retired but formerly the progressive and imaginative chairman of the Rugby League Council and of Salford, thought of the Australians as 'super-fit and strong athletes battering their way down the middle of the field and boring the pants off a decreasing number of spectators'. To diminish the opposition in the hope of increasing the morale of one's own men might be all very well if it is grounded in truth, dangerous if based on false precepts. When the 1982 Australians arrived in England one unpalatable truth remained; not since 1970 had Great Britain beaten Australia in an Ashes series ... and that was not something that could easily be explained away.

That 1970 triumph, made all the more satisfying for having been achieved in Australia, was in the days of Frank Myler, Mick Shoebottom, Keith Hepworth, Alan Hardisty and the young, brave Malcolm Reilly. Players of such quality seemed readily available to Britain in those days, but by the end of the 1970s most of the world's best players were Australian. Changes had already been taking place, and after the defeats of 1970 the rethinking and the reorganizing gathered pace. In 1978 in England, 1979 in Australia and 1982 in England again, Australia demonstrated clearly how successfully their game was evolving.

It would not have required a Nostradamus to predict the calamities of 1982. Australia's tour of 1978 and Great Britain's forlorn traipse around Australasia in 1979 showed unequivocally where the power now lay. Between 1979 and 1982 nothing had seriously materialized to suggest that that power might be usurped. No truly outstanding young players had emerged in Britain, and Great Britain's performances in the intervening years had offered no more than occasional hope.

The Australian Tour

The confrontations with Australia in 1978 and 1979 were particularly relevant to the events of 1982 and are therefore worth recalling in some detail. Australia won the 1978 series 2–1, but Great Britain were competitive enough to ensure that the post-tour inquests were kept suitably brief. Besides, as well as losing the second Test, the Australians were beaten in two club games, those against Warrington and Widnes—comforting victories for those who refused to see signs of decline in the British game and especially for those who steadfastly refused to accept Australian omnipotence.

Peter Fox, the Bradford Northern coach, was in charge of that Great Britain side, and failure to recapture the Ashes cost him his job, a sacking which history has shown to be somewhat harsh. In the first Test at Wigan, Great Britain's play was dull and predictable but efficient enough to keep Australia's victory (15–9) to a modest margin of six points. Ten minutes from the end of the second Test at Bradford, Britain led 18–4, were stretched and embarrassed by a late flush of Australian points, yet won 18–14; but in the final Test Australia's fast, youthful side led 19–0 at half time and 23–6 at the end.

A victory of such scope could not easily be ignored. It was clear that Australia had an enviable number of talented players at their disposal, although Frank Stanton, their coach, admitted that the number of young players taken on tour had been the result more of accident than of design. When Brian Lockwood had to withdraw from the last Test because of injury he was replaced by Vince Farrar, playing his first game for Great Britain fourteen years after signing professional. Farrar played with credit, but his selection was symbolic of the ageing, sluggish direction in which British Rugby League was going compared with the youthful, optimistic paths being taken by Australia.

The results of that series, nevertheless, were to throw into even sharper relief the thrashings of 1982; except in the final Test perhaps, there was never quite the same degree of one-sidedness in 1978 as there was to be four years later. Australia's narrow win at Wigan was deserved, but Great Britain claimed afterwards that the sendings off of the scrum-halves, Steve Nash and Tom Raudonikis, had caused more damage to Britain than it had to Australia. 'That was the turning-point,' Fox claimed. 'Up to that point Nash had been one and a half times a better player than Raudonikis. He had tackled him out of the game.'

Great Britain even took the lead after the dismissals, but the gaps that Nash's devoted tackling had helped to close in midfield began to reappear with alarming frequency. The British pack, Jimmy Thompson in particular, showed no fear of hard work, but if defensively wholehearted, the British forwards were limited in attack, rarely forcing the Australians back into their own '25' and rarely threatening to open a gap in their opponents' defences. In contrast, the Australians, displaying reserves of energy in the final phases of the game, scored two tries in the last ten minutes.

A number of changes were made in the Great Britain side for the second Test and were justified by a remarkable victory, 18–14. Not often has a British coach in recent years been able to claim, as Peter Fox did afterwards, that 'everything went according to plan.' The success of that plan owed much to the recall of Brian Lockwood, whose intelligence and clever hands brought more variety to the pack. Playing for Great Britain for the first time in five years, Lockwood had a rewarding match in spite of receiving considerable attention and some hard physical treatment from the Australians. It was unlucky for him and for Britain that damaged knee ligaments sustained in the game kept him out of the side for the third Test.

In spite of ten anxious final minutes, this was Britain's most convincing all-round performance for a long time. In addition to Lockwood's weighty contribution there was a lot of purposeful running from Phil Lowe and Paul Rose, who replaced Steve Norton. George Nicholls showed a vast improvement on his form of the first Test, while Jim Mills made a clever job of drawing in the opposing pack. Tony Fisher, the 35-year-old Bradford hooker, who had not played Test football for eight years, was a contentious choice but justified himself.

There was the opportunism of Stuart Wright, the Widnes right wing, some classy touches from the young John Joyner, making his first appearance for Great Britain, craft and hard work from the half-backs, Steve Nash and Roger Millward (and similar qualities from John Holmes, who replaced Millward), and six goals from seven attempts by George Fairbairn. It was no surprise that Fox felt pleased with life.

Since that 1978 Test Great Britain have not once beaten Australia. Had it been realized just how many failures lay ahead, the two tries by Wright and the six goals by Fairbairn would have been savoured like a rare wine. Britain even led 18–4 at one stage, but again the Australians displayed a disturbing—and significant—capacity for throwing heavy punches over the final rounds. In this instance Ray Price and Steve Rogers scored tries in the last ten minutes, and Britain were left with little room for manoeuvre at the end.

The third Test, at Leeds, was the emphatic start of Australia's modern supremacy. Britain, not without justification, trusted largely to the players who had performed so well in the second Test but by half-time were floundering against an Australian side full of youthful running (though directed masterfully by the guile and experience of Bobby Fulton and Tom Raudonikis). Australia can rarely be accused of complacency, but it is possible that they felt they had done enough by the interval, leading as they were by 19–0. Surprisingly, Britain had the better of the second half, scoring tries by Millward and John Bevan to one by Raudonikis, and if George Fairbairn's

The Australian Tour

kicking had been less wayward, Australia's victory might have been less emphatic.

Harry Womersley, who was to be the tour manager in Australasia in 1979, made some predictable observations afterwards. Britain had not, he said, looked beyond the next Test in selecting a team for that series. It had been thought that the Ashes would be won by employing experienced players but now was the time to look to the future. More young players must be given their opportunity. Such cries, of course, were to be heard again four years later.

Peter Fox meanwhile was prepared to defend himself and his policies for as long as anyone was prepared to listen, but his final words on the subject—which one day might act as a suitable epitaph—were terse. 'I did my job,' he said. Universally popular Fox was not, but his devotion and his thoroughness were qualities that might arguably have earned him a longer run in the job. However, when the saviour for the tour of Australasia was sought the Rugby League hierarchy turned to Eric Ashton.

The tour of Australasia should have stripped away the last of the illusions. Although Britain's results overall were no disgrace (they won twenty-one of twenty-seven games, including two of three Tests in New Zealand), the defeats in the three Tests in Australia were so thorough, so overwhelming, that results elsewhere could not distract attention from them. Britain lost the first Test 35–0 in Brisbane, offered a semblance of competition in Sydney, when they were beaten 24–16 in the second, and were then routed again in Sydney 28–2 in the final Test. These must have been painful results to bear for Ashton, an outstanding player in his time and a successful coach. But he was powerless, as were his outclassed players, to prevent the advance of Australian rugby.

Ashton had to join the party ten days late because his daughter had been involved in a car crash; in that short period some observers could detect a crumbling of discipline. Some time later a Hull Kingston Rovers official, who had joined the tour briefly, claimed that the players had been living in a 'holiday camp'.

Such allegations were strenuously denied by management and coach, but there is little doubt that Ashton had a difficult task sustaining the levels of enthusiasm and dedication required for a lengthy, demanding tour. A considerable number of injuries—Britain sent for three replacements in John Burke, George Fairbairn and David Topliss for Jim Mills, Tommy Martyn and Roger Millward—failed to help, and after the first Test at Brisbane the tour was practically doomed.

Mick Cronin's performance alone in this game would have been more than enough to beat Britain. The Australian centre gave an astonishing display of place kicking, distances and angles proving no deterrent as he landed ten out of eleven kicks. In addition there were five tries from a side too powerful, quick and imaginative for the British. The dismissal of Trevor Skerrett five minutes from time completed the glum picture. Tom Raudonikis offered Britain cold comfort by suggesting that had Nash played, Australia's margin of victory might have been reduced by at least ten points. Nash was absent, injured.

There was also some encouragement to be found in history. In 1958 Britain had lost the first Test in Sydney 25–8 but then won the next two in Brisbane and Sydney 25–18 and 40–17. Again in 1970, the last time they had won an Ashes series, they were beaten in the first Test 37–15 in Brisbane but won their next two Tests in Sydney 28–7 and 21–17.

But although there was an improvement on the first Test—things could scarcely have got worse—and indeed a spirited performance in a second half, which saw Britain progress from 17–4 to a defeat of 24–16, history was not to be repeated. Britain were particularly unfortunate to lose Norton on the morning of the match because of a calf injury, but interest in the series was already waning and an attendance of 26,807 was the lowest at Sydney Cricket Ground for an Anglo–Australian Test. The attendance for the final match promised to be much lower. It was, by almost 10,000.

Again, as at Brisbane, Britain were thrashed. Norton was sent off fifteen minutes from time, but his absence could not excuse a pitiful British performance. Australia had already demonstrated their total supremacy before Norton's dismissal, and Eric Ashton neither sought excuses nor made them afterwards. Deficiencies in fundamental skills were evident in a match in which Graham Eadie, Ray Price, Rod Reddy and Les Boyd scored tries and Mick Cronin kicked another eight goals, giving him fifty-four points in the series.

A number of recommendations were made after the party returned home from New Zealand, but they were designed primarily to ensure that future tours to Australasia were more compactly and efficiently organized. They did little to attack the real problem—simply, the discrepancy in fitness and ability that now existed between the countries. A number of urgent words were uttered about Britain's future prospects, but the investigations into this morale-draining and financially costly tour were quickly concluded.

Even the sound of the old shibboleths could still be heard: that Australian rugby was an obsession with speed and brute force: that Britain still monopolized the skills and the subtleties. The creed was losing some of its followers but still, like the Flat Earth Society, retained a surprising amount of support.

By the following year, when New Zealand toured England, Johnny Whiteley, one of Britain's finest post-war forwards, and Colin Hutton were in charge of affairs as coach and manager. Here were two honest, well-intentioned, enthusiastic men whose credentials, experience and integrity demanded respect. But their two years in charge were disappointing—for them as much as anyone. The New Zealanders were the more fluent, imaginative side in their three-match Test series with Great Britain, even though they had to be content with an equal share of the spoils from a draw, a win, a defeat. The chief comfort for Whiteley and Hutton in that series was that Britain—almost exclusively thanks to two tries from Des Drummond—looked slightly less bankrupt at the end of the third Test than they did after the first and second.

Nor did events of the following season do much to dispel the pessimism, although when Great Britain beat France 37–0 at Hull in early December hope ran higher than for some time. Britain's two black wingers, Des Drummond and Henderson Gill, scored five tries between them—there were seven in all—and the side ran and handled with confidence and enterprise. But Hull was to prove a false dawn. Two weeks later in Marseilles neither the French, never a predictable side, nor Britain, were recognizable from the Boulevard match, and France won 19–2. For Hutton and Whiteley this was a deflating defeat. The Australians would be arriving in ten months' time, and they were now short of time and opportunity to rectify some glaring weaknesses.

The response to that defeat was, at least, constructive. A squad system—the idea for which had been germinating during the New Zealand tour—was initiated, with the objective of bringing some thirty prospective Great Britain players together during the summer for concentrated and specialized fitness training and also, of course, to foster a sense of purpose, unity and team spirit.

Pre-season games were arranged, one of them an international against France in Venice, an exotic exercise that suited Britain's ambitions and was also designed to help attempts to revive the sport in Italy. Defeat (France won 8–7) was not part of the plan. It was hard to fault the intentions behind that game or those against Hull Kingston Rovers (which Britain won 30–0 against a very weak side), Leeds (who won 22–21) and Widnes (who spread further gloom by inflicting another defeat, 13–5, upon the international side) but, set against later events, these matches proved of minimal value.

As the coming of the Australians drew near, Rod McKenzie, the senior lecturer in physical education at Carnegie College, Leeds, who earlier had been recruited to help with Britain's fitness programme, maintained that the fitness of the players had improved significantly over the summer. The players themselves expressed their enthusiasm for the squad system, and morale was clearly high.

But the mood in Rugby League circles elsewhere was less optimistic. There was keen anticipation of the Australians' arrival but also anxiety at the prospects for Britain. One newspaperman summed up the mood accurately soon after the tourists arrived: 'I feel a tremendous sense of excitement at the

Australians being here,' he said. 'I'm also terrified at the thought of what they will do to us.'

THE AUSTRALIANS IN BRITAIN

An accepted fault of Great Britain's tour of Australasia in 1979 was that the party was announced too far before the event, almost seven weeks in advance. A consequence of this was that players who did not want to miss out on an inviting trip went to Australia 'hiding' injuries. It was an encouragement for players to lose form and concentration, and it denied the selectors the opportunity of assessing the form of prospective tourists in such important matches as the Challenge Cup final.

Australia, of course, did not make the same mistake. A larger squad was announced well in advance of the tour, but the final party was named only the week before they were due to arrive in England:

Manager: Frank Farrington
Assistant manager: Tom Drysdale
Coach: Frank Stanton

Captain: Max Krilich (Manly, Sydney), hooker
Vice-captain: Wally Lewis (Fortitude Valley, Brisbane), stand-off
Chris Anderson (Canterbury-Bankstown, Sydney), wing
Kerry Boustead (Eastern Suburbs, Sydney), wing
Les Boyd (Manly, Sydney), prop or second row
Greg Brentnall (Canterbury-Bankstown, Sydney), full-back
Ray Brown (Manly, Sydney), hooker
Greg Conescu (Northern Suburbs, Brisbane), hooker
Steve Ella (Parramatta, Sydney), full-back, centre or stand-off
Eric Grothe (Parramatta, Sydney), wing
Rohan Hancock (Toowoomba Wattles, Queensland Country), prop or second row
Brett Kenny (Parramatta, Sydney), stand-off or centre
Paul McCabe (Manly, Sydney), second row or loose forward
Don McKinnon (North Sydney), prop
Mal Meninga (Southern Suburbs, Brisbane), centre

The Australian Tour

Gene Miles (Wynnum-Manly, Brisbane), centre
Rod Morris (Wynnum-Manly, Brisbane), prop
Steve Mortimer (Canterbury-Bankstown, Sydney), scrum-half
John Muggleton (Parramatta, Sydney), second row
Mark Murray (Fortitude Valley, Brisbane), scrum-half or stand-off
Wayne Pearce (Balmain, Sydney), loose forward or second row
Ray Price (Parramatta, Sydney), loose forward
Rod Reddy (St George, Sydney), second row
John Ribot (Manly, Sydney), wing
Steve Rogers (St George, Sydney), centre
Ian Schubert (Eastern Suburbs, Sydney), utility
Peter Sterling (Parramatta, Sydney), scrum-half
Craig Young (St George, Sydney), prop

Trainer: Alf Richards
Medical Officer: Dr Bill Monaghan

It was a squad that was not greeted with unanimous approval by the Australian press, and there were inevitably accusations that some choices were 'political', but it had been predictable enough for Colin Hutton to guess twenty-two of the twenty-eight names. Some familiar figures were absent—Graham Eadie and Mick Cronin in particular—but to English eyes it looked a formidable enough party.

It was clear that Australia would be fielding a highly experienced pack. Ray Price, acknowledged as the finest loose forward in the game, Les Boyd, Rod Morris, Rod Reddy, Craig Young and Max Krilich had been members of the 1978 party; so too had Chris Anderson and Kerry Boustead, the wingers, Ian Schubert, a utility player, and Steve Rogers, the centre, one of the most highly paid and most popular of Australian footballers.

The majority of the squad, though, were newcomers, although the reputations of such as Greg Brentnall, the full-back and a former Australian Rules footballer, Wally Lewis, who had been a member of the Australian Rugby Union side that had toured Japan, Europe and the British Isles in 1977, Mal Meninga, the powerful centre from Brisbane, and Steve Ella, the full-back or centre and a cousin of the Rugby Union Ella brothers, had, to a modest degree, preceded them.

A tour, be it cricket or Rugby League, will inevitably claim its casualties and, more often than not, produce successes that were not predicted. Some players, for whatever reason—lack of opportunity, injury, loss of form or even some flaw in their character—will subside into anonymity. Others will respond to the challenges, capitalize on their good luck and establish or enhance their

The Australian Tour

reputations. This was true of Australia's 1982 tour. At the end of it, it was safe to assume that some Australians had been seen for the last time in Europe, whereas others, barely known at the start, were familiar, established figures who had won standing, respect and admiration.

Peter Sterling was one of the first of the new, young school to impress himself deeply on English minds. He was in England, according to the publicity material, as understudy to Steve Mortimer, but it was evident after the first match against Hull Kingston Rovers at Craven Park that more performances of that quality and Sterling would soon be indispensable—which he became. The extraordinary energy that was to characterize his play throughout the tour was immediately apparent in a game in which the tourists won 30–10 after trailing (a rare experience!) 8–5 at half-time.

But originally Sterling was not the main point of interest in that opening game. There had been considerable discussion in England about the tactics that the tourists would employ; particularly there had been speculation about the tourists' use of the 'bomb'—a high, searching kick designed primarily to test the nerves and technique of the opposing full-back. Colin Hutton, the Great Britain manager and Hull Kingston Rovers chairman, who had watched Australia play two Tests against New Zealand, had warned his players that they were likely to be subjected to these aerial attacks, and the first game suggested that the high kick was to be an important part of the Australian armoury.

From the kick-off Brentnall fielded the ball and immediately sent a long kick downfield to Fairbairn. The Hull KR full-back returned the ball. Brentnall sent it back again. Such duals were once a feature of the game but had long since gone out of fashion, which possibly explained why the less patient members of a crowd of 10,000 resorted to jeers and whistles ... and why Fairbairn looked so perplexed.

The crowd soon had reason to be upset. The first half was little more than a public exhibition of ill temper. Liberal use was made of fist and boot, and after nineteen minutes Rod Reddy became the first tourist to be dismissed, sent off for punching Steve Crooks. Les Boyd was to follow him, accused by the referee, Fred Lindop, of not choosing his words with enough care. Boyd, in fact, was cleared of the charge of foul language when he appeared before the Disciplinary Committee later that month, but he was a prominent figure in those early bouts of pugilism. Between times the Rovers hooker, David Watkinson, had been dismissed for an attack on Ray Price, and a distasteful half ended with Rovers leading 8–5, Steve Hartley and Gary Prohm scoring tries after Craig Young had scored the first try of the tour early in the game.

Possibly the Australians had anticipated trouble and decided to get their retaliation in first. Before the game Roger Millward, Hull KR's coach, had

1. The Australians' discipline was, with a few exceptions, admirable. However, this was not the case during the first half of the first game of the tour against Hull KR at Craven Park, a match that sorely tested the control of the referee, Fred Lindop. Here Price and an apparently contrite David Watkinson (who was later sent off) are given a forceful reminder of the rules of the game.

vigorously rejected a suggestion that his club would deliberately pursue a policy of physical intimidation in an attempt to 'soften up' the tourists.

He was no doubt telling the truth, but it did not appear that the Australians believed him. They were clearly determined to take this early opportunity to show the English clubs that they were grown-up lads and well able to look after themselves. They made the point with all the subtlety of a rubber cosh, but it had the doubtful merit of succeeding. Moments of violence were to flare again

The Australian Tour

before the tour was through, but never again were there excesses of behaviour to compare with those of that first half.

There was some gloomy speculation during the interval. Was this to be the shape and nature of the tour? The second half did much to dispel the fears. The Australians had chosen an extremely strong side for this first game—almost their Test side, as it was to prove—and as the game progressed, they displayed all the qualities that had been predicted of them: speed, skill and enviable fitness—this, too, less than a week after arriving in England.

Sterling had remained aloof from the shabby events of the first half and in the second was the inspiration of what was, to English eyes, an ominously assured display of running and handling. The scrum-half scored two tries, running 25 yards and vigorously handing off Rovers' young winger, Garry Clark, for one of them and showing an alert eye for opportunity for his second. He was then significantly involved in the approach play to two other tries.

But perhaps most worrying of all for English followers was the thrilling end that Mal Meninga gave to the game. After gaining possession on the left side of his own half, Meninga ran 70 yards to score in the right corner. George Fairbairn was the final obstacle before the try line, but Meninga swept through the Great Britain full-back's despairing diving tackle. Wholehearted and courageous, Fairbairn for once cut a forlorn figure. In a single instance Australia had established an important physical and psychological advantage. **(Final score: Hull KR 10   Australia 30.)**

A week later and the Australians had scored more than 100 points. Steve Hartley, the Hull KR stand-off and a strong candidate for a place in the first Test, and Gary Prohm, the New Zealand forward, scored tries in the first half of the match at Craven Park. Though it was not appreciated at the time these two players were the founder members of an exclusive brotherhood. By the end of the tour only seven players performed the feat. Henderson Gill managed it in the tourists' second game at Wigan, but in their next eight games the Australians conceded only one more try, to Brynmor Williams, the former Welsh Rugby Union international, in the match against Wales at Cardiff.

Wigan were always likely to provide resilient opposition, but it was in retrospect, as the Australians moved from one overwhelming victory to another, that their performance in this match increased its value. Wigan possibly went closer to beating the Australians than any other club side—apart from Hull—although for this game the tourists had made considerable changes in the powerful side that had beaten Hull KR. Price and Rogers, in the fifteen as substitutes, were the only links with Craven Park.

Alex Murphy, who the previous season had coached Leigh to the league championship, was now in charge at Wigan, a suitably expansive stage for a man of such ambitions. Murphy's powers of persuasion were beginning to work too. Wigan were developing, after a long period of mediocrity, into one of the game's more enterprising sides. The club's followers, used throughout a distinguished history to individuals and teams of brilliance, were being drawn irresistibly back to Central Park. A crowd of 12,000, more than double the average (and the tour's second highest club attendance), was given a performance worthy of the side's rising status.

Frank Stanton must have had a shrewd idea what his Test side—give or take the odd position—would be from the start. He must have been slightly perturbed, nevertheless, at the early evidence of his reserve strength. Wigan began the game enthusiastically, looked likely to subside when McCabe and Muggleton scored tries before half-time and Boustead after it, but rediscovered their momentum when Danny Campbell, a New Zealand forward who might lack some of the game's subtleties but is not short of determination, replaced Lee Bamber.

Wigan, indeed, ended the game camped only yards from the Australians' line and threatening to snatch victory. On attack the Australians dropped a number of important passes, and in defence they were severely stretched at times and might have been even more hard-pressed if the Wigan forwards had shown variety as well as determination.

The Australians again used the high kick—but not to excess—and such a kick was directly responsible for the first try when the young and inexperienced Wigan full-back, Barry Williams, seemed unnerved by the tactic. Ian Schubert kicked downfield, and the Australians moved up swiftly. Williams fielded the ball, chose to find touch rather than run with the ball, failed to do so, and a weak kick put the tourists in possession. The ball was worked down the left, an inviting opening materialized and McCabe scored.

A half-time lead of 10–6 was stretched to 13–6 when purposeful running, first by Gene Miles and then by Paul McCabe, provided an opening for Kerry Boustead to score in the right corner. But although Wigan were a little too predictable forward, they gave their followers visions of victory when Henderson Gill—after Campbell had punched the initial hole in the tourists' defences—accepted his only opportunity of the match to score muscularly in the left corner. The final minutes were anxious ones for the Australians. Not often were they to experience such pressure as Wigan exerted over that tense final phase. (**Final score: Wigan 9   Australia 13.**)

Two nights later the Australians travelled to one of Britain's Rugby League outposts, Barrow, once in Lancashire but now part of Cumbria. Barrow are not

The Australian Tour

one of the most fashionable of clubs; their geographical position often leaves them excluded from mainstream rugby life. Too rarely, unfortunately, is their presence felt, which is a pity, for they have a deserved reputation for playing adventurous, skilful rugby. Nobody at that time typified their character better than Ian Ball, who was excluded from this game because of injury. This was unfortunate, for he is the type of player, individualistic and unpredictable, who might have set the tourists some problems.

Barrow, to their credit, did exactly that—in the first half at least. They threw the ball about, carelessly at times, but with an appealing sense of enjoyment, and they had a splendid first forty minutes. It was Barrow too who, devilishly, gave the Australians some aerial troubles by employing the 'bomb'. When Schubert came under pressure from two such kicks in the first half he was left floundering on both occasions.

The confusion the second time was such that the tourists conceded a penalty, from which Tickle, in front of the posts, scored. Schubert made some amends, scoring the only try of the first half, but it was curious to see the full-back so unnerved by a tactic meant to confound the English. Not that Greg Brentnall, who was full-back in the three Tests, ever showed similar vulnerability.

The Australians were sloppier in that first half than at any other time on the tour, but Barrow's flame was soon to be snuffed. The purposeful running of Derek Hadley, the strength of Eddie Szymala and the energetic work of their half-backs, Mel Mason and David Cairns, evaporated against the superior pace, strength and fitness of the Australians. Tries came steadily, and finally with a rush, as Schubert, Ella and Rogers scored in the last minutes to add to tries scored earlier in the second half by Conescu—one of his rare contributions to the tour—Pearce and Murray. Three points in the first half, twenty-six in the second ... that was an accurate measure of how much the Australians improved in this game. **(Final score: Barrow 2   Australia 29.)**

The tries, eight of them, continued to flow the following Sunday at Knowsley Road, where St Helens were hopelessly ill-equipped to cope with a side now gathering unmistakable momentum. But then St Helens never gave themselves the remotest chance of winning this game. They were due to play Warrington in the final of the Lancashire Cup the following Saturday and they fielded a side—a pack especially—well below strength. It was a decision they were to regret.

Medical certificates were later produced on behalf of the injured players, but the fact that the club was to apologize publicly for its team selection was evidence enough of guilt. The episode was an insult to the tourists, who, expecting this to be one of their harder games, had chosen an exceptionally

The Australian Tour

strong side; it was an embarrassment to the club; it alienated their supporters and brought condemnation from the League and the threat that St Helens might forfeit future games against the Australians. Not surprisingly, Frank Stanton forcefully expressed his disenchantment afterwards.

Even allowing for the absences of such experienced forwards as Harry Pinner, Peter Gorley, Graham Liptrot and the younger, talented Gary Moorby the Australians were impressive. St Helens had little to offer in attack and only once seriously threatened to cross the Australian line. Inevitably, they were preoccupied with defensive duties, which, to be fair to them, they performed with considerable devotion.

But devotion was not nearly enough. There were two tries each for the Australian wingers, Boustead and Grothe, whose first was the result of a powerful 65-yards run down the left after he had gathered the ball in his own half from a St Helens kick designed as a relief from pressure. There were two tries too for Les Boyd—playing, significantly, in the front row—and one each for Rogers and Sterling. **(Final score: St Helens 0   Australia 32.)**

Meninga burst a blood vessel in the St Helens match; Price needed stitches in an eye wound; and Boyd suffered a pinched nerve in his shoulder. But none of these injuries was to prove serious. The worst the Australians had suffered was the hamstring damage Rohan Hancock had sustained at Barrow. It was feared that he might have to be sent home, but this proved unnecessary. The Australians could feel gratified with their preparations so far and even more optimistic after their next match with Leeds. Two days before this game the Great Britain side for the first Test had been announced. It contained three Leeds players, Les Dyl and David Ward, a centre and a hooker respectively of considerable experience, and David Heron, a young, promising loose forward who had been numbered among the substitutes. These selections gave additional interest to a fixture that was expected to provide the Australians with much their sternest examination so far. Leeds were then leading the first division, having won nine of their first ten games.

Instead the match confirmed what was becoming increasingly evident: that Great Britain would find the Australians extremely difficult to beat. It was possible to have reservations, however inconsequential, about all the tourists' games up to this stage but difficult to find much fault with this performance, made all the more significant by the quality of the opposition. There were still the occasional handling lapses, but then the speed and force of so many of the tourists' moves made some error almost inevitable.

The Australians' strength was best demonstrated by Eric Grothe, who collected a try similar to one he had scored at St Helens four days earlier. Again

The Australian Tour

the ball came to him from a relieving opposition kick, this time by John Holmes, who, from close to his own posts, sent a long ball upfield. But if Holmes thought that his kick would bring some welcome respite, he was badly mistaken. Within seconds, after three players had been thrust aside effortlessly, Grothe was touching down in the left corner—a formidable example of opportunism, strength and pace.

That was one of many good things in a game in which Leeds were overwhelmed by opponents for whom all the pieces were now neatly falling into place. The Australians supported one another with the dedication of zealots. Brilliant individualism flourished not for its own sake but invariably as the product of some selfless piece of teamwork. Boustead scored a try that owed much to the pace of a sprinter but as much to a sudden change of direction that must have left the Leeds full-back, Neil Hague, feeling foolishly inadequate.

Meninga, enhancing his reputation with every game, once more demonstrated his awesome power. Ella showed what quality there was among the reserve strength by coming on for Sterling and scoring two tries. Wayne Pearce was at loose forward in this game, and John Muggleton and Paul McCabe formed the second row behind Young, Krilich and Boyd. It was a fine pack but one that could be strengthened. Stanton must have known at this stage precisely what his side would be for the first Test, now just over a week away, even though there was still a match against Wales to be played at Cardiff. **(Final score: Leeds 4   Australia 31.)**

On their previous tour the Australians had beaten Wales 8–3. That was a defeat narrow enough to be regarded as a moral victory—the Northern Ireland soccer team used to claim a monopoly on 'moral victories'—by a side whose Rugby League future is frequently the subject of speculation. There was, however, no hint of a contest this time. Wales offered a traditional quality—passion—for the first twenty minutes but then subsided as the Australian tries began to arrive.

There were four of them from Steve Ella, playing at full-back and timing his runs into the attack with perfection, two from John Ribot and one each from Mark Murray, Don McKinnon and Wally Lewis. Wales at least had one try to show for their somewhat laboured and limited efforts, Brynmor Williams, to rapturous appreciation from 5,600 spectators, forcing his way over for a try in the second half.

Wales were poor, but even allowing for their limitations it was obvious that Australia were not short of reserve strength and that for certain positions they had enviably powerful cover. Ella's performance earned him the job as substitute the following week, but of the players who started this game only

The Australian Tour

Reddy was chosen for the Test side. One newspaperman, a Rugby Union reporter who had been drafted in late to cover the match, steadfastly refused to believe, when told, that it was possible that not a single player of this side might appear in the first Test. (**Final score: Wales 7   Australia 37.**)

**First Test
Boothferry Park, Hull, 30 October
Great Britain 4   Australia 40**

The first Test at Boothferry Park, Hull, was to confirm all the worst English fears about the state of the domestic game. Those fears had been mounting as the match approached. Australian preparations had gone smoothly; the tourists had suffered no serious injuries to leading players, and every man chosen for the game had shown encouraging form. Some of the players—Peter Sterling, Eric Grothe, Mal Meninga and Wayne Pearce especially—had been outstanding, giving performances that were all the more welcome coming from such young and still largely unknown players.

Most of the forecasters thought that Australia would win. Those who did not could be accused of excessive patriotism or blindness. It was illogical to anticipate anything other than a victory for Australia. History and the evidence of the first seven tour games insisted on nothing less.

Frank Stanton could have had few problems in selecting his side. His choice of Les Boyd, a second-row forward, at blind-side prop was analysed in some quarters as a sign of the weakness of reserve forward strength at his disposal. But such a move, which Stanton possibly had in mind from the beginning, allowed him to bring in Wayne Pearce in the second row. Pearce had arrived as understudy to Ray Price at loose forward but had done enough against Wigan, Barrow, St Helens and particularly Leeds to suggest that he was good enough to play anywhere in the pack, and certainly enough to suggest that he was far too good to be left out.

One of Stanton's few worries in the week before the first Test was the Disciplinary Committee meeting on the Thursday. Rod Reddy and Les Boyd were both making personal appearances at this meeting after having been dismissed in the first match of the tour, Reddy for alleged punching and Boyd

The Australian Tour

for use of unparliamentary language. Both were cleared. Boyd, indeed, was found to be the victim of mistaken identity.

The Great Britain team meanwhile, which had not been greeted with universal approval when it had been announced almost two weeks earlier, had endured some anxious days leading up to the Test. Trevor Skerrett, the Hull blind-side prop, had had to withdraw from the previous week's international in Cardiff because of knee ligament trouble. Skerrett was considered indispensable to the side at this time, and so it was with relief that he and his Hull colleague, Steve Norton, who had been suffering from a badly bruised hip, were passed fit.

It now remained to be seen if some of the selectors' more contentious choices could be justified. This unenvied body of men were not lacking sympathy because the difficulties of their job were well appreciated. Their chief problem was not a shortage of players but rather a shortage of players of outstanding quality. For most positions there were at least two or three players demanding recognition. A selector's job is much easier when most positions have no more than one man offering an irresistible claim.

Even so there was considerable scepticism about the selectors' policy. They opted solidly for experience, with George Fairbairn at full-back, Eric Hughes and Les Dyl in the centre and Jeff Grayshon, David Ward, Trevor Skerrett, Les Gorley and Steve Norton in the pack. Steve Nash, who had not played for Great Britain for four years, was recalled as scrum-half and captain, and that choice above all seemed to reflect a failure to come to terms with reality on the selectors' part.

It was not that Nash was not a good player; at his best he had been a superb practitioner, intelligent, creative and an almost recklessly brave tackler. But he was now 33, playing second-division football with Salford, and he had suffered the previous season from an eye injury serious enough to threaten a premature end to his career. Whiteley and Hutton had praised his attitude in training. But at the very least the choice of Nash was a risk.

Nor was the logic of choosing Steve Evans on the left wing easy to grasp. Evans was a talented 24-year-old who had toured with Great Britain in Australia in 1979. (He was indeed one of the few players to emerge from that tour with much credit.) His market value had been established the previous season when Hull had paid Featherstone Rovers £70,000 for him, but Evans was regarded first as a centre, secondly as a stand-off and thirdly as a winger. It was in this position that he was playing for a powerful Hull side in which competition for places was keen ... but on the right. The only suggestion of adventure came with the inclusion of Lee Crooks, a 19-year-old Hull second-row forward who had helped to secure his place by producing a wonderful performance for his club in a league game against Leeds. In one of Hull's

2. David Heron showed more enterprise than some other Great Britain forwards when he replaced Lee Crooks in the first Test match at Hull, but he is not going to make progress here. He has been taken low and firmly from behind by the first Australian tackler, while Rogers moves in higher to ensure that the ball is smothered.

outstanding displays of the season Crooks had scored three tries and kicked seven goals.

Optimistic British noises were made beforehand. It would have been surprising if they had not been, and Steve Norton offered the opinion that as long as Britain got their tackling and their defensive work right, they could win. Australia, he said, had not been put under pressure so far on tour—which was largely true—and that if they were, there was no saying how they might react.

Norton's optimism proved ill-founded. English—and Welsh—audiences had already seen the full extent of the tourists' attacking abilities. What the first Test was to prove conclusively was that the Australians' attacking strength was based on defence so sound as to be near-flawless. After the second match of their tour the Australians went through games against Barrow, St Helens and Leeds without conceding a try. The impregnability they had shown against the clubs was now demonstrated even more emphatically against Britain.

The match was in the charge of a French referee, Julien Rascagnères, who had done well when given control of a league match between Leigh and Castleford. He had a good overall game and was especially impressive in the opening stages, when tempers were likely to be most volatile. He was particularly quick to punish off-side at the play-the-balls, insisted on properly formed scrums and acted so efficiently and quickly that physical confrontation was kept to a minimum.

By half-time the semblance of a contest remained. Australia led 10–4, but the assurance with which Meninga and Boyd had scored their first-half tries and the sterility of the British tactics, particularly from the forwards, had held out no great promise for the home team in the second half. Crooks had opened the scoring for Britain in the second minute with a penalty; Meninga had replied with a penalty four minutes later; and then, midway through the half, came the first of Australia's eight tries, Meninga once more demonstrating the forceful finishing that had already won him a handsome reputation.

Before Meninga gained possession Sterling had decisively changed the point of attack, switching from left to right, and giving the ball to Young. Although under pressure, the prop worked out a high pass to Pearce, wisely missing out Rogers, who almost certainly would have been halted by Dyl had he been given the ball. As it was, Dyl now had to turn his attention to Meninga, racing up on the outside on to Pearce's pass. Dyl closed in on his opposite centre but suddenly found himself going back in the direction from which he had come, as he was forced off his feet by the strength of Meninga's hand-off. The way to the line was now clear.

Australia's second try owed much to the imagination of Sterling, who stepped effortlessly off his left foot and then darted into the heart of the British defence before slipping out a choice pass to Rogers. Boustead took up the move, and then Pearce, now sprinting down the right, turned the ball inside to Boyd before being knocked off his feet by a deplorably late tackle by Dyl. All the hard work had been done and Boyd scored unhindered. At the interval the Australians ran briskly from the field. The British players trudged off. It was a small enough point but significant.

The Australian Tour

There had been a certain dogged quality to Britain's play in the first half, if no great imagination. But the second half exposed mercilessly the barrenness of British rugby compared with the fluent, exciting play of the Australians. They provided an unanswerable case against those British coaches who would claim that bold, sweeping rugby is impossible under the six-tackle rule. It was a fortunate thing for Britain that Australia were not playing to the old unlimited possession rule because it is unlikely that Britain would ever have seen the ball. As one old cynic remarked at the end: 'That crowd were really given their money's worth today. They saw two games ... one when Britain had the ball and another when Australia had it.'

It is true that much of the British tackling was feeble, but it was also possible to argue that the sheer weight and persistence of the Australian attacks made it so. This, however, was no consolation; there was no consolation. Fairbairn had a wretched match at full-back; Drummond, Britain's one player of true quality, was preoccupied with defence (although he did come agonizingly close to scoring a try, the ball squirting out of his hands just as he was about to place it over the line), as indeed were the rest of a laboured three-quarter line; Woods played with more purpose than he was credited with, but Nash, though honest and hard-working, was unable to offer anything remotely to compare with the tireless Sterling. Nash's greatest battles had been with Raudonikis. It had been unfair to ask a man past his best to compete with someone as young, and as good, as Sterling.

Forward, there were simply no comparisons. Skerrett and Norton showed obvious signs of distress from their injuries, raising doubts about the wisdom of selecting them at all. Grayshon, in his deliberate way, tried to be constructive, but Skerrett, Ward (who surprisingly lost the scrums 7–3 to Krilich) and Gorley were painfully predictable. Little emanated from Norton. Crooks had a useful first appearance and landed both his penalties before departing injured soon after half-time. His replacement, the young David Heron, showed some enterprise, but Britain found nothing from which to draw comfort, not even a penalty count (21–7) heavily in their favour.

The Hull crowd, described at first as a capacity crowd of 32,500 (a figure later revised to 26,771) was an admirably fair-minded multitude. It encouraged Britain in the first half, spared them any slanders when they were overrun in the second half, and stayed to the end to savour and applaud the brilliance and the skills of the Australians. In a second half of six tries and thirty points it was given much to ponder and to appreciate. Australia's play was exhilarating. Practically every move threatened a try; their finishing was ruthless and every move, every try, was a demonstration of their superiority over the British. The true width of the divide between the countries was beginning at last to be appreciated.

The Australian Tour

Grothe gathered from Norton an untidy pass intended for Hughes in the forty-third minute, forced off Norton when the loose forward moved across to try to retrieve his blunder and accelerated effortlessly past Fairbairn. He grounded the ball short of the line, but his momentum took him over it. The British possibly had some justification for their claim that the try was illegal, but it stood.

Next, alertness close to the British line brought Price a simple try after he had gathered the ball at acting half-back, exchanged short passes with Sterling, broken effortlessly through an unconvincing tackle by Grayshon and dived over. The Australians never lacked support—such a glaring difference between them and all their opponents throughout the tour—and the fifth try was yet another example of teamwork, although this score, from Boustead, was significant also for the raw power and determination that Rogers displayed in the building of it.

When Kenny fed Rogers, the Australian centre extricated himself from a clinging tackle by Dyl like an escapologist wriggling free of a straitjacket. Dyl, to his credit, attempted to snuff out the danger a second time, but by then Rogers had returned Kenny's pass, the stand-off had plied Boustead and the winger had dived over the line, with Dyl hanging vainly to his legs.

Pearce, in his first international for Australia, was voted man of the match, and the next two tries showed why. As the tour developed, Pearce's ability to burst through tackles became less of a source of wonder because he displayed it so often, but at this stage Pearce was still relatively unknown. By the end of this game his reputation had been firmly established. Pearce, exploding through a joint tackle by Nash and Norton, both of whom made the mistake of trying to tackle him round the chest, set up a try for Kenny, who took the ball at blistering speed, brushing off a despairing tackle by Drummond and touching down to the left of the posts; and it was Pearce who scored the next try after a move that demonstrated the sweep of Australia's football.

This try came after the Australians had been subjected to one of their few moments of anxiety. Nash put up a kick that was fielded by Brentnall in his in-goal area. Four tackles later Pearce was touching down beneath the posts, a move of adventurous audacity. Brentnall and Boustead made the initial advances, then Krilich slipped out a superb pass to Young, even though Norton was hanging on to the hooker with the persistence of a drowning man. Pearce was now in full stride down the centre; Young timed his short pass inside to perfection; and Fairbairn, rushing up to try to block Young's pass, was barging wildly into Young when Pearce passed him at speed down the other side.

The final try provided a breathtaking example of Australia's close-passing skills, with Sterling, Rogers and Kenny first exchanging passes; the move then developed when Brentnall joined the attack and arrowed in towards the posts.

3. Eric Grothe in full stride was an unforgettable sight, and he scored remarkable tries against St Helens and Leeds. In the first Test at Boothferry Park, Hull, as he leaves George Fairbairn (and a touch judge) trailing, he shows that his pace, strength and opportunism were no less effective at Test level.

A swift pass from the full-back was followed by an even swifter one from the scrum-half to Reddy and the second-row forward was through the last line of the defence. This was football played at the speed of a pinball machine, and it was compelling.

Meninga's place kicking was near-perfect. He added the goal points to seven of the tries and landed a penalty besides. With his try he collected nineteen points in all. Shades of Mick Cronin and Graeme Langlands....

Great Britain: Fairbairn (Hull KR); Drummond (Leigh), Hughes (Widnes), Dyl (Leeds), Evans (Hull); Woods (Leigh), Nash (Salford) captain; Grayshon (Bradford Northern), Ward (Leeds), Skerrett (Hull), Gorley (Widnes), Crooks (Hull), Norton (Hull)

Substitutes: David Heron (Leeds) for Crooks after 47 minutes, Ken Kelly (Warrington) not used

Scorer: goals—Crooks (2)

The Australian Tour

Australia: Brentnall (Canterbury-Bankstown, Sydney); Boustead (Eastern Suburbs, Sydney), Meninga (Southern Suburbs, Brisbane), Rogers (St George, Sydney), Grothe (Parramatta, Sydney); Kenny (Parramatta, Sydney), Sterling (Parramatta, Sydney); Young (St George, Sydney), Krilich (Manly, Sydney) captain, Boyd (Manly, Sydney), Pearce (Balmain, Sydney), Reddy (St George, Sydney), Price (Parramatta, Sydney)

Substitutes: Ella (Parramatta, Sydney), Muggleton (Parramatta, Sydney) not used

Scorers: tries—Meninga, Boyd, Grothe, Price, Boustead, Kenny, Pearce, Reddy; goals—Meninga (8)

Referee: J. Rascagnères (France)

Attendance: 26,771

The next game should have been one of the Australians' more difficult encounters, but in fact it proved to be one of the easiest and brought them forty-four points, their biggest haul from any one game. Leigh, under the guidance of Alex Murphy, had won the league championship the previous season, securing the title excitingly by defeating Whitehaven in the last game of the season. But decline had set in quickly. Murphy had departed for Wigan, and his place had been taken by Colin Clarke, the former Wigan and Great Britain forward.

That night Leigh were made to look something less than champions. Indeed, they were more like small boys, armed with no more than their school blazers, desperately trying to extinguish grass fires. No sooner was one blaze quelled than another one, more serious, would flare in some other part of the field. Ray Tabern, the Leigh hooker, expressed this sense of hopelessness when he said afterwards: 'You could stop them on one side of the field, look up, and somebody would be racing in at 90 miles an hour on the other side.'

The Test side, with the exception of Meninga, whose place kicking possessed little of the accuracy of the previous Saturday, had been given a night off, but that was no comfort to Leigh. Confronted with such pace, handling skills, support play and emphatic finishing, they conceded twelve tries, three each to McCabe, Anderson, and Ribot, two to Muggleton and one to Lewis. McCabe's tries were the most significant, for one theory gathering some strength was that if the Australian Test pack could be strengthened at all, it might be by McCabe's replacement of Reddy in the second row.

Before the first Test Johnny Whiteley had pondered hopefully the significance of Australia's switching of Boyd from second row to front row... a

The Australian Tour

sign of weakness of the reserve forward strength, perhaps? Possibly, but the display that McCabe gave in this game showed the options that Stanton had available to him. McCabe did eventually play in a Test—the final one—but only because of injury to Ray Price. But what wouldn't Britain have given for a forward of his purposeful running and finishing abilities?

Leigh played well in the first half—well enough to restrict the Australians to a lead of 11–4 at the interval—but were overwhelmed in the second, as they conceded tries literally left, right and centre. In the end the victory was too emphatic to be of great significance, marvellously entertaining though the play had been.

If this match offered one outstanding lesson, it was the value of discipline. Trevor Court, the referee, penalized the Australians to an excessive degree, but the tourists never once resorted to dissent. Tempers did run high at one stage in the second half, and after a brawl in which practically every player was swinging a boot or a fist Rod Morris and Eddie Hunter (who had been on the field for only six minutes as a substitute for Eric Chisnall) were sent off. The Australians may have wondered with some justice, however, why when Mr Court was so keen to punish so many things, he ignored a dreadful foul by the Leigh scrum-half, Ken Green, on Steve Ella. When Ella went to field a high kick by John Woods, Green, chasing a kick that he had no hope of gathering, followed through with his boot, catching Ella a sickening blow on the head. These were, though, no more than brief, seedy sub-plots. The Australians had received a standing ovation from the Boothferry Park spectators. They now received another one from an appreciative Leigh crowd. (**Final score: Leigh 4   Australia 44.**)

A surprise awaited the Australians at their next venue, Bradford. The tourists won, and they had seven points to spare at the end from a 13–6 victory, but until the final eight minutes they were repeatedly repulsed by the fervour and speed of Bradford's tackling. Half-time tactical talks at Bradford are held on the pitch more often than not because the dressing-rooms are so far away and Stanton, talking ceaselessly to his men, actually looked concerned. With an interval score of only 7–4 in the Australians' favour, his expression was understandable.

Bradford, like Leigh, were recent champions who were experiencing hard times. Northern had won the league title in 1980 and 1981, but their dour, cramped style had not endeared them to the game at large. Directing the side's fortunes was Peter Fox, who had been coach to the Great Britain side in 1978 but had been overlooked in favour of Eric Ashton for the job in Australia the following year.

The Australian Tour

Fox was convinced that he had suffered an injustice. He was suspicious of the national press which, he believed, had played a sizeable part in his sacking four years before. Fox frequently invited criticism. He was outspoken to a degree that inevitably attracted resentment; his manner was often brusque. But if he had his detractors, he also had his admirers, and this game was a vindication of his beliefs and methods. In spite of his side's losing, the match must have given him some personal satisfaction.

Leigh and St Helens, Leeds and Great Britain had been unable to cope with the pressures to which they had been subjected. What Fox's side now illustrated was that through proper mental and physical preparation, unflagging physical effort and the pursuit of an understood policy the Australians could be restricted, if not beaten. Fox had a limited side at his disposal, but he got the best out of it. There never seemed any great likelihood that Northern, after some early flourishes from Alan Rathbone, would score a try, but their defences were so good, the barriers erected so swiftly and efficiently, that the breadth and sweep of the Australian attacks were repeatedly reduced to manageable proportions—although there was one astonishing run by Grothe that started close to the corner flag in his own half and almost finished in a try in the far right corner. The play of a side clearly inferior in so many departments but so utterly determined and repeatedly thwarting such talented opposition made riveting watching.

The tourists' concern had been shown early in the first half when only a wild lunge by Brentnall—it was one of the very few occasions on which he committed an ugly act—on Alan Rathbone prevented the loose forward from breaking free, and again Rathbone had to be obstructed to relieve another anxious moment. McCabe, scoring his fourth try in two games, took advantage of one of Northern's rare defensive lapses in the first half, but not until eight minutes from the end did the tourists penetrate Northern's line again, and then Brentnall and Miles made the game secure for the tourists.

Keith Mumby and Alan Rathbone played impressively enough in this match to earn places in the Great Britain side for the second Test. But of deeper significance was the lesson that the match taught Britain. It was evident enough after the first Test that Britain did not possess a side remotely good enough to defeat the Australians. But Bradford—against a powerful side, stronger than the one Wigan had held to four points—had given a timely and welcome reminder that the Australians could be made to work much harder for their victories, that although it might not be possible to beat the tourists, they were fallible. (**Final score: Bradford Northern 6   Australia 13.**)

The Australian Tour

The next match, against Cumbria at Carlisle, brought the Australians forty points for the third time. The Cumbrian side included Dean Bell, a 21-year-old New Zealander, who had brought quality to a struggling Carlisle side. One argument suggested that as Bell was a New Zealander, he should not have been chosen; a more persuasive argument was that he was playing for a Cumbrian club and was too good to leave out.

The problems of bringing together a Cumbrian side had been seen the previous week when the county's coach, Phil Kitchen, had had to cancel a training session at Workington because not enough players were able to travel there. This was frustrating for Kitchen, who had already voiced his disappointment at having been given so little time in which to prepare his side. A local newspaper recalled Kitchen's achievement in guiding the Cumbrian side of two years before to a worthy win over the New Zealanders but also, with a sense of balance, reminded Cumbrians of the thrashings that the side had received from previous Australian tourists in 1973 and 1978.

Great Britain's side, extensively reconstructed for the second Test, had been announced the previous day, and there were no Cumbrians in it. Had it been delayed for a couple of days, the selectors might have discussed at least the credentials of David Cairns and Derek Hadley, two players of talent who both suffered from the disadvantage of playing with an unfashionable club, Barrow. Both contributed generously to a Cumbrian performance that was thoroughly commendable but also hopelessly inadequate.

As in so many of their matches up to this point, at half-time the Australians allowed their opponents to believe that they still had a match on their hands. They led 16–2, a convincing enough score but not sufficient to demoralize the Cumbrians. But their abundant skills, allied to unrivalled fitness, so often left sides panting in pursuit in the second half. Cumbria were no exception. For sixteen minutes of the first half they played with characteristic determination but had conceded tries to McKinnon, Sterling and Ribot (two) by the interval. Five tries after half-time for Rogers, Ella, Boustead, Meninga—this after a 60-yard run—and Pearce (after an even longer dash) confirmed the remorselessly widening gap between the sides.

Late in the game the Cumbrians rediscovered the fervour that had characterized their play for the first quarter-hour, and expectation among the crowd of 5,750 began to mount as the possibility of a home try increased. The Australians had not given away a try in three previous games and in nine matches had conceded only four altogether. They were becoming collectors' items, and judging by his efforts in the late stages of this game, Dean Bell desperately wanted one. He jinked, burrowed and wriggled in an attempt to find a way through from a number of plays close to the Australian line, but without success. The Australians, who appreciated the rarity value of tries just as much as Bell, obviously begrudged giving one away. (**Final score: Cumbria 2   Australia 41.**)

They did concede one in their following match, against Fulham, the second-division London club then in their third season of existence. It was a pity that it was such a miserable day, for Fulham officials had hoped that the Australians, now belatedly receiving the nationwide recognition that their skills had earned, would give Fulham a record attendance. But a cold, wet, windy day kept the crowd down to 10,430—good but slightly disappointing.

Somehow the game never quite captured the imagination in the way that others of the tourists' games had done. A greasy ball and slippery conditions underfoot presented new problems for the Australians, and in the first half alone they probably dropped the ball more times since their ghastly first half at Barrow. It was in keeping with their attitude, though, that they should come to terms with their problems, if not with their place kicking.

Fulham, like Bradford the week before, had obviously been well prepared for the game by their player-coach, Reggie Bowden, who had inspired Widnes to many a trophy before joining Fulham. They tackled with unwavering dedication in the first half, won possession often through John Dalgreen's hooking skills and were only six points in arrears at the interval. They had suffered the misfortune, though, of losing their loose forward, Joe Doherty, with a leg wound that required forty stitches.

Murray and Ella scored tries in the first half and McCave, Muggleton, McKinnon and Ribot in the second, when Fulham's energy began to drain away. In the sixty-fourth minute, however, arrived the moment for which English audiences had waited for more than four and a half games: a try. It was scored by Hussein M'Barki, the former Moroccan Rugby Union captain, who had brought forceful running and many moments of skill to the Fulham left wing since his signing from the French Rugby Union club Cahors the previous season.

The try was well conceived and executed but it could almost certainly have been prevented. Steve Diamond's long, low, diagonal kick set M'Barki running for the line. Ella, moving to his right to counter the danger, could probably have kicked the ball dead but chose to try to drop on it, which in the slippery conditions proved to be a little too adventurous. He failed; M'Barki made the touchdown and was greeted as if he had just settled a cup final. (**Final score: Fulham 5   Australia 22.**)

The Australian Tour

Only one match now remained before the second Test at Wigan the following week. The Australians were convinced that the match, against Hull at the Boulevard, would be their most taxing of all, and they were right. Whereas Bradford had organized an admirable defensive blockade, Hull now added another dimension, putting the tourists under sustained pressure for the first time.

Important matches at the Boulevard are occasions to be savoured. A crowd of 16,049, approaching capacity and the largest outside of the Tests, was given a display by Hull that Great Britain never matched. Australia paid Arthur Bunting the compliment of playing their strongest side. There was the risk of injury, of course, but the Australians accepted that. The ambition to become the first side to go undefeated through a full tour was now increasingly important to the Australians, and Hull—even more than Great Britain seemed the side capable of depriving them of that objective.

Hull lost, but in doing so gave a marvellous performance. The Great Britain players, if only they had been there to watch it, might have derived some encouragement from the contest and garnered some ideas, but they were too preoccupied with their preparations for the second Test. It seemed an opportunity wasted although they did attempt to catch up later in the week by studying the game on video.

Hull's pack lacked three established and experienced members in Steve Norton, Trevor Skerrett and Charlie Stone, but their absences did not impair Hull's efficiency. Mick Crane had an outstanding game at loose forward, running selflessly and intelligently, passing creatively and frequently trying to disrupt the Australians' defensive formation by following up a series of accurately placed grub kicks. These tactics did not always succeed, but they were a sign that Hull had given some thought to the game and made a welcome change from the all too familiar head-down one-man charges so beloved of British forwards.

Elsewhere in the pack Paul Rose and Lee Crooks were unflagging, while Keith Bridges showed that he had lost few of his hooking skills, out-heeling Max Krilich 12–5. At open-side prop the veteran Mick Harrison was playing his first game for almost a year, while in the second row Hull had little alternative but to use the inexperienced colt, Wayne Proctor.

There was nothing makeshift about the Hull pack that night, however. Encouraged by an enthusiastic and vociferous crowd, the Hull forwards ran and tackled like fanatics. Tony Dean and Dave Topliss were energetic and inventive half-backs, while Gary Kemble repeatedly made himself available from full-back, joining his attack with well-timed, long striding runs. In the centre Steve Evans showed a determination not always apparent in his play;

The Australian Tour

James Leuluai, one of three enterprising New Zealand signings made by Hull the previous season—Dane O'Hara and, of course, Kemble were the others—made a number of penetrating runs but suffered a broken jaw early in the second half; and O'Hara and Prendiville on the wings completed a Hull side with which it was difficult to find much fault.

At the end of a first half of punishing effort Hull led 7–0, and the chances that the Australians might lose for the first time were far from outrageous. Hull had enjoyed an extraordinary piece of luck early in the game, when Sterling had kicked through low with, it seemed, mathematical precision. Price ought to have scored, but as he stooped to gather the ball, it struck the base of a post and rebounded to a grateful Evans. Such an escape did no harm to Hull's confidence, and six minutes before half-time Topliss scored the try that Hull's efforts had merited.

An excellent try it was too, very much Topliss's own work, with the stand-off chipping the ball over the heads of three Australian defenders, following up his kick with single-minded devotion and plunging on the ball at the back of the posts. Crooks had earlier landed a penalty and took full advantage of the simple task of extending Hull's lead.

The pertinent question now was whether Hull could maintain their supremacy. They tried hard to do so but failed to sustain their efforts of the first half. There were, nevertheless, only sixteen minutes remaining when Australia edged ahead for the first time. Their first try, from the alert Boustead, was created by one of those bewildering changes of direction at which Sterling was so adept. Then Meninga embarked on a blistering run up the wing, was tackled low and hard by Kemble but managed to slip out the ball—and support, inevitably, was waiting. Grothe collected the pass and ran strongly to the line.

Hull were now clinging to a lead of only one point, and it was not enough; the game was slipping tantalizingly from their grasp. A harsh penalty hurried the process, Meninga's kick striking the post and dropping over the crossbar. Hull were now in arrears. They had few reserves of energy to call upon, and five minutes from time Grothe's second try, and the goal for it by Meninga, gave Australia a lead of six points. That was sufficient for their purposes, but they would not have wanted it any closer which it might have been had not Hull, crucially, had a 'try' by O'Hara disallowed early in the second half. **(Final score: Hull 7   Australia 13.)**

Second Test
Central Park, Wigan, 20 November
Great Britain 6   Australia 27

The agitated state in which British Rugby League had been left by the Australians' victory in the first Test was apparent in the Great Britain side selected for the second Test at Central Park, Wigan. Ten changes were felt necessary, and another was forced upon the selectors when David Watkinson, the Hull Kingston Rovers hooker who had replaced David Ward, was injured in a game against Widnes the previous Sunday and had to withdraw. This brought in John Dalgreen, from the second-division club Fulham, a player who, with a nice sense of timing, had given a typically hard-working display for his side against the Australians at Craven Cottage seven days earlier.

Great Britain's side for the first Test had been criticized for relying too heavily on experienced players, some of whom, unarguably, had enjoyed their best days. Many followers of the game were disappointed that more young players had not been given their opportunity. That opportunity was now granted, although ten changes inevitably suggested that the selectors had reached a state of desperation. As Trevor Watson observed in the *Yorkshire Evening Post*: 'The axe appears to have been not so much swung as thrown.'

One theory suggested that the selectors would have done much better to choose a predominantly young side for the first Test. If that side had taken a thrashing, the selectors could then have opted for players of experience. As it was, young players were drafted in now, with the Australians already leading 1–0 in the series and with their confidence running high. It was expecting too much perhaps that inexperienced players such as David Stephenson, Henderson Gill and Bob Eccles should attempt to make good the blunders of the first Test. There was, nevertheless, greater sympathy for this team than for the first; an effort had been made, it seemed, to inject the side with some youth while at the same time retaining a liberal amount of experience.

The discarding of George Fairbairn was inevitable after his wretched performance at Boothferry Park, and Keith Mumby, the Bradford full-back, was introduced in his place. Henderson Gill, the black Wigan left-winger, was recalled. He had shown considerable promise (in spite of supposed defensive deficiencies) in two full internationals against France the previous season but had fallen from favour after absenting himself from summer training with the Great Britain squad. He was one of the few players to have scored a try against

4. Ray Price was widely admired by the rest of his colleagues. In addition to his creative skills, he possessed a hardness and determination that few British forwards could match. Having broken mercilessly through this tackle by Grayshon in the first Test, Price has the try line firmly in his sights. 'How could you play badly with men like him around you?' asked Wayne Pearce.

the tourists, and he was now brought back as Des Drummond's opposite winger.
    Mike Smith and David Stephenson replaced Dyl and Hughes in the centre, and there was a new half-back pairing of John Holmes and Ken Kelly. Holmes was 30 and had not played for Great Britain for three years; he had been, in his day, a gifted stand-off, an intelligent and classical passer of the ball. It was now

hoped that his passing abilities and his keen sense of timing would bring some much needed breadth to the British attack.

The chief doubt about him was whether his appetite for football at this rarified level still remained. Holmes himself had almost certainly considered his Great Britain career to have finished. Ken Kelly, his half-back partner, might also have been a little surprised to find his international days revived, even though he was substitute in the first Test. He had played his first Great Britain international a year after Holmes, in 1972, and his last a year later than Holmes in 1980.

Of the forwards only Skerrett and Grayshon remained from Hull. Norton and Gorley, Ward and Crooks had gone, to be replaced by David Heron and Bob Eccles, John Dalgreen (after Watkinson had been excluded because of injury) and, surprisingly, Chris Burton, the Hull KR second-row forward. Burton's selection was completely unexpected and inevitably led to some whispered accusations of bias towards Hull KR, where Burton was not always assured of a first-team place.

There was, of course, considerable debate and speculation about this revamped side, all of which was in stark contrast to the peace of the Australian camp. They had quietly, no doubt contentedly, announced that they would be fielding the same side that had played in the first Test, the only changes being the substitutes, Lewis and Brown replacing Ella and Muggleton.

History offered Britain some hope. In 1963 they had suffered their heaviest defeat ever against Australia, losing 12–50 at Swinton. They had been reduced to eleven men in that game, but even before that the Australians had been by far the superior side. Changes were made—ten of them—for the next Test at Leeds, and Great Britain won 16–5. But Johnny Whiteley did not think it necessary to delve nineteen years into the past to find some encouragement. He was looking back no farther than a fortnight, to the Australians' match with Bradford. 'The Australians are a good side,' he said, 'but, as we saw at Bradford, they are not so happy when the pressure is put on them. Two or three of their players are not all they have been cracked up to be.' Soon after making that statement he was left to contemplate another ruthless Australian victory.

Not the least remarkable aspect of Australia's win (27–6) was that it was achieved from the thirty-fifth minute with only twelve men. One of the most vulnerable men in the Australian side—or, more accurately, the man with the most inflammatory temper—was Les Boyd, a formidably powerful player with an unusually low boiling point. One of the many commendable qualities exhibited by the Australians was their discipline. Boyd was one of the exceptions. If there were signs of trouble, Boyd could not resist becoming involved. If there was no trouble, Boyd would frequently make it. Had the Australians not been such an excellent team, Boyd's excesses could have been a

The Australian Tour

serious flaw. In the event they failed to matter—apart from tarnishing the tourists' image slightly. Boyd's offence on this occasion warranted dismissal, and Julien Rascagnères, who was to control all three Tests, did not have to think twice about sending him off.

Boyd lashed out at Dalgreen with his boot—gratuitously, it seemed—while the hooker lay on the ground. In fact, the television replays showed that Dalgreen had first stabbed a boot at Boyd, which to the naked eye, and from a press box at the back of the stand, had not been immediately apparent. The replay also showed that Boyd's kick was less brutal than it had at first appeared, Boyd clearly checking the power of the kick before he made contact. But it was a hard enough kick, nevertheless, and a foolish act of violence—and Boyd departed.

Yet Australia without Boyd were even better than they had been with him. His departure seemed to induce a hardening of concentration, if that were possible. There was simply no impairment of the tourists' defensive efficiency and, as they showed as the game wore on, no restriction on their attacking capabilities either. Nor was the loss of Boyd their only problem. Eric Grothe injured a knee in the first half and failed to appear after the interval; Meninga moved from the centre to the left wing, with Lewis replacing him in the centre.

Australia's victory was a triumph for, above all, selfless, ceaseless support play, the like of which British rugby had not seen for a long time. Afterwards Frank Stanton was probably close to identifying the source of his side's success when he said: 'The way the players discipline themselves to play for each other is probably their greatest quality of all.' That was it. The Australians possessed brilliant individualists, but no exhibitionists.

Keith Mumby gave a fine display on his first appearance for Great Britain. His anxiety in dealing with high kicks on the tour of Australia of 1979 had hindered his international progress. But the tourists, who had been expected to use the tactic frequently, gradually abandoned it as the tour progressed, probably because they found little need for it. But in any case Mumby looked as if he could have dealt with anything that day, including balls dropping from the heavens. His defence was flawless. He did not miss a tackle and a number of his efforts almost certainly prevented tries. He also kicked three penalties from three attempts, a particularly commendable effort since he was no longer place kicking regularly for his club.

Mumby was a clear British success. There were not many others. Drummond and Gill on the wings occasionally hinted at what they might have achieved if only they had received a semblance of service. Three of the younger players, Smith and Stephenson, the centres, and David Heron, the loose forward, found it as much as they could do to survive; Burton was floundering in depths obviously beyond his experience. Dalgreen let no one down, but the pack as a whole was depressingly limited. Skerrett, as usual, had a lot of courage and effort to offer but little imagination, and his dreary one-man barges down the middle appeared embarrassingly outdated by comparison with the fluency and mobility of the Australian forwards.

Ken Kelly emerged with more credit than most, especially after suffering a jarring crash tackle from Brett Kenny in the first half. He could remember little about the game afterwards, so shaken had he been, but although his defence could be faulted, on attack he looked to be one of few British players capable of making some advance. Holmes's recall was not entirely a failure, but nor was it particularly auspicious. Hopes that the British players would run wide failed to materialize; little was created from Holmes's efforts, and the Leeds stand-off was unable to instigate any moves to surprise the Australians. Holmes was substituted by John Woods just after the hour but seemed reluctant to leave the field. Perhaps it crossed his mind that this could well be his final appearance for Great Britain.

Much the most disturbing aspect of Britain's play, though, was the predictability of the forwards. Nothing seemed to have been learned from the first Test. It was obvious then, and indeed during most of the tour, that athletes as hardened and as fit as the Australians, tacklers as fast and as accomplished, could have coped indefinitely with the one-man barges so slavishly pursued by the British forwards. But they persisted in their dull-witted ways, going nowhere. Sisyphus eternally pushing his boulder to the summit of Hades hill would know how it felt.

To appraise the Australians one by one would simply be to recite a litany of virtues. To put any department of the side under scrutiny was to find excellence. Ray Price was given the man-of-the-match award, but it might have gone to anyone, and such awards tend to be something of a nonsense in a team game, especially when the teamwork is of this standard.

Krilich was beaten 7–3 at the scrums, but the penalty count was 17–13 in Australia's favour. The truth was that if Krilich had never won another scrum on tour, the results would not have altered materially. Krilich and his men had learned to live without this source of supply; and the Australian captain more than compensated for any scrummaging deficiencies with his work in the loose, his speed and inventiveness at the play-the-balls and his leadership. He was an inspiring captain.

And what a talented pack he had at his command. English spectators could do no more than watch with a deep envy not only the power but also the ball-handling skills of Craig Young. The name of Brian McTigue must have passed through many a Wiganer's mind as Young repeatedly blasted holes in the British defences and then took advantage of those gaps by slipping out balls of timing and subtlety. Was Young not the type of forward Britain once possessed

5. Eric Grothe was capable of covering enormous distances at times. In the second Test at Wigan he appeared on the right wing as acting half-back. Seconds later he turned up on the left wing and provided the pass for Sterling to score a try. Grothe also scored a try in the second Test but injured a knee in doing so and missed the final Test a week later.

in abundance? Such a question must have been asked many times that day.

Young was outstanding, but so too was Price, tireless, sinewy, determined, the very embodiment of lean strength; and Pearce, so strong-running that he would burst powerfully through tackles; and Sterling, a man of astounding energy and creativity; and Meninga, collecting another eleven points to go with his nineteen of the first Test and reaching 100 points for the tour.

The Australian Tour

In the second half came a moment to cherish, when the Wigan spectators responded to a show of Australian virtuosity with the sort of spontaneous and deafening applause that Sydneyites might have given to Joan Sutherland singing at the Opera House. Meninga started it when he collected a British kick deep in his own half and then broke forward. He put Kenny in possession, and the stand-off was tackled. Then, from Krilich at acting half-back, the ball looped from Lewis to Sterling to Rogers to Boustead to Sterling to Reddy to Pearce to Lewis to Kenny to Lewis to Price. At that point a British tackle brought down the curtain on this particular act. But there was not a spectator who had wanted to see it end. There was no try to celebrate at the end of it, but rarely in sport can a team have won such ungrudging admiration from their opponents' supporters as Australia received then.

Perhaps this was a slight indulgence, but Australia could afford it because by then the match had been won emphatically. Victory was theirs by half-time, and even against twelve men there was not the slightest chance of Britain depriving the Australians of it. In the second half it was difficult to remember Great Britain advancing once into the Australian '25'. Thirteen men against twelve should prove an unequal contest, but on the evidence of this display the Australians would have had to be reduced to ten men before any kind of equality was established.

The tourists led 15–6 at half-time, with Price, Sterling and Grothe scoring tries. The try by Price was the product both of opportunism by the loose forward, who collected the ball from acting half-back and dived over, and of intense Australian pressure close to the British line. Those by Sterling and Grothe were the results of the sort of sweeping movements that the spectators had come to expect and to admire. Sterling's try gave an illuminating insight into Australian versatility, for it began on the right with Grothe, their left-winger, gathering the ball from acting half-back. The move was worked back across the field, down the left wing and finished with Grothe giving the final pass to Sterling.

Grothe injured a knee in scoring his try in the twenty-sixth minute, and that was the end of his contribution to the British section of the tour. It was a fitting end, if painful, another excellent try from a player whose powerful running and sense of opportunism had made him, at times, the most exciting player in the side. It was a try which demonstrated not only Grothe's pace but also his strength, for on his run to the line he knocked Bob Eccles, the tall, strong British second-row forward, off his feet, and he had Ken Kelly clinging to him uselessly when he went over.

There were two more tries in the second half, one from Meninga and one from Rogers, who was unfortunate to have another one disallowed. He was adjudged off-side when he ran on to Sterling's measured, angled kick, but M.

The Australian Tour

Rascagnères, an alert referee, was almost certainly wrong on this occasion. Meninga's try was simple enough but was made possible by an astonishing pass from Lewis, who was not far from the centre of the pitch when he threw out a precise, beautifully weighted spun pass to the left wing. It took Drummond completely by surprise, caught him out of position and made Meninga's task that much simpler. Nine minutes from the end Rogers punished some weak covering by Kelly, and the Ashes were once more safe in Australia's possession.

Great Britain: Mumby (Bradford Northern); Drummond (Leigh), Smith (Hull KR), Stephenson (Wigan), Gill (Wigan); Holmes (Leeds), Ken Kelly (Warrington); Grayshon (Bradford Northern) captain, Dalgreen (Fulham), Skerrett (Hull), Eccles (Warrington), Burton (Hull KR), David Heron (Leeds)

Substitutes: Woods (Leigh) for Holmes after 61 minutes, Rathbone (Bradford Northern) for Burton after 74 minutes

Scorer: goals—Mumby (3)

Australia: Brentnall (Canterbury-Bankstown, Sydney); Boustead (Eastern Suburbs, Sydney), Meninga (Southern Suburbs, Brisbane), Rogers (St George, Sydney), Grothe (Parramatta, Sydney); Kenny (Parramatta, Sydney), Sterling (Parramatta, Sydney); Young (St George, Sydney), Krilich (Manly, Sydney) captain, Boyd (Manly, Sydney), Pearce (Balmain, Sydney), Reddy (St George, Sydney), Price (Parramatta, Sydney)

Substitutes: Lewis (Fortitude Valley, Brisbane) for Grothe at half time, Brown (Manly, Sydney) for Reddy after 69 minutes

Scorers: tries—Price, Sterling, Grothe, Meninga, Rogers; goals—Meninga (6)

Referee: J. Rascagnères (France)

Attendance: 23,216

Only one club game now remained, against Widnes, and the chance that the Australians would win all their fifteen games was now probable rather than possible. Widnes, nevertheless, represented a difficult obstacle. They were no longer the side that had moved so powerfully and successfully through the 1970s; they were certainly not as good as the 1978 team that had been one of only two clubs to beat the Kangaroos that season. Their vulnerability had been shown the previous Sunday when they had been beaten in a league game

The Australian Tour

against Halifax, who were then second from the bottom of the table; but they remained strong opposition.

Perhaps the most notable aspect of the game was that for some ten minutes after the interval the Australians were unable to escape from their own half. Widnes were not at full strength, but they played with great determination and spirit and, unlike Great Britain, varied their tactics in an attempt to disrupt the Australians. Those tactics consisted chiefly of a variety of kicks from Andrew Gregory, some high, some low and short, and they caused the tourists problems, although Ella, playing at full-back, caught two high kicks with cool assurance.

There was never much doubt, however, that the Australians would win. On a drenching night, handling mistakes were inevitable, and the Australians made their share, but they also produced some flowing moves and a lot of forthright rugby. Mortimer, who had arrived in England as first-choice scrum-half, had a fine game, and his alertness at play-the-balls close to the Widnes line twice brought him tries. It was an adventurous pass from the scrum-half too that enabled Ribot to score late in the game.

McCabe again showed the determination of his finishing (a determination that was equalled by the local junior band, which steadfastly refused to leave the pitch after half-time until it had completed all its routines and numbers), and Rogers, who reserved his best moments for the Tests, fashioned an individualistic try seven minutes from time. There were, though, a number of disappointments for the tourists. Meninga's place kicking, which throughout the tour tended to veer between extremes, was poor, and the centre finished the match limping. Young had to retire with a shoulder injury, and his replacement, John Muggleton, was sent off after punching David Hulme to the ground in an off-the-ball incident.

The Australians' objective was achieved easily enough, nevertheless. Mick Burke, who had played with such promise at full-back for Great Britain in games against France the previous season, did no harm to his reputation with a sound defensive display, some enterprising forays forward and three goals. But at half-time the Kangaroos were on course for their fourteenth win when they led 11–4. An excess of bad temper threatened to ruin what was a vigorously contested game, but after Muggleton's dismissal the tourists settled and played some of their best rugby. **(Final score: Widnes 6   Australia 19.)**

The Australian Tour

Third Test
Headingley, Leeds, 28 November
Great Britain 8   Australia 32

The week of the third and last Test at Headingley, Leeds, must have been as unfortunate as any in Britain's Rugby League experience; and for the selectors it was an acute embarrassment. They had seemed like men in despair when they had announced their side on the Monday, and the events of the following days did nothing to dispel this unfortunate impression. Injuries to Mumby and Gill scarcely made a thankless job any easier, but the eight men on the selection committee will break into cold sweats when they look back at this ghastly week.

Six more changes were made to the side beaten in the second Test, with Mumby, of necessity, being replaced by Fairbairn. David Topliss became the third stand-off (and also the third captain) in three games; Peter Smith, of Featherstone Rovers, was brought into the second row in place of Burton; Mike O'Neill, a young Widnes forward, replaced the injured Grayshon; and Brian Noble, the Bradford hooker, took the place of the unfortunate Dalgreen, dropped for no satisfactory reason. Lee Crooks, to the exclusion of Bob Eccles, was recalled to the re-formed second row, and Mick Crane took the place of David Heron at loose forward.

After announcing the side, the selectors discovered that Topliss had departed for a mid-winter holiday in Majorca. Cynically, it was suggested that that was as good a place as any to be when opponents to face Australia were being sought, but although contact was quickly made with Topliss, who as quickly made arrangements to return home, the episode did not reflect well on him, or on the selectors—or, for that matter, on a squad system that could allow one of its players to take a holiday at such a time. In the meantime the selectors had made another blunder by announcing that the captaincy would be transferred to Ken Kelly. But when Topliss returned home they seemed so grateful to see him that they gave him back the captaincy. Kelly, not surprisingly, was bitterly disappointed.

The following day Gill withdrew from the side because of a damaged shoulder, and Kelly also announced that he was not available. The Warrington scrum-half claimed that he was still suffering from concussion, the after-effects of his collision with Kenny the previous Saturday. That had certainly been a violent encounter, one which had badly shaken Kelly, but inevitably it was suggested that Kelly's disenchantment with the treatment he had received from the selectors over the captaincy had played a part in his withdrawal. Kelly's place went to Andrew Gregory who, many critics felt, should have been in the side in the first place, while Evans was restored to the left-wing position that he had occupied anonymously in the first Test.

Neil Courtney, the Warrington prop, was the next player to have his loyalty tested. He was now drafted into the team in place of the ailing Trevor Skerrett who, it was decided, required a cartilage operation. Courtney was gratified to be given this unexpected international opportunity and dutifully promised that he would give of his best. His Warrington coach, Kevin Ashcroft, also expressed his pleasure at seeing Courtney in the side and said that he would not let anyone down. On Friday evening, by which time no more twists to a dismal week seemed possible, it was decided that Paul Rose would play at blind-side prop, with O'Neill switching to field-side. The hapless Courtney now found himself relegated to substitute.

Australia had had their problems, too, though nothing to compare with this. They were without Ray Price, who had broken a hand early in the second Test, Craig Young, who had injured his shoulder, and Eric Grothe, who had damaged a knee. There was also the possibility that Les Boyd, who was appearing before the Disciplinary Committee for the second time on tour, might be excluded. However, a reciprocal arrangement had existed for some time between the countries whereby players sent off on tour would not be suspended. This spirit prevailed, although Boyd was fined £500. It was felt that he had suffered some provocation when sent off at Wigan.

Astonishingly, after all the fumblings and the embarrassments, Great Britain gave by far their most encouraging display of the series. They lost heavily enough (8–32), but 18 of Australia's points came in the final ten minutes, and before that late flood Britain fought with a determination not often apparent in the first two Tests. They played some good rugby at times. They even scored a try, their first in four Tests against Australia, and although the game ended with spectators once again marvelling at Australian expertise, there was at least a feeling that Britain's future prospects were not perhaps as depressing as they had once seemed. As Frank Stanton remarked afterwards: 'That was a true Test.'

Although Britain's performance fell some distance short of greatness, it was, until the subsidence of the last ten minutes, sometimes skilful, always wholehearted. Collectively, the side discovered for the first time a sense of purpose and some pride; individually, there were a number of worthwhile contributions. Unlike the first two Tests, it was not easy this time to compile a list of obvious failures.

Not the least of the British successes was Fairbairn. His limitations had been

6. One of Peter Sterling's many assets was his ability to switch the point of attack, quickly and frequently, to the consternation of the opposition. In the third Test at Leeds, Mike O'Neill optimistically attempts to halt the scrum-half, but Sterling is already contemplating his next attacking option.

cruelly exposed in the first Test, and he must have known that he would be dropped for the second Test. Recalled in place of the unlucky Mumby, Fairbairn always had been a transparently honest player. Now, clearly under considerable personal pressure, he displayed a wealth of physical and moral courage, and in emerging so creditably from this encounter he went far to restoring a diminished reputation.

Both British centres played with promise—and with much more maturity than in the previous week at Wigan. Mike Smith at last justified some of the

The Australian Tour

expansive claims made for him in Hull quarters, while David Stephenson discovered a much needed toughness to go with his other undoubted, though often flimsy, skills. Evans was sometimes suspect on defence, but he took his try well, the result of a move with which the Australians would have been pleased.

Topliss could scarcely be considered a long-term investment for Britain, but he brought a lot of energy and determination to stand-off. It would be charitable perhaps to say that it was an excess of enthusiasm—no great fault—which caused Topliss twice to concede valuable ground by querying the referee's decisions; and at scrum-half Gregory played with unfailing enthusiasm. He was constructive and maintained his discipline, something he does not always find easy to do. He did enough to make many people wonder why, in these lean times, such an obviously gifted player had been overlooked.

Brian Noble was another unqualified success. It would have been difficult to have found anyone who could have matched Krilich's form on this tour, and Noble inevitably suffered by comparison with the Australian captain. He had nothing like Krilich's mobility in the loose or his creative powers, but he did get the better of the scrums—there were only seven of which Noble won five—and he did compare with Krilich for energy. Here was a young man grasping his first, unexpected, opportunity gratefully, almost greedily. To English eyes it was a fine sight.

The young Widnes prop, Mike O'Neill, had a less distinguished first appearance for Great Britain, although he had his moments; but Peter Smith, in his unobtrusive, honest but vigorous fashion, poured in a lot of effort. Crane had played outstandingly for Hull against the Australians, and he now recaptured a sizeable amount of the form of that game. He was tireless and experimental—a refreshing contrast to much of the predictable forward play seen in the series. With his socks rolled down to his ankles, he had an impish, rascally air, a welcome ingredient for a British side that had known nothing other than relentless, grim-faced toil.

Over the final ten minutes the Australians produced a memorable spell of rugby and a breathless surge of scoring, in which thirteen points were accumulated without Britain touching the ball, other than to restart the game. There were images to treasure from that final phase—of Lewis throwing out passes of incredible length; of the guts and power of Meninga; of the searing speed and penetration of Kenny, finding sublime form in the last match of the tour; of the remarkable power of Pearce; and, yet again, of the depths of Sterling's energy.

Before those final riches, though, a crowd of 17,300 saw a genuine contest. In the first fifteen minutes Britain displayed more ideas and cohesion than in the previous two Tests. It would be untrue to say that Australia looked

The Australian Tour

discomposed. They were much too well-disciplined and well-organized for that, but at the last they had been given something to think about.

The first half was brought to a close by a brawl in which there were few bystanders. Boyd began the trouble by crash-tackling Topliss, and almost immediately fists and boots were swinging. As tempers subsided and bodies became disentangled, it was possible to contemplate a remarkable interval score of 6–4 to Australia, with Meninga kicking three penalty goals to two by Crooks. When Crooks, with a measured and coolly taken dropped goal, reduced the lead to a single point soon after the interval, the expectations and excitement of the crowd began to rise.

Then, in the fiftieth and fifty-third minutes, Australia scored tries, Meninga added the goal points for one of them and swiftly the uncomfortable lead of one point had been extended to the reassuring one of nine points. Ribot was perhaps the only Australian with whom it was possible to find serious fault. Stanton must have thought so too, for Ribot was replaced four minutes after scoring his try; but at least before departing he had the satisfaction of putting Australia on course for their fifteenth successive win.

Missed tackles had cost Britain dearly all the way through this series, and when Pearce broke through Evans allowed him to escape. Alex Murphy, helping with the televised commentary of the match, had made the point at the interval that Pearce had been running into the wrong places in the first half. He could not be accused of any such misdirection in the second half, throughout which the 21-year-old, playing at loose forward in place of Price, was startlingly effective. After bursting past Evans he fed Reddy, who in turn supplied Ribot, who went over in the left corner.

Pearce was again heavily involved in the second try scored, to considerable Australian jubilation, by Krilich, showing speed over 30 yards that would not have disgraced a centre. Pearce this time burst through the joint tackle of Crooks and O'Neill. Kenny took his pass and whipped the ball inside short to Krilich, now generating full power through the middle. The line was some distance away, but Krilich was not to be denied this final opportunity of a try. The cover was closing in on him fast by the time he arrived at the posts, but he had the legs and the pace to secure his objective.

Boyd and Crane had spent ten minutes in the sin bin for the parts they had played in the brawl of the first half and now Britain lost Crooks for good, sent off for his unnecessary involvement in a skirmish following the Australians' second try. This was a foolish display of temper by Crooks, who had played so well up to this point. It meant that a side that was already beginning to find it difficult to confine the Australians now had to do so a man short.

The anticipated British collapse was a long time materializing, however. In fact, the next phase of the game, during which Brentnall and Rose also spent

The Australian Tour

ten minutes in the sin bin, was by far Britain's best of the series. They put Australia under real pressure, were twice held just short of the line to the right of the posts and then worked a move which ended in a try in the left corner.

Crane played a major part in it. He was deeply involved in a move which was brought to a halt near the right-corner flag. The ball was then worked left, and Crane came into the move with telling effect, throwing a superb pass to Stephenson, who was given some room in which to work. He in turn gave a fine pass to his left wing, Evans, who still had a considerable amount of work to do before touching down. But Kenny, who had taken the place of the temporarily absent Brentnall at full-back, was forced back by Evans's momentum and was unable to prevent the Hull player from touching down. It was the first time in four Tests that Britain had had the satisfaction of scoring a try.

That, however, represented the zenith of Britain's achievements. Five minutes later, after a move of blistering pace down the right wing, Kenny gave a stunning reverse pass to Boustead, who raced over. Four minutes later Boustead was the supplier, and this time Rogers went in vigorously.

The next try is worthy of a detailed description. It was arguably the best of the series and possibly of the tour. It showed Australian rugby at its finest, and contained many of the qualities that had so impressed an appreciative British public. When Britain kicked off after Rogers's try, Sterling caught the ball, moved forward and was tackled. Brown (who had come on for Boyd four minutes earlier) took the ball at acting half-back and was tackled. Now Krilich moved to dummy half, and a memorable manoeuvre began to gather momentum. Krilich fed Sterling, who then plied Lewis, whose incredibly long pass inside sent Kenny on a blistering run of 20 yards. Meninga came into the move. Drummond tried to tackle him twice and bounced off him both times, as though he were trying to run through an oak door; and when Rose tried to halt the centre he was knocked clean off his feet as Meninga simply turned his shoulder to meet the charge.

McCabe now appeared for the first time and, when he was tackled, Meninga, at acting half-back, brought Lewis into play. Again Lewis found Kenny with another astonishingly long pass. The ball came inside short, and a glorious move ended with Pearce racing round Smith and sprinting away to score beneath the posts. There was still time, after an opening engineered by Lewis, for Kenny to race down the centre, subtly switching direction as he went, to score the final try of the game ... and of an unforgettable campaign.

Great Britain: Fairbairn (Hull KR); Drummond (Leigh), Mike Smith (Hull KR), Stephenson (Wigan), Evans (Hull); Topliss (Hull) captain, Gregory (Widnes); Mike O'Neill (Widnes), Noble (Bradford Northern), Rose (Hull), Peter Smith (Featherstone Rovers), Crooks (Hull), Crane (Hull)

Substitutes: Courtney (Warrington) for O'Neill after 70 minutes, Woods (Leigh) not used

Scorers: try—Evans; goals—Crooks (2); drop goal—Crooks

Australia: Brentnall (Canterbury-Bankstown, Sydney); Boustead (Eastern Suburbs, Sydney), Meninga (Southern Suburbs, Brisbane), Rogers (St George, Sydney), Ribot (Manly, Sydney); Kenny (Parramatta, Sydney), Sterling (Parramatta, Sydney); Boyd (Manly, Sydney), Krilich (Manly, Sydney) captain, Morris (Wynnum-Manly, Brisbane), McCabe (Manly, Sydney), Reddy (St George, Sydney), Pearce (Balmain, Sydney)

Substitutes: Lewis (Fortitude Valley, Brisbane) for Ribot after 54 minutes, Brown (Manly, Sydney) for Boyd after 70 minutes

Scorers: tries—Ribot, Krilich, Boustead, Rogers, Pearce, Kenny; goals—Meninga (7)

Referee: J. Rascagnères (France)

Attendance: 17,318

THE AUSTRALIANS IN FRANCE

There never seemed any great danger that the Australians would not emulate in France what they had achieved in Britain and win all their games. Their biggest concern was history. In 1978, after a successful tour of Britain, Australia went to France and lost both Tests, much to Stanton's chagrin. He had obviously brooded on those games in the meantime, and he spoke of them as if some outrage had been perpetrated. 'There is well documented evidence to tell you what happened,' he said. 'We will not be caught out a second time.' And, of course, he was right.

What had happened, in fact, was that France won both games by narrow margins, the first 13–10 at Carcassonne, after Michel Naudo had scored what almost certainly was an illegal try—the evidence suggests that he touched down well over the dead-ball line—and 11–10 at Toulouse, where Jean-Marc

The Australian Tour

Bourret, who was later to find the financial charms of French Rugby Union too great to resist, had gone on as substitute and dropped the winning goal in the final minutes. Stanton probably had good cause to feel upset after the first Test, not only at Naudo's highly dubious try but also at the bewildering refereeing of André Breysse. But France played well, nevertheless ... and even better in the second Test.

The French had prepared for the Tests of 1982 by organizing a three-match tour of England earlier in the season. It is doubtful if these games, against Oldham, Featherstone Rovers and Wigan, did much to further Anglo-French relationships, for they were all ill-tempered affairs, but they seem to have benefited the French. In both Tests, the first at Avignon and the second at Narbonne, the Australians were presented with more problems than they had encountered in Britain, and the corporate spirit of the French was excellent.

All the games outside the Tests were won with ease by the Australians, who started their remorseless accumulation of points with a huge win over Roanne. The curiosities of this game were that the side was captained from full-back by Chris Anderson, while John Ribot kicked ten goals (he scored nineteen points in all). Eric Grothe, recovered now from the knee injury which had prevented him playing in the third Test in England, scored five tries. **(Final score: Roanne 0   Australia 65.)**

After the first Test the Australians met an Aquitaine selection side and found points even more readily forthcoming. This time they collected sixty-seven, with Ella scoring seven tries, Ribot four—he also kicked another four goals— three from Mortimer, two from Grothe and one from Muggleton. **(Final score: Selection Aquitaine 2   Australia 67.)**

Another old score was settled in the following match, against the French Under-24 side at Toulouse. The corresponding fixture on the 1978 tour had brought the French victory by 20–5 (although a penalty count 33–2 in favour of the French is perhaps significant!), with Alain Touchages giving an almost perfect display of place kicking, landing ten out of eleven kicks. There was nothing similar this time. The Australians won 42–3. The Test apart, however, this was the first game in France in which the tourists experienced a suggestion of competition. Maury, one of a number of respected figures in the French team, scored a try but again the Australian points flowed. Mortimer was in irrepressible form and collected three tries; so too did Anderson. There

The Australian Tour

were two for Ella and one each for Miles and Grothe. Ribot continued to help himself to goals—six of them. **(Final score: France Under-24 3   Australia 42.)**

The following Sunday the Australians ran up another fifty-three points against a Catalan selection in the delightful setting of the Gilbert Brutus stadium in Perpignan. An official attendance of 4,676 was given, but an unofficial estimate put the figure at more than double that. Members of the Catalan side that had beaten the Australians in 1948 were paraded before the crowd, but a weak home side—though not short of some talented individuals such as Sebastian Rodriguez and Guy Delaunay, Marc Ambert, Guy Laforgue and Phillippe Fourcade—was no match for the Australians. Three players each scored three tries—Ella, Sterling, and Ribot—and Meninga and Muggleton (playing in the centre) two each. Meninga was back and kicking goals (seven), so that Ribot had to be satisfied with his tries. **(Final score: Catalans de France 2   Australia 53.)**

Pamiers, the venue for the Australians' final game against a local side, a Midi-Pyrénées selection was not quite what the tourists had anticipated. They had insisted that this fixture be switched from Albi to Pamiers, believing they would be spared a long, inconvenient bus ride. This was one of the few blunders made throughout the tour. Pamiers was farther away from their Narbonne base than Albi ... and much less accessible. The coach got lost along the back roads, and a game which should have started at 8.30 p.m. began half an hour late. Playing conditions were appalling. It was cold, and the pitch was a morass. Forgivably, the tourists did little more than was required to keep some 1,000 spectators satisfied and themselves from suffering from hypothermia. Grothe and Kenny scored two tries each, and there was one each for Rogers and Conescu. Rogers added four goals. **(Final score: Selection Midi-Pyrénées-Rouergue 0   Australia 26.)**

The Australian Tour

First Test
Avignon, 5 December
France 4   Australia 15

Australia started this game at Avignon with almost precisely the formation that had finished the final Test against Great Britain at Leeds. In that game Ribot had been taken off soon after scoring his try; Meninga had moved to the left wing and Kenny into the centre, with Lewis easing in at stand-off. Australia had ended the match with a flood of tries, and Stanton now retained a formation that had obviously impressed him. The variations were that Young had returned at open-side prop, and Boyd was back in the second row in place of the injured Rod Reddy.

What most British observers would have found hard to believe, particularly in view of the damage that Grothe had done to so many defences in Britain, was that Stanton could afford to name him as substitute. Only a few days earlier he had scored five tries against Roanne, admittedly not the most powerful side on earth. As it transpired, Australia were indebted to Grothe's strength and opportunism in a punishingly hard but absorbing, entertaining contest.

After twenty-five minutes Grothe was needed when Wally Lewis was involved in a fair but painful shoulder charge with Christian Macalli and was led away holding his arm stiffly by his side, his collarbone damaged. It was an unfortunate end for Lewis, whose international opportunities on tour had been limited because of the precocious brilliance of Kenny but who had provided English audiences with some memorable moments—not least his pass to Meninga in the Wigan Test. The injury did not, however, cause the Australians any serious disruption. Meninga and Kenny simply reverted to their more familiar positions of centre and stand-off, and Grothe came in on the left wing. The French, in retrospect, were probably sorry to see Lewis depart. Only eight minutes after his arrival Grothe, from a move which owed much to Krilich's alertness, raced on the outside of Patrick Solal and André Perez, and scored in the corner.

When, four minutes after the interval, Grothe scored his second try after Pearce and Sterling had joined forces and Young had slipped the left-winger the important pass, even Stanton might have wondered why Grothe had not been in from the start. Grothe enjoyed the French section of his European tour twice as much as the English part—in terms of tries, that is—for in five

The Australian Tour

appearances in France he scored fourteen tries to seven tries in seven appearances in England.

These were considerable contributions to a comparatively low-scoring game, one in which French determination was nicely blended with skill. It was only over the final ten minutes—how many times we had seen the Australians impressive in this phase!—that the French began to find their stamina and resolve beginning to evaporate in the warm, mellow sunshine, and there was a sustained period after the interval when the Australian defences were subjected to more stress than they had experienced for a long time.

Robin Whitfield, the British referee who controlled the match to the satisfaction of both sides (but found himself less popular after the next Test), said afterwards that during this period of intense pressure the Australians, for the first time in his experience, were under genuine strain. In the next Test at Narbonne tempers began to fray seriously. That did not happen at Avignon, but Whitfield said that the Australians were becoming impatient with one another—the unmistakable sign of a team under stress. To their credit, though, they allowed neither their composure nor their defences to disintegrate, and in the last ten minutes it was the exhausted French who were struggling to remain united.

There were two instances in the first twenty-five minutes which crystallized the nature of this distinguished French performance. After only six minutes Jacques Gigue set the right defensive example for his colleagues when he halted a potentially dangerous run by Kenny with a committed tackle. Then Christian Macalli, a splendid hooker, provided the rare sight of a player bursting clean through the Australians' first line of defence. Had support been available, France might well have scored a try; with the score at the time only 4–2 to Australia, the course of the game might have changed.

This incident, though, also showed a typical French characteristic: unpredictability. After Macalli had made his break he had to wait for support. When Yvan Gréseque arrived, however, Macalli promptly threw out a wild pass, which the scrum-half had no hope of gathering. Instead the loose ball was picked up by Krilich, who promptly initiated the move which brought Grothe his first try. Thus rather than finding themselves 7–4 in arrears, the Australians were now 7–2 ahead.

Charles Zalduendo, who had been injured in a car crash, was missing from the French pack, which was a pity because this hard-running prop had caused the British a lot of problems the previous season in Marseilles. His absence, however, did not seriously weaken a French pack led with unquenchable spirit by the captain, Joel Roosebrouck. This player, we had been informed the previous season, had retired from the game after enjoying a distinguished international career. His talents would be missed, of course, but France appeared to have a more than adequate replacement in the young Roland Puech. Now here was Roosebrouck, resurrected and looking far from ready for a pair of slippers, a pipe and a place by the fireside. The French captain was an inspiration, tackling with the commitment of a man ten years his junior and ceaselessly probing in attack for a gap in the Australian defences.

Although the French three-quarters were allowed only limited opportunities on attack, there was more determination generally, and certainly more enterprise, from their pack than Britain had mustered; but, to be fair, the Australians never reached the heights of Hull, Wigan or Leeds. There was a jaded look about them at times which suggested that, with the tour now drawing to its close, minds were beginning to turn increasingly to Brisbane and Sydney.

Passes were dropped, and tackles were missed—though no crucial errors were made. But in spite of everything, and in spite of the excellence of the French performance, Australian weakness was comparative. They had their anxious moments, but they never seemed likely to lose; and after resisting that early second half pounding they had plenty to spare at the end.

Grothe's opportunism, his two tries, made him perhaps the most influential Australian, but Sterling and Pearce, who scored Australia's third try after Krilich and the forward substitute, Brown, had exchanged passes in a move which opened a gap through the middle, now showed a French audience the full range of their youthful powers. Sadly, that audience was disappointingly small, just above 8,000, of which almost half had been allowed in with complimentary tickets.

France: Perez (Toulouse); Solal (Tonneins), Guigue (Avignon), Delaunay (XIII Catalan), Fourcade (Le Barcarès); Guiraud (Lezignan), Grésèque (XIII Catalan); Daniel (Pia), Macalli (Villeneuve), Chantal (Villeneuve), Ambert (Pia), G. Laforgue (XIII Catalan), Roosebrouck (Villeneuve) captain

Substitutes: Caravaca (Limoux) for Ambert after 71 minutes, Laumond (Villefranche) for Fourcade after 73 minutes

Scorer: goals—Perez (2)

Australia: Brentnall (Canterbury-Bankstown, Sydney); Boustead (Eastern Suburbs, Sydney), Rogers (St George, Sydney), Kenny (Parramatta, Sydney), Meninga (Southern Suburbs, Brisbane); Lewis (Fortitude Valley, Brisbane), Sterling (Parramatta, Sydney); Young (St George, Sydney), Krilich (Manly, Sydney) captain, Morris (Wynnum-Manly, Brisbane), McCabe (Manly, Sydney), Boyd (Manly, Sydney), Pearce (Balmain, Sydney)

Substitutes: Grothe (Parramatta, Sydney) for Lewis after 27 minutes, Brown (Manly, Sydney) for McCabe after 60 minutes

Scorers: tries—Grothe (2), Pearce; goals—Meninga (3)

Referee: M. R. Whitfield (Great Britain)

Attendance (estimated): 8,000

Second Test
Narbonne, 18 December
France 9   Australia 23

The French had been greatly heartened by their performance at Avignon, and while they may have realized that they did not quite possess the resources to beat the Australians, they knew they were capable of giving them a game. Louis Bonnery, the French director of coaching, said with some conviction that he was seeking a win in Narbonne. 'In Avignon our defence was good,' he said. 'In Narbonne I am looking for more attack and combined play.' His optimism was not totally misplaced. The French lost again, 9–23, but once more the Australians were made to work harder for victory than at any time during the Tests in Britain.

There were signs at Avignon that the Australians were beginning to lose concentration. By the time Narbonne arrived, many of their players were suffering from acute boredom. Although it is discourteous to the French to say so, the Australians regarded their three weeks in France as an appendage to their main mission. The primary objective, to beat Britain, had been achieved. There was still, however, that fierce determination on the part of the Australians to settle the account for 1978 and, of course, an equal determination to become the first touring side to win all their games.

It was clear that a considerable amount of tension had built up in the Australian team. It was now released in a strong physical display that severely taxed Robin Whitfield's powers of control. Curiously, Max Krilich, who had been such a model captain so far, showed the hard, uncompromising side to his

The Australian Tour

7. Guy Laforgue (no. 11) made this forceful break in France's second Test with Australia at Narbonne. A try seemed certain, but a second later Laforgue was stopped by a quite brilliant tackle by Brentnall, the Australian full-back, who hit Laforgue so hard that the ball was forced from his grasp.

nature. At 32 years of age, he was unlikely to make many more appearances in Europe, and he seemed determined to leave the French with something to remember him by—bruises, if necessary.

Whitfield awarded twenty-three penalties against the Australians, many of them for scrum offences but a number for over-vigorous tackling. Not until two minutes from time, however, did he make use of the sin bin, sending Craig Young there for punching Christian Macalli while the ball was elsewhere. Whitfield had won praise at Avignon. He was now castigated both by the French and, especially, by the Australians. 'It was the worst display of refereeing I have seen at international level,' said Stanton. It was a pity that such a successful tour should end in condemnation.

The Australian Tour

In spite of the physical excesses, there were more examples of Australian excellence on a bitterly cold afternoon of wind, dark skies and flurries of snow and sleet. Peter Sterling, even after eleven weeks of ceaseless effort, had still not used up all his supplies of energy; Brentnall, a player whose contributions to the side in England had perhaps not been fully appreciated, was again a flawless full-back; Meninga and Grothe formed a powerful and potentially destructive left-wing partnership. There was quality from Kenny at stand-off and speed from Pearce at loose forward.

Above all there was a fine last performance from Rod Reddy. He too, like Brentnall, had been one of the less obviously compelling figures in England, but in this game—and at 28 he could be making his final European tour—he displayed the full range of his talents. He played a major part in Grothe's tries before and after half-time and scored a marvellous individualistic try in the second half himself. Krilich seemed to have abdicated his role as captain and organizer in pursuit of physical retribution, but Reddy now assumed these parts admirably. He was at the heart of Australian organization in the middle of the field: he carried the ball, set up the passes and deployed the defence.

Once again Roosebrouck was an inspiring French captain, even though afterwards he admitted that he was not in perfect physical condition. Nor, for that matter, was Charles Zalduendo, the experienced prop pressed prematurely back into international football when Henri Daniel withdrew from the side. He had been recovering from the effects of his car accident and, during the final phases of the game, was reduced to walking pace.

Zalduendo had not been over-impressed with the Australians. 'I was not fit and neither was Roosebrouck, but we gave them a game. I cannot understand why Britain were beaten by such big scores. To me their front row was not anywhere near as good as those I faced in the 1972 and 1975 World Cups. Then there were O'Reilly and Beetson,' he said. There was truth in Zalduendo's observations, but while the French performance in these two Tests is not to be underrated, the Australians did not reach in France the sustained levels of excellence that they achieved in the Tests in Britain.

Australia's early tackling had an almost maniacal intensity to it, and the French were repeatedly forced back by two- and three-men driving tackles. Laforgue made early inroads into the Australian defence, and Gréseque should have been given a penalty when he was cynically taken out of the game by Brentnall. France's early attacking position was lost, however, when Guiraud's attempted drop goal sailed wide of the posts. Australia took possession for the first time and immediately worked a try, a fine one too, even if the crucial pass from Pearce to Meninga was probably forward.

Five tackles were used in driving the French back hard to the half-way line. Then on the sixth tackle Krilich, from acting half-back, found Pearce striding wide into a gap in the French defence. His pace took him round his immediate opponent. It seemed that his speed would also carry him to a try at the right corner flag, but he was halted by an alert and unexpected cover tackle by Guigue. However, before Pearce was brought to the ground he turned and, from a seemingly impossible position inches from the turf, fed Meninga, who went over. The support, as always, had been there.

France's handling in the stiff wind was nervous; they struggled when they had possession and were unable to make ground; and their problems were compounded by the fierce battering that their forwards took from the aggressive Australians. They met spirited resistance, Roosebrouck marshalling his defences courageously.

The place kicking of Etienne Kaminski was to cost France dearly in this game. With André Perez injured, France had no recognized goal kicker, and Kaminski, reluctantly, had accepted the job. He had brought the score to 2–5 when he landed a penalty, against the wind, but was then to miss two penalties directly in front of the posts. Had he succeeded with those simple kicks, France would have led at the interval. Instead, they were 10–7 in arrears.

A chest-high tackle by Brentnall on Laforgue—the ball being forced out of the Frenchman's grasp—prevented a likely try after Roosebrouck and Macalli had combined to put the second-row forward in the clear. That splendid piece of defensive work was then emulated by Delaunay, who halted Grothe with a fine cover tackle. This was the nature of the first half, fluctuating and exciting, and French anticipation was never higher than when Grésèque gave them the lead at 7–5.

France, using as pivots Guiraud and Grésèque, their half-backs, had employed close passing tactics. The Australians, by contrast, were always ready to open the game out, even in their own '25', a policy that proved expensive when Rogers was crash-tackled by Solal and the ball shot high out of his grasp. Grésèque took the ball on the full and scurried 20 yards to the posts. Kaminski found that kick within his compass. By half-time, however, Australia had regained the lead, but again their score had an element of doubt about it.

After Brentnall had gained 60 yards with an accurate kick to touch downwind, Reddy broke left and threw a speculative pass inside. The ball went astray over the line and Grothe, following up, scored. France claimed that Grothe had punched the ball forward; the referee ruled that it had touched a French arm and the try stood. Meninga increased French disappointment by landing a fine goal from the touchline. The Australian play in the first half had its vulnerable moments, but there was now little likelihood of France depriving the Australians of the twenty-second, and final, win of the tour.

Soon after half-time Reddy's individualism brought Australia another try,

The Australian Tour

and they were now beginning to draw remorselessly away. Their football began to develop smoothness and confidence; the ball was passed at speed and the direction of the attack switched constantly. Sterling was at the heart of so many attacks, and after another passage of fluent Australian play Reddy sent Grothe over in the corner.

The French, as at Avignon, were now tiring, a process quickened by the disappointment of a disallowed 'try' by Guiraud and another missed penalty by the hapless Kaminski. He was to score the final points of the tour from a penalty, but before then Kenny had intercepted Guiraud's pass to Grésèque and raced 40 yards to the posts.

France: Guigue (Avignon); Solal (Tonneins), Delaunay (XIII Catalan), Laumond (Villefranche), Kaminski (Le Pontet); Guiraud (Lézignan), Grésèque (XIII Catalan); Zalduendo (Villeneuve), Macalli (Villeneuve), Chantal (Villeneuve), Cologni (XIII Catalan), G. Laforgue (XIII Catalan), Roosebrouck (Villeneuve) captain

Substitutes: Caravaca (Limoux) for Cologni after 63 minutes, Laville (Villeneuve) for Laumond after 66 minutes

Scorers: try—Grésèque; goals—Kaminski (3)

Australia: Brentnall (Canterbury-Bankstown, Sydney); Boustead (Eastern Suburbs, Sydney), Rogers (St George, Sydney), Meninga (Southern Suburbs, Brisbane), Grothe (Parramatta, Sydney); Kenny (Parramatta, Sydney), Sterling (Parramatta, Sydney); Young (St George, Sydney), Krilich (Manly, Sydney) captain, Boyd (Manly, Sydney), McCabe (Manly, Sydney), Reddy (St George, Sydney), Pearce (Balmain, Sydney)

Substitutes: Ella (Parramatta, Sydney), Brown (Manly, Sydney) not used

Scorers: tries—Grothe (2), Meninga, Reddy, Kenny; goals—Meninga (4)

Referee: M. R. Whitfield (Great Britain)

Attendance (estimated): 7,000

The Australian Tour

LESSONS

Before the start of the season Colin Hutton returned from an investigative visit to Australia, where he watched two Test matches against New Zealand, as well as other club games, and declared that he had seen nothing to fear. Did he really believe that? If so, here surely was the sporting equivalent to Neville Chamberlain's returning from Germany, waving his useless scrap of paper and proclaiming, 'Peace in our time.' Hutton could still find nothing to impress him after the opening match of the tour, when his own club, Hull KR, became the first of the Australians' victims.

Such apparent short-sightedness—especially in view of later results—might easily have cost Mr Hutton all vestiges of credibility. But Mr Hutton was neither stupid nor blind, and in private he was offering opinions rather different from his public utterances. He and Johnny Whiteley knew that Great Britain had little or no chance of beating Australia, but Hutton, as team manager, felt that he could not possibly admit anything so damning in public. His job was to try to build morale, not destroy it. To have admitted his true thoughts (and these were that Britain were now playing a style of rugby that had been abandoned in Australia seven years previously), he believed, would have been to betray his players and his own position. Whether Mr Hutton spoke with the greatest diplomacy is debatable, but there was no doubting his good intentions.

Great Britain's coach and manager must have realized after the defeat against France in Marseilles the previous December that the possibility of finding a side good enough to compete with Australia was remote. Unfortunately, there was then little time in which to correct things. Laudable attempts were made to do so, but it was like trying to swot on the eve of an important examination. It was too late. Hutton and Whiteley were not without a sense of pride, nor short of a supply of optimism, but they were given no opportunity to indulge either, and their worst fears were soon realized.

It was evident after Great Britain had been beaten 40–4 in the first Test at Boothferry Park that the Australians were vastly superior in practically every department of the game.

Hutton pleaded that defeat should not be attributed to the choice of the team. It would be deluding to do so, he claimed; it would be to miss the point. He was right to a degree because any side the selectors dreamed up would almost certainly not have been good enough to challenge the Australians. But the selection process, nevertheless, deserved to be examined. Difficult though their job was the selectors did not emerge with great credit.

Although from a British point of view the Ashes series was depressing, it would have been a mean spirit that could not acknowledge the quality of the opposition; and the lasting impression of the tour will be that of the brilliance of the rugby played consistently by the Australians and particularly in the Tests. The shame of it was that they were given so little publicity, certainly nothing like the amount their excellence deserved. Before the game with Fulham the club's managing director, Harold Genders, made the bold but justifiable claim that the Australians were 'The fittest, finest side that had ever visited Britain ... at any sport', while David Watkins, outstanding as a Rugby Union stand-off for Wales and as a back for Wales and Salford Rugby League, maintained that they were easily the most entertaining side he had seen in all the years he had been associated with rugby of both codes.

Acknowledgement of the Australians' excellence came from other Rugby Union quarters. Writing in the *Observer* on the first Test, Geoffrey Nicholson said:

> The great Alex Murphy has said that the Australians are from another planet. After their victory at Hull it would be hard to deny them another, and scarcely more modest title, as the most efficient national rugby side, of either code, in the world.

In the same newspaper Clem Thomas, covering the second Test, wrote:

> It appears that British Rugby League football simply does not have a 'roobar' big enough or strong enough to fend off these remarkable Kangaroos who are being hailed as the best rugby team of any code to visit the United Kingdom—an extravagant claim which they fully lived up to at Central Park.

In the *Guardian* Carwyn James, the late, outstanding Welsh RU coach who guided the British Lions to their memorable wins over New Zealand in 1971, declared:

> The Australians left no one in Britain in doubt as to their athleticism, superb fitness, teamwork and flawless handling. Whereas the curse of the Union game is nine- or ten-man rugby, the curse of the League is the blinkered, bulldozing tactic of one-man rugby. The Australians, however, have clearly restored the art of collision rugby allied to support play which leads to thrilling, sustained movements.

The Australians were not magicians, however, even though many a British player must frequently have felt like the victim of legerdemain during the

The Australian Tour

Tests. There were moments of perfection from the Australians; there were movements at Boothferry Park and at Wigan which failed to bring tries but will remain indelibly impressed on the mind; but they were the product of qualities that everyone could appreciate—pace, fitness, support play, selflessness, skilled handling. There was no mystery to it. But when all these qualities are brought together with such coherence, the one purpose being the good of the team, the results can be unforgettable.

For Britain the experience was demoralizing, although the game can be so insular in this country that even such merciless lessons as these were in danger of being minimized or even ignored; and the most obvious lesson was that Britain no longer had a monopoly in skill. This was a tired old myth that had persisted for generations. It was possibly true once. It was still passionately believed in some British quarters. Certainly, there were still fanatics who clung to the creed, though a few believers must have resigned membership after this tour.

The British game had been warned against this false religion after the tour of Australia in 1979. Raymond Fletcher, the *Yorkshire Post*'s correspondent, writing after the third Test at Sydney, said:

> The simple fact is that Australia are fitter, faster and play better football. Yet even now British officials will not concede the latter. Yet if by football we mean running and passing at speed, backing up and slipping the ball out of tackles, then Australia are in a different league.... Britain has done little right even at half-pace.

The same critic was still offering valid advice before the start of the 1982 series:

> With four six-footers in their back division [he wrote], there is no doubting the power of the Australian side which opens the most eagerly awaited tour for years at Hull Kingston Rovers. But it would be a mistake for British officials to keep underselling the skills of the Australians. In winning a record nine successive Test matches Australia have scored thirty-eight tries to three. On those figures alone it is discrediting the game as much as the Australians to keep insisting that they lack Britain's skills.

The Australians vividly bore out the truth of that observation.

At no time throughout the series was there any evidence of superior British skill. Britain's only try, scored by Steve Evans in the second half of the final Test, was the result of good, very good rugby, but, by comparison with much of the Australian play, it was not exceptional. There were no collective moments to compare with the tourists' best moves, no moments of individualism to set beside those provided by Kenny and Sterling, Meninga and Rogers, Boustead

The Australian Tour

and Grothe, Price, Young, Pearce and Krilich.

In contrast to the mobile, forceful, imaginative Australian pack, the British forwards, until the final Test—and then only to a limited degree—were laboured and predictable. The sterility of the British game had been thrown into sharp relief by the New Zealanders of 1980. The leanness, fitness and mobility of such men as Mark Broadhurst and Mark Graham, the desire of the New Zealand team as a whole to keep the ball 'alive', challenged the slow-moving, unimaginative British pack. Colin Hutton realized then how glum the situation was, for it was after that series that the squad system was announced. 'It was apparent during the Test matches [against New Zealand] that this country had fallen behind in world standards,' he said. 'Positive action is needed if we are to challenge the Australians in 1982.' Hutton also added the rider that there was 'tremendous potential' for improving the fitness of British players after the results of tests taken at Carnegie College, the physical education centre in Leeds.

Therein lay another alarming discrepancy between the sides. Australia were markedly fitter than the Great Britain side, an inescapable truth demonstrated generally and specifically by the floods of points that Australia produced in the second half of the first Test, when they ran in thirty points, and in the final Test—Britain's best performance!—when eighteen points were plundered in the final ten minutes. Even the Australians' modest twelve second-half points at Wigan were scored with the help of only twelve men!

Only in scrummaging could Britain claim some superiority over the Australians, and a big improvement in this department was promised by the time Great Britain are next in Australia in 1984. It was not to prove that important a difference, however. Krilich, in fact, beat David Ward at the scrums 7–3 at Boothferry Park but then lost them 5–2 to John Dalgreen and 7–3 to Brian Noble but Great Britain were rarely able to capitalize on this source of possession. The Australians, by contrast, exploited their possession to the full.

The Australians tackled harder and with far better technique, their low, fierce tackling being much more effective than the often sloppy high tackling of the British. Their support play was vastly superior. An Australian scarcely ever, and certainly never crucially, lacked support. A British player making a break was rarely given it. Des Drummond made a fine break in the final Test from acting half-back. It was one of his rare opportunities and he attempted to make the most of it, bursting forward with characteristic determination. But to freeze the video just before he was tackled is to understand one of the most significant differences between the teams. Drummond is to be seen surrounded by green-shirted Australians. There is not a glimpse of British white in the frame.

The Australian Tour

Australia were mentally tougher than Great Britain and showed far greater discipline, Boyd excepted. When Max Krilich and David Ward became the first players in a game in Britain to be sent to the sin bin—in the first Test at Hull—Krilich simply turned his back and ran smartly away; Ward went quickly enough but not before throwing his arms wide in a gesture of appeal and wounded innocence to M. Rascagnères, the referee. It was rare to see the Australians give away foolish penalties, show signs of dissent, or allow their concentration to be upset.

If this examination of the differences between the teams appears laboured, it is to make this point: that the Australians were so obviously the products of a much more efficient system of Rugby League. They were full of good habits and rarely exhibited bad ones. The British were full of bad habits and all too rarely showed good ones. The difference was emphasized constantly at the play-the-balls, which were a repeated reminder of how much more attention the Australians paid to technique and how much more alert and better organized they were.

The play-the-ball is one of the simple skills in the game, yet it is commonplace to see British footballers performing this play sloppily or incorrectly or even not at all but just allowing the ball to roll between the legs to the acting half-back. Such untidiness is almost always allowed to go unpunished by the referee. The skill is often performed so slowly when a side is attacking that little unusual results from it. When the British team lined-up at an Australian play-the-ball they were frequently disorganized, moved up too slowly and were put in trouble by the speed of the opposition's play. What a contrast to the Australian methods! So many times Krilich, from acting half-back, initiated some startling moves against a British team slow to appreciate the dangers. The simple skill of playing the ball was invariably done correctly, in a manner that a young player could have been encouraged to follow.

When Colin Hutton and Johnny Whiteley presided over their summer camps they imagined that they would be able to go through some advanced routines with their players. They were frequently dismayed to find it necessary to explain fundamentals. Such elementary deficiencies were symptomatic of the flaws in a club system that for too long had paid too little attention to good coaching—to standards of fitness and the best methods of attaining fitness, discipline, technique, individual and unit skills, scrummaging and tackling (the tackling shields used by the Australians in training were unheard of in England).

Australia's present supremacy can almost certainly be attributed to their National Coaching Scheme, which was started in the 1960s and which at the time of writing has produced some 7,000 accredited coaches. A scheme as

The Australian Tour

comprehensive as the Australian system, designed to encourage as many players as possible to take up the game and to instil in those players good habits that eventually become second nature, must have an advantage over a country in which coaching, as the Australians know it, is still regarded with indifference, even distrust. One of the faults of the British club system is that too many coaches who were outstanding players in their day imagine that they have nothing new to learn about the game. Such an obtuse attitude has prevented the investigations of other sports—American grid-iron football, Rules football, soccer and athletics, for example—that Australian coaches have made in an attempt to broaden their horizons.

British Rugby League is at a disadvantage compared with the Australian game. It does not enjoy the importance given to it in Brisbane and Sydney. It wins nothing like the same press or television coverage. The players are less fêted and less well paid. There is scarcely a single British Rugby League player now playing who would be widely recognized outside his own sport. The competition in Australia is fiercer, the rewards greater, and so the standards tend to be far more demanding. During the 1970s a number of English players—Reilly and Millward, Bishop, Topliss and Ashurst, to name a few—were welcomed into Australian Rugby League. Even if there were now no international ban in operation, it is difficult to think of too many British players that the Australians would be desperate to sign.

It would be interesting, nevertheless, to see if the soaring standards of Brett Kenny, Peter Sterling or Wayne Pearce would survive the draining effects of a long English winter, to find out if their dedication to training would remain as enthusiastic on cold, winter nights at Watersheddings, Oldham, or Post Office Road, Featherstone, as it would in Sydney's inviting climate.

These are valid points in defence of the British Rugby League footballer, but they are not, emphatically, offered as excuses. At the end of a demoralizing Ashes series no one connected with Rugby League in Britain—administrators, officials, players, or coaches—should have been seeking excuses. There was only one honest thing to be done: admit to the deficiencies and try to correct them.

The series possibly brought about the end of the old selection system whereby the team was chosen by a selection committee of eight. Such a system, whatever its advantages, was in need of review. In English soccer a similar system had long since been discarded and all authority invested in the team manager. When Frank Myler, captain of the victorious Great Britain tour to Australia in 1970 and an outstanding player for many years with Widnes and St Helens, and Dick Gemmell, formerly a Great Britain international with Hull and now a director of that club, were appointed coach and manager respectively in place of Whiteley and Hutton, it was they who selected the

The Australian Tour

Great Britain Under-24 side to meet France at Carpentras. The team was then ratified by the selection committee, a significant departure from normal procedure.

Eight selectors from various parts of the north should in theory produce a team that is not susceptible to charges of bias, something less easy to achieve when one or two men choose a side. Frank Myler immediately encountered this problem when he picked his first Under-24 side, for it contained four players from his own club, Oldham. There is possibly no perfect system, but the wild changes made by the selectors for the Tests gave an impression of uncertainty, helplessness, even panic. There is little chance of finding a successful side when so many changes—thirty-three different players were used in the series, and only Drummond played in all three games—are made, and the damage done to players' confidence and loyalty is difficult to calculate. In the end the selectors arrived at a team which, for seventy minutes at least, acquitted itself with credit. But they seemed to have done so not through logical consideration but through dangerous experimentation.

However, amid all the investigations and inquests, amid all the British disappointment and even anxiety, it was important not to overlook the brilliance of the Australians. Many eminent critics were prepared to concede that they were the finest Australian side to visit Britain. Others might have disputed such a claim, but a British side of any generation would have been hard-pressed to have contained them.

They were a credit to themselves and to the game. They had five players sent off during the tour—Reddy, Morris, Muggleton and Boyd twice—and Boyd's lack of control was one of their few serious weaknesses. But in spite of isolated ugly moments they showed almost military discipline. Their public relations and their public image were good. On the field they were unforgettable, providing spectators with a tremendous amount of pleasure. There cannot have been too many instances in the history of these confrontations when the British public has responded to an Australian side in the way the spectators at Hull and Wigan did. Too much virtue can be a bore. As Tolstoy observed: 'Happy families are all alike; unhappy families are all unhappy in their own way.' Yet the Australians were a happy party without being in the slightest bit uninteresting. It will be a fortunate touring party in future that will get so many things so absolutely right.

When a side is as good all-round as were the 1982 Australians it is slightly invidious to select individuals for special appraisal. All the Australian players used in the Test series would have readily found a place in the Great Britain side; only Des Drummond might possibly have been worthy of a place in the Australian team. That was one measure of the divide between the teams. In selecting Max Krilich, Peter Sterling and Brett Kenny, Mal Meninga, Steve

The Australian Tour

Rogers and Wayne Pearce—and Frank Stanton!—for special attention, one is simply choosing a group of players who embody the qualities that made the Australians such a memorable side—energy, pace, power, culture and fitness.

That is not to say that the players omitted did not also display similar qualities. They did... and more. For example, one will remember the finishing of Kerry Boustead, who probably never wasted a scoring opportunity throughout the tour and certainly not in the Tests; on the other wing there was the compellingly powerful running of Eric Grothe, who gave to the tour some of its most riveting moments—his tries at St Helens, Leeds, the Boulevard and Boothferry Park, Wigan, and in both Tests in France; there was the cool, flawless play of Greg Brentnall at full-back, in defence rarely under pressure in the Tests and scarcely making a mistake throughout the tour; there was the hungry drive of Ray Price, one of the older players who showed an appetite for the game that was an example to younger members of the party; there was the subtle mixture of power and deftness that Craig Young brought to his work; there were the selfless contributions of Rod Reddy; and there were inevitably some explosively effective moments from Les Boyd, even if he was one of the few Test players perhaps who failed to enhance his reputation.

It will be a surprise if Sterling, Kenny, Meninga and Pearce do not tour Europe again. They are young enough and good enough to do so, another reason for assessing their value. English followers could only watch such precocious talents with envy. It was not simply their skills either that made them the object of so much admiration. Throughout the tour there was never the suggestion of a mean act from the four of them.

When the Australians arrived one of the first things that their manager, Frank Farrington, spoke of was his concern that his Australian players should project a good image. That good image was certainly projected most forcefully by four of the young members of the party. Presiding over all, though, was the omnipotent **Frank Stanton.**

There is not a coach in the British game who would have paid as much attention to detail as Frank Stanton. His thoroughness was one of the most impressive of his qualities. Frank Farrington and Tom Drysdale, his assistant manager, were important members of an administrative team that included Dr Bill Monaghan and Alf Richards. But Stanton was in control, and it was to him that the players went with their problems.

Stanton had completed a lot of his homework before he left Australia. Like Whiteley and Hutton, he had to accept a system of selection of which he was critical but while he may have objected privately to some of the players made

8. Frank Stanton established himself as one of the finest coaches in the game—arguably the finest. He paid as much attention to detail as an engraver. His planning before and during the tour was rewarded by an unforgettable series of performances by his team.

available to him, he knew that from his squad he could probably find a Test side good enough to retain the Ashes. He believed that the side which beat New Zealand in two Tests in Australia could be improved. Before departing for England he knew and understood his players' personalities and appreciated their capabilities. He made it his business to know and understand.

Stanton was a firm believer in psychology as an important part of coaching. His room at the Dragonara Hotel in Leeds was full of coaching aids, video equipment and books with such titles as *Sports Psyching*. He had had the personalities of his players assessed before leaving Australia. This exercise told him which players might be best put together—for example, Ian Schubert, outgoing and buoyant, with Eric Grothe, introverted and meditative, and Les

The Australian Tour

Boyd with John Muggleton. These two players had been on opposite sides in the Australian Grand Final between Manly and Parramatta, and there had been some bad blood between them. Stanton was determined that it would not be allowed to spill over into the tour. Two other players on opposite sides in that final, Ray Price and Paul McCabe, also shared rooms. Two close friends, Peter Sterling and Brett Kenny, were kept apart. Stanton's aim was to foster friendships. In this instance it was not necessary.

He was a disciplinarian. Rules were laid down by Stanton before the start of the tour, and the Australian coach introduced fines for lateness, bad or rowdy behaviour, sloppiness and any misdemeanour that might bring discredit to the party. To help alleviate boredom he split the squad into four teams, and throughout the tour these teams would compete at touch rugby, soccer, volleyball, darts and pool. Each week the players would be provided by Stanton with a weekly schedule, running from Monday to the following Sunday so that the players knew each day precisely what their programme was at practically every hour of the day. Halfway through the tour Stanton changed the schedules so that the players did not become jaded by the routine.

Eager to learn new things about the opposition or about his own party, Stanton encouraged his players to remember and to write down the gist of conversations they might have with, for example, English coaches. The information would then be given to him. In this way he gained insights into what the opposition thought about him and his players and was able to use the information, sometimes for motivational purposes. These activities, though they may not constitute an offence under the Official Secrets Act, perhaps seem extreme, but they illustrate his thoroughness and his desire to discover, and possibly to make use of, new information.

Stanton left his players in no doubt about their objectives in Britain. They were there to win the Ashes, and everything was directed towards that end. At the start of the tour he intensified the fitness training because he believed that this above all would concentrate his players' minds and make them understand their brief. As the tour wore on, Stanton realized that Australia's fitness was far superior to Britain's, and the intensity of the training was relaxed slightly.

It was soon evident that his squad had become divided into first and second teams, and Stanton spent a lot of time encouraging players that he knew would never gain a Test place. He made sure that the players were well mixed in training, in an attempt to allow his charges to retain a sense of equality. Stanton found boredom a problem and did everything he could to vary the training.

The corporate spirit was fostered in other ways. Players had to perform menial tasks, so that it was no surprise to see Steve Rogers and Les Boyd sweeping out the dressing-rooms after the game at Cardiff or Max Krilich acting as timekeeper in the smoke-filled Widnes press box. Ray Price's broken hand did not prevent him carrying out the bucket of sand for use in place kicking in the final Test. On match days, indeed, all the players who were not involved in the game were assigned tasks—two kept the tackle count, others worked on a game analysis chart, some checked the turnstiles. There were no idlers.

Stanton was fortunate that his players did not suffer many serious injuries. Price, Young and Grothe missed the last Test, but by then the Ashes had been won. Stanton maintained that the natural fitness of his players was partly responsible for the lack of injuries, but he was a great believer in flexibility exercises as a means of avoiding them, and he insisted on intensive medical treatment if a player was hurt.

Statistics were of great interest to Stanton, but he made them work for him. Some months before he left Australia he began to study videos of Sydney and Brisbane club games—standard practice for Australian coaches—and to work out a tackle count for each position. By the time he arrived in England he had a good idea of the amount of tackling each player should be achieving over a fifteen-match tour. The tackle count for each game was charted on the wall of the hotel's medical room, as was each player's tackle count for the tour.

Stanton's statistics told him that his only serious problem was lack of possession. He knew which players were gaining possession and which players were losing it. One of those losing it, of course, was Krilich, but Stanton had complete faith in his captain and was prepared to tolerate Krilich's weakness in the scrums for his many other admirable qualities. To compensate for this particular lost supply of ball, however, Stanton demanded that his side win 85 per cent of the loose balls. Many English coaches would consider it a waste of time to have players continuously dropping on loose balls in training. Not Stanton. He made his players work at this exercise until they had perfected it, and it proved yet one more department of the game in which Australia were superior to Britain.

Although Stanton must have had a shrewd idea of what his Test team would be even before he left Australia, he could not be completely sure how certain players would respond to English conditions or to the demands of the tour; and of course he could not know how fortunate or otherwise he would be with injuries. Yet his team selections and any experiments he made proved to be unerringly correct. The players who best illustrated this were Peter Sterling and Brett Kenny, who, English audiences had been told, were the understudies to Steve Mortimer and Wally Lewis, and Wayne Pearce, a player primarily available to provide cover for Ray Price. Yet at the end of the tour these three youngsters were great players in their own right. Stanton can take his share of the credit for their development.

Sterling and Kenny were the half-backs in the first match at Hull Kingston

Rovers. Stanton was known to have considerable admiration for Kenny, who had been playing outstandingly for Parramatta before the tour started, but was his decision to play Sterling designed principally to make Kenny feel at ease, partnering his young Parramatta club colleague as he was? Whatever his thinking, Stanton must have realized after that first game that the pair were Test material. Sterling was outstanding, and although Kenny's reputation was yet to be established, here immediately was a young and highly promising alliance.

Then there was Pearce. Had Pearce been pressed too early or too quickly, Stanton might have been accused of favouritism towards the young loose forward (Pearce was the only player from Balmain, Stanton's own club, in the party) so he left him out of that first game. As he was one of the first players to emerge from his own youth policy at the club, Stanton possibly felt more affection for Pearce than for any other member of his squad. But long before the first Test it was obvious that Pearce had to be in the side on merit, not as the result of favouritism.

Even then Stanton could not be sure that these three young players would repeat their form of club games in the Tests, and to get Pearce into the side Stanton had to take the slightly daring risk of playing Boyd in the front row. The British camp, perhaps rightly, read this as a sign of Australia's forward reserve weakness, but to have laid too much store by it would have been foolish. Boyd's switch to the front row was never a noticeable weakness, while Pearce's inclusion immeasurably strengthened the pack.

Stanton had the confidence of his players. Each week a team meeting was held, and the players would be encouraged to air any grievances or criticisms they might have—of colleagues, if necessary. Only Stanton and his players attended these meetings—a mixture of the confessional and the complaints counter. Frank Farrington, the manager, said later that he would have loved to know what transpired at these meetings. But it was a measure of the mutual trust that existed between players and coach that he never did find out. A confidence was never broken.

The Australian coach made ample use of video for studying the opposition and for correcting faults. An example of how he would make video work for the benefit of an individual and of the team came in the Leeds game. John Holmes, the Leeds stand-off, twice got Les Dyl racing on the outside of Steve Rogers and dangerously into the heart of the Australian defence. Rogers was not sure why this had happened. The video was studied to find out why. Having established the reason, the Australians then took steps to ensure that any such mistakes were not repeated. Stanton was not prepared to be caught out twice.

Although Stanton would use video as an aid to arousal, he also believed in allowing players to motivate themselves in the way they liked best. He was a martinet, but he achieved his ambitions as much by persuasion and encouragement. He was not a shouter. English coaches could learn a lot from him. Stanton never pretended that he had a monopoly on knowledge, and that was one of his great strengths. He had an enquiring mind. He was never satisfied.

After coaching Australia through two successive tours of Europe as well as the 1979 series in Australia, Stanton might well decide that he has had his fill of international football. If that proves to be the case, and whatever happens to him in the future, he is assured of an influential place in the game's history. A few events in the 1978 tour rankled with Stanton—particularly the two Test defeats in France—but he settled all the old debts this time. There is simply not a great deal more you can do than be the primary force behind a side that wins all its twenty-two games.

In **Max Krilich** Australia possessed an ideal captain. He was good-humoured and articulate off the field, and there was no doubting who was in control on it. In some respects he represented one of Australia's weaknesses because he was so often beaten at the scrums. This weakness even cost him his place at home. In Australia's Grand Final of 1982 Krilich was substitute for Manly, with Ray Brown hooking. But his qualities were seen at their best on this tour. They more than compensated for any flaws.

Although there were signs that his self-discipline and objectivity were wavering in the second Test in France, there was no hint of any such failings in England; and while Stanton must take credit for the thoroughness with which the side were prepared off the field, Krilich earned much admiration for the firm way in which he maintained control on it. Great Britain used three different captains, Steve Nash, Jeff Grayshon and David Topliss, and all suffered by comparison with Krilich.

Stanton had complete trust in Krilich, and this investment of faith seemed to give Krilich great self-confidence. That Stanton was prepared to overlook Krilich's lack of possession at the scrums and work on other areas to compensate was evidence of the high regard in which he held his captain. His trust was not misplaced. Even in a side of so many fine players Krilich's authority was always evident.

Having such an authoritative and efficient organizer on the field was heartening enough; but Krilich had much more to offer. In contrast to the majority of British hookers, he was remarkably quick and mobile. He invariably went acting half-back, and his alertness and vision, his quick, darting movements, almost always caused problems for Britain at the play-the-balls.

9. Max Krilich was an inspiring Australian captain throughout the tour. He was frequently beaten at the scrums, but his leadership, his example, and his often brilliant play in the loose more than compensated for any deficiencies. He frequently broke tackles, and this stretching effort by David Watkinson in the first match of the tour against Hull KR is unlikely to stop the Australian hooker.

    The discipline of the side was often exemplary, and credit for this is due to Krilich. His players never questioned his decisions or those of the referee, and he in turn rarely became frustrated with his own players, although Wayne Pearce did earn some sharp words from his captain when he dropped the ball, a rare mistake, in the first Test. His own players would have struggled to find flaws in their captain's attitude. He never avoided work, never shirked a tackle and not once throughout the British tour showed any desire for revenge when he was the victim of rough treatment. It would have been hard to imagine him shamming injury in any way. When he was helped from the field with an

The Australian Tour

injured ankle in the match against Cumbria one knew that he must be hurt.

Krilich was a dangerous player in the loose, with a deceptive side-step. He possessed that enviable Australian quality of being able to burst out of tackles, often getting out a pass when it did not seem possible to do so. A good example of this occurred in the first Test, when Australia scored their seventh try (a move started by Brentnall after he had caught a high kick from Nash in his in-goal area), Krilich slipping a lovely pass to Young even though he had the powerful Skerrett clinging to him.

His own moment of glory, of course, came in the final Test, when he scored his one try of the tour, a splendid one. The way in which his colleagues greeted this try was testimony to his popularity. When Krilich burst on to Kenny's inside pass, the line was still some distance away, but Krilich had the pace and the stamina to reach it. Raelene Boyle, winning the women's 400 metres at Brisbane, might have been speaking for Krilich as well as herself when she said: 'I had me teeth together and me bum up and I was really running.' The British cover was closing in by the time he had arrived under the posts but too late to stop the 32-year-old Australian from touching down.

In the final Test little time remained when **Peter Sterling,** as usual heavily involved in an Australian offensive, received a pass from a colleague, turned quickly to his right and slipped a pass to David Stephenson, the Great Britain centre. A mistake ... after fifteen games and seven weeks! The sense of disbelief could have been no greater if Jack Nicklaus had stepped up to the first tee at Augusta, swung and missed.

Sterling was as close to perfection on this tour as made no difference, a scrum-half of inexhaustible energy, a player of endless enthusiasm. He was the popular choice as the best player of all, the jewel in the crown. From his first impressive performance at Craven Park to the last Test at Leeds, he was a source of inspiration. No matter how much scrutiny he might come under, the flaws simply refused to appear. His maturity, for a 22-year-old, was astonishing.

At the start of the tour Stanton said that Australia were in England to win the Ashes. 'If in the process of doing so we provide entertainment as well, so much the better,' he said. That hinted perhaps at a dour approach—but that never materialized, and Sterling above all characterized the side's sense of enjoyment. Here was a young man who was supremely fit, gifted and revelling in his youth and talent. He would have been impatient if he had not been involved in every minute of every game.

The sheer physical presence of Meninga and Grothe offered the more compelling sight. Sterling, indeed, was not of a physique or an appearance to

10. Peter Sterling was adept at penetrating deep into the British defences and then slipping out a telling pass. Here, in the first Test match at Hull, he is watched helplessly by Grayshon and Skerrett. Inevitably support, in the shape of Ray Price, is there, but on this occasion Sterling is looking elsewhere.

prompt a Hollywood movie mogul to rush forward for his signature. Slight of build, with fair hair longer than that of the rest of his colleagues, he operated on a pair of legs slightly bowed. He looked human enough, but the physical energy he poured into this tour was a constant source of wonderment.

One of his most appealing qualities was his complete selflessness. Not once was there the suggestion of his seeking glory for himself. Everything he did was for the benefit of a better-placed colleague and for the team. Close to the opposition line, he would often give the ball to a colleague when he might have tried to reach the line himself.

The Australian Tour

Sterling's appetite for the game was illustrated many times during the Tests. But it was particularly significant that whenever Britain started or restarted a game it was usually Sterling who caught the ball. He would stand in the middle of his pack and invariably he would be the player rising to catch the ball. British policy would be to leave this job to a forward so that the scrum-half could be protected. That was not part of Sterling's thinking. He would stand where he knew he would get the ball. He was greedy for it but never with it.

In attack he was superb and no less so in defence. He was always available. He was prepared to take his share of the bruises and would tackle any opponent, no matter what his size. His tackling, indeed, was as forceful as that of a man half as heavy again. He did not appear to be particularly quick, although this might have been a deception as he showed when he broke from a scrum and easily held off the challenge of Garry Clark to score a try in the first game at Hull KR. But if he was fractionally short of pace, it mattered not because his quick thinking, vision and acute sense of timing meant that he was always acting at speed.

There is not a coach anywhere who would not be grateful to have Sterling in his side. Everything he did was right, and it was always Sterling who was looking to make good the mistakes of others. He was ever alert. Stanton believed that the longest a player could concentrate fully was twenty minutes, but Sterling never suffered from loss of concentration—not until that pass to Stephenson! His passing was almost always flawless; his changes of direction and his darts into enemy territory were a joy. It was just such a foray that brought Australia their second try of the first Test, with Sterling making a quick break, feinting left, pushing hard off the left foot to launch himself into a sharp run to the right and then putting Rogers into space with an acutely angled pass.

Steve Rogers was one of the most interesting of the tourists. It might be assumed that one of the highest paid Australian Rugby League players would not want to exert himself unduly on a European tour of twenty-two games. He was one of the most experienced players, one of the most respected, with an established reputation, yet in the British section of the tour he played in nine of the fifteen games and was substitute in three others. He wanted to be involved.

Curiously, in games outside the Tests, though frequently exhibiting his pedigree, Rogers made a number of mistakes. He took his eye off the ball, missed tackles, lost concentration and dropped passes. In the Tests he was flawless. Here was an example of someone who was likely to foul up rehearsals but who could be guaranteed to be word-perfect on the night. He was the player for the important occasion.

11. Steve Rogers was a player who needed to be reassured and pampered before big matches. Frank Stanton was only too willing to minister to his needs. While Rogers was sometimes prone to carelessness in the less important games, he was near flawless in the three Tests.

Rogers was full of quality. All his work had about it the stamp of the craftsman. He does not look especially powerful, yet he broke an exceptional

The Australian Tour

number of tackles—not with brute force but rather with a steely determination—with bewildering regularity. In the second half of the first Test he burst out of a tackle by Les Dyl, no weakling, to play a major part in Boustead's try.

In the second Test he brushed off Kelly's challenge like a man casually dusting a speck of dust off his lapel and scored the first of the two tries that he collected in the series. In the final Test he crossed the line with three British tacklers clinging to him like paper streamers.

Krilich was an admirable captain but he was given faithful support by Rogers, who organized the backs. Rogers was, after all, surrounded by young players in Brentnall, Meninga, Grothe, Kenny, Sterling and Boustead (even though he was on his second tour), who could not have failed to respond to his classy promptings. In the third Test Rogers was often the player who made the initial break, and it was his pace that once enabled him to catch Drummond from behind—no little feat, for Drummond on this occasion was, for once, in full flight.

Rogers was blessed with pace and on one occasion was too quick for his own good. When Sterling put through a perfectly timed angled kick Rogers left his mark like a sprinter leaving the blocks. He touched down but was ruled off-side by M. Rascagnères, the referee. Television showed M. Rascagnères to have been surprised by Rogers's pace. There were no complaints from Rogers or his colleagues, even though Australia appeared to have been denied a legitimate try.

Like Peter Sterling and Brett Kenny, **Wayne Pearce** played with a maturity that belied his twenty-one years. It is possible that Stanton had Pearce in mind for a Test place early on, but the young Balmain forward arrived as understudy to Ray Price. He did not play in the strong side that opened the tour at Craven Park but performed so impressively in the next four games at Wigan, Barrow St Helens and Leeds that he became an inevitable selection for the first Test. In three of those games Pearce was in his familiar position of loose forward, but the idea of moving Boyd into the front row to accommodate Pearce in the second row in the Test side probably came to Stanton early in the tour.

Pearce's attitudes on and off the field were exemplary. A non-smoker and non-drinker, he surprised even his colleagues by his devotion to fitness. As one of the first and brightest products of the youth policy that Stanton was operating at Balmain, Pearce had the respect and admiration of his coach. That faith in Pearce was amply repaid. When the Australians used boxing in their training Pearce was the most impressive practitioner. He looked as if boxing might have been his second trade. He showed that controlled aggression so

12. Along with Peter Sterling and Brett Kenny, Wayne Pearce was one of the revelations of the tour. His pace and his ability to burst through tackles made him extremely dangerous. His fitness, too, was extraordinary, his discipline exemplary.

evident on the field. Rogers had the ability to drag himself out of tackles. Pearce simply used to burst straight through them. His power, fitness, and remarkable pace made him a formidable forward.

His ability to break through tackles was seen in the first Test at the sixth try scored by Kenny, Pearce bursting through a joint high tackle by Nash and Norton as if he was running through a paper hoop. That was followed by a

The Australian Tour

lovely pass to Kenny. Then at the next try he showed his anticipation and his pace when he sprinted on to Young's pass and scored beneath the posts.

There were similar efforts from Pearce in the final Test. This time O'Neill and Crooks paid the price for trying to tackle Pearce too high. Playing at loose forward in place of the injured Price in that game, he burst through the pair of them and then fed Kenny who turned the ball inside for Krilich to score his memorable try. Then when Pearce scored his try he left the British second row forward, Peter Smith, flat-footed as he raced in under the posts.

Pearce was unspoiled. He was honest, modest, dedicated, and his commitment to the team was absolute. He tackled hard and fairly, and never displayed any temper. He was floored by a dreadful late tackle by Dyl in the first Test after he had slipped the ball inside to Boyd—who scored—but showed no signs of resentment when he recovered. It certainly failed to halt either his punishingly hard attacking play or his uncompromising defence. He attributed a lot of his success to Ray Price. 'How can you be a bad player when you are mixing with players like him?' he asked.

Mal Meninga had his vulnerable moments in defence and was chiefly to blame for the only try that Australia conceded in the Tests when he failed to gather a British kick. He was, too, likely to miss the occasional tackle. But this powerful centre from Brisbane was also responsible for some of the most exciting attacking moments of the tour. The try he scored in the first game when, from the left side of his own half, he ran 70 yards to touch down in the right corner, was an early statement of his danger and of his strength and pace.

Meninga's discipline, like that of so many of his colleagues, was admirable. The only time that he showed the slightest loss of temper was when Krilich scored his try in the third Test and Crooks went barging into the celebrating Australians. When Meninga gained possession the crowd's anticipation sharpened. For such a big, powerful man his running was remarkably smooth, and this combination of strength, pace and style made him a compelling sight. Distances were no object to him; opponents were there to be bounced out of the way. Meninga provided English audiences with some of the most gripping running of all.

His strength made him a fearsome opponent. In the first Test Les Dyl, a hard, seasoned, determined professional, was twice made to look a weakling—when Rogers dragged himself out of the Leeds player's tackle in the second half and, once before that, in the first half, when Meninga broke clear down the right and scored the first try of the series. Dyl came across at pace to cover his opposite centre but was stopped in his tracks and forced back off his feet by the strength of Meninga's hand-off. 'Don't blame Dyl,' Alex Murphy appealed to his

13. No player excited English spectators more than Mal Meninga. The sheer power and physique of the man made him a compelling sight when he was on the move. Meninga's value was increased by his place kicking, which was sometimes erratic but rarely let him down in the Tests. His 'straight-on' method of kicking is rarely seen in Britain these days. He would take as much care with a kick from in front of the posts as he would with one close to the touchline.

television audience. Certainly Dyl deserved sympathy. There was little he could do against that sort of resistance.

The Australian Tour

The best example of Meninga's strength, however, came in the final Test during the build-up to Pearce's magnificent try. Twice in this movement Meninga resisted determined tackles by the gutsy Drummond, who simply bounced off the centre, and then Paul Rose, a big, strong forward, can never have been knocked off his feet so spectacularly as he was when he came into contact with Meninga, who simply turned his shoulder to meet Rose's challenge.

On his first appearance for Australia against New Zealand Meninga's contribution was brief. Injury—to which he was not accustomed—forced him out of the contest. His first appearance against Great Britain compensated for that disappointment. He scored the first try of the series and landed eight goals, giving him nineteen points in all. His place kicking was not always as accurate as it was at Hull, though he would take as much care with a kick in front of the posts as he would with one from the touchline. It never let him down in the Tests, however, and eight goals in the first Test were followed by six at Wigan (and a try) and seven at Leeds for a total of forty-eight points in the Tests.

Brett Kenny entered many Australian moves with the sudden brilliance of an action painter hurling paint on to canvas. Australia were never placed in a position from which they had to retrieve a game. Had they been, Kenny might well have been the player who could have done it for them. Some doubts were expressed early in the tour about how Kenny would respond to hard physical treatment, but his appetite for work was insatiable and his acceptance of physical blows beyond criticism. He never tried to 'hide' in a game, nor showed any inclination to do so. He proved himself to be a totally honest player, who could tackle uncompromisingly hard. He took Brentnall's place in the final Test, while the full-back spent ten minutes in the sin bin, and never flinched during one of Britain's few periods of ascendancy. He was unable to prevent Evans from scoring his try, but Brentnall would probably not have stopped it either.

His discipline was absolute. It was hard to remember him losing his temper or showing signs of retaliation. He showed himself to be a sensitive person too. Having ousted Wally Lewis from the stand-off position that the Queenslander had been expected to fill Kenny seemed determined to show at every opportunity his concern for and his warmth towards his deposed colleague. When Lewis threw out the stunning pass that gave Meninga his try at Wigan Kenny ran not to congratulate the scorer but the provider; and when Lewis was injured in the final club match at Widnes it was Kenny who ran on to help him from the field.

14. When given the opportunity to run over a distance Brett Kenny would produce blistering pace. This was such a run, bringing him his try in the first Test against Great Britain. Fairbairn, Woods and Dyl can do nothing to stop him. Norton was already out of the race, and Drummond is given a look of contempt as Kenny swerves inside the Great Britain winger.

Kenny handled the ball skilfully and timed his passes to perfection. His defensive qualities were proven on this tour but it was his attacking skills which made him such a dangerous player. There was nothing better in the series than the searing break he made down the right in the final Test followed by a remarkable reverse pass to Boustead who then sent in Rogers. That was one occasion when Britain could justifiably feel that they were the victims of sleight of hand.

That was followed just before the end by a try from the young stand-off that was the result of scintillating pace, a try scored with nice timing to a tannoy announcement that Kenny had been voted the man of the match. It was the perfect ending for Kenny on his first tour of Britain.

2

THE INTERNATIONAL SEASON

An international flavour was brought early to the season, though it is doubtful if very many people noticed. Gatherings of 1,160 at Watersheddings, 840 at Post Office Road and 3,700 at Central Park saw a French XIII beat Oldham and Featherstone Rovers and lose to Wigan. All three matches had a common theme—violence—and it is doubtful whether they did much to promote Anglo-French relationships. The object of these games, as far as the French were concerned, was to give them some meaningful competition in preparation for the Tests against Australia in December. For that purpose they were possibly of some value, but as a public relations exercise they were an embarrassment.

The trouble with the French is that they often seem unable to make up their minds whether they would prefer to fight or to play football. That, admittedly, is not a characteristic to which they have exclusive rights—as a disgraceful Test between Great Britain and France at the Boulevard all too graphically illustrated—but to the outsider especially the French can be infuriating, so often allowing their natural ball-handling skills to become submerged by darker desires. Just how good they can be was shown in their two Tests against the Australians, when their aggression, skill and determination were mixed in equal proportions.

When the French take a retrospective look at this season, they will probably do so with a mixture of frustration and disappointment. Logic will have told them that they had no chance of emulating their 1978 successes against Australia, but the standards they achieved at Avignon and Narbonne gave them justifiable grounds for thinking that they would defeat a reshaped Great Britain side, at least at home. Perhaps they were a shade too optimistic. Certainly the consistency of their performances against Australia was not repeated against Great Britain, and they lost 20–5 at Carcassonne and 17–5 at Hull after an appalling match.

There were not even any small consolations. In the Under-24 international at Carpentras, Great Britain won 19–5 and met surprisingly unconvincing

15. When Tony Myler played in the two Tests against France there was criticism that his name and not his ability had won him a place, his uncle being Frank Myler, the Great Britain coach. However, Myler played well in both games, and later was to give a performance in the Premiership Trophy final against Hull which persuaded even the severest critic that he was one of the best youngsters to emerge in 1982–83.

resistance, Garry Clark, the 18-year-old Hull Kingston Rovers winger, scoring three good tries on a highly promising first appearance. Whether the French would have found more enthusiasm in the return match at Oldham will never be known. Oldham was the victim of some of the severest weather of a generally mild winter, and shortly before the start a heavy fall of snow left the ground unfit for play. In a sport in which international opportunities are

The International Season

limited, the cancellation of that match was frustrating. For a number of reasons, it was not possible to rearrange it.

France's best result was their 12–12 draw from the Colts international at the small, open, wind-swept ground at Apt near Avignon, a game in which the British could derive more satisfaction from the result than the performance. The French were the more skilful, handled more enterprisingly, ran with greater purpose and showed a keener appreciation of support play. In Didier Lacourt they possessed a persistently inventive stand-off, in Robert Mercadal and Pierre Montgaillard two forceful props, and in Francis Lope a fine second-row forward.

The British were commendably dogged, which enabled them to level the scores at 12–12 after the French, now with the advantage of a forceful wind, seemed to have the game won when Lope scored a try that was the result of excellent support play. But there was little satisfaction to be derived from seeing British forwards so often embarking on those one-man drives so beloved of the senior players in the matches against Australia, support glaringly absent. Easily the outstanding British player, nevertheless, was a forward, Keith England, displaying maturity and, with two tries, opportunism. Castleford have produced some of the best young forwards in the British game in recent seasons, and England appears likely to sustain the tradition.

There was even less to admire in the return match at Leigh. This time Britain won easily, 24–10, against a French side showing little of the teamwork that had characterized their play at Apt. The French opened in the most enterprising manner, with Eric Salgado testing his opposing full-back, Wayne Atherton, with a long kick downfield. The tactic worked perfectly. Atherton, unfamiliar with the full-back position, fumbled the ball; Lope was first to it, picked it up and ran through for a simple try. Lacourt added the goal, kicked a penalty and France were seven points to the good, but the confidence of that bright opening was soon to evaporate.

Phillip Eden and Kevin Jones scored tries in an undistinguished first half, and only a point separated the teams at the interval. The French, however, had lost their hooker, Alain Bartello, and their winger, Phillippe Gril, in the first half, and by the time the influential Lacourt had also limped out of the contest Britain were on course for a comfortable win. The French belatedly discovered some spirit when Montgaillard scored after a sweeping movement, but before this Keith Atkinson, Wayne Atherton and Keith England, again impressive, had scored tries, and there was another try from Gareth Ingham three minutes from the end.

It was inevitable that under the new regime of Frank Myler and Dick Gemmell there would be a change of personnel in the full Great Britain side. Under Johnny Whiteley and Colin Hutton, players from Humberside provided

16. Great Britain had good cause to respect the Tonneins winger, Patrick Solal. He had inflicted considerable damage on them at Marseilles the previous season and scored this splendid try in the international at the Boulevard. Hull were so impressed that they signed the Frenchman before the end of the season.

the nucleus of the team—and this was especially true of the side that played Australia in the third Test. Now the emphasis switched west of the Pennines to Widnes, Myler's old club, which supplied five players for the British side in Carcassonne and four for the return match at Hull. Accusations of bias were levelled at Myler, of course, but there was also a general satisfaction at seeing the average age of the side fall sharply.

If Britain had played as well at Hull as at Carcassonne, Myler and Gemmell would have had just cause to feel satisfied with the way the remodelled side was progressing. That performance, however, was wretched enough to make them wonder if any progress at all had been made. The discipline that had been such a rewarding British feature at Carcassonne evaporated in a display of vengeful violence. The referee was poor and the players dismal, showing little skill and even less self-control.

After Carpentras and Carcassonne stock-taking had been a reasonably rewarding job. Suddenly it had become a glum business. Were Britain really on the right lines after all? Were players available who were good enough to test the Australians in 1984? If so, who were they? The international matches showed that Britain had some promising, youthful material, but it was difficult to discern among it a latter-day Alex Murphy or Malcolm Reilly. Certainly, there was no evidence of a budding Wayne Pearce, Peter Sterling or Brett Kenny.

Garry Clark, with his three tries in Carpentras, probably made as much of an impact as anybody, and it was a pity that injury prevented him from appearing in the full internationals. Clark's place at Carcassonne went instead to a surprised but grateful Joe Lydon of Widnes, who barely six months before had been a member of the England Under-19 Rugby Union squad. Lydon, Ronnie Duane, the Warrington centre, Tony Myler, the Widnes half-back, and Andy Goodway and Terry Flanagan, two Oldham forwards, made their first full RL international appearances. They acquitted themselves well, too, without suggesting that they would be the new youthful leaders of a British renaissance.

One player who did enhance his reputation was Andrew Gregory, the Widnes scrum-half. His lack of discipline against France at Marseilles the previous season had been costly both to himself and to his side. He needed to prove after that disappointing performance that he had the maturity to complement his undoubted talents. In the three Tests that he played in 1982–3 he showed that he had. Gregory seems to be a player who provokes extremes of opinion, either fulsome admiration or heated condemnation, but in an age short of genuine talent he deserves encouragement and sympathetic treatment.

Carpentras, 16 January
France Under-24 5   Great Britain Under-24 19

The wind that had brought up swirls of dust the previous day at Apt where the Colts had played had not abated on the Sunday at Carpentras—but as far as

The International Season

Britain were concerned it was no ill wind. Garry Clark showed a fine turn of speed and an acute sense of opportunism, and he scored three good tries; John Fieldhouse and Ronnie Duane also went over, and Frank Myler and Dick Gemmell could view the start of their stewardship with some satisfaction.

It would not have been difficult before the kick-off to argue a strong case for a British victory. Since the revival of Under-24 fixtures in 1976, Britain had an impeccable record against the French, having won all previous ten games against them. Indeed, their only defeats in this period under the control of Johnny Whiteley had been against the senior sides of Australia in 1978 and New Zealand in 1980. It was a surprisingly easy victory, nevertheless, particularly as the French had a number of full internationals in their side.

The French are never easy to predict, but they were unusually subdued, for which Britain, of course, can take credit. Apart from some isolated flare-ups, John Holdsworth, the Leeds referee, enjoyed a relatively peaceful afternoon. That he did so was probably due to the fact that the British established a firm ascendancy in the first fifteen minutes. Britain's defence in this period was sound and their tackling so uncompromising that the French appeared to lose spirit.

By half-time Clark had scored two of his three tries. His first, the completion of purposeful approach play by Tony Myler, Ronnie Duane and Mick Burke, was a good one; his second was especially impressive. Terry Flanagan, the British captain, was constructive and involved throughout, and it was from one of his many passes that Clark raced away to score. This particular pass, though, was not one of Flanagan's best, and the Hull KR winger had to stoop and stretch to gather the ball, but he did so without breaking stride, racing past three French defenders on his way to the line.

Burke was successful with two of his place kicks in the first half, landing a penalty and a goal, but kicking successfully into a capricious wind in the second half was practically impossible, and in all five attempts were missed by the full-back. They were not to prove serious. By the time France had scored their only try, Britain were beyond catching.

The previous season, in Tonneins, Des Drummond had scored three tries for the Under-24s. Soon after half-time Clark equalled that feat, completing another enterprising move in which Flanagan and Duane were involved, Flanagan earning credit for a delightfully subtle reverse pass and Duane for showing assured handling under pressure. Almost immediately John Fieldhouse, the only member of the pack not to do himself full justice, burst on to Joe Lydon's pass and possessed the stamina and pace to reach the line from 45 yards—much the best moment of the game for the Warrington forward, who was suffering from concussion at this stage and had to be replaced by Ronnie Smith of Salford on the hour.

The International Season

There was a brief change in the pattern of the game when the experienced Christian Schiccitano accepted a well disguised pass by Phillippe Marty, took advantage of a lapse in Britain's concentration—and a gap at the heart of their defence—and scored under the posts. This was not enough, however, to upset the balance of power, and strong running by Duane just before the end brought Britain their fifth try.

Myler and Gemmell announced at once that the same side would play against the French in the return match at Oldham two weeks later. They had in fact to make one change, bringing in Ronnie Smith of Salford in place of the injured Mick Worrall. It would have been interesting to see how Smith, steadily winning a reputation for himself as a hard-running, fearless forward and a very useful place kicker, would have performed and, indeed, if the side as a whole would have confirmed the promise of Carpentras. But the heavy snow that fell at Watersheddings shortly before the start of the return game put an end to all speculation and debate.

France Under-24: Dauphin (Cavaillon); Fourcade (Le Barcarès), Fourquet (Toulouse), Maury (Cahors), Criottier (Le Pontet); Berge (Le Pontet), Schiccitano (Carpentras); Rabot (Villeneuve), Bernabé (Le Pontet), Storer (St Gaudens), Balez (Albi), Carpène (Toulouse), Marty (Lézignan)

Substitutes: Puech (Albi) for Carpène after 50 minutes, Gomez (Pia) for Balez after 59 minutes

Scorers: try—Schiccitano; goal—Berge

Great Britain Under-24: Burke (Widnes); Clark (Hull KR), Duane (Warrington), Lydon (Widnes), Moll (Keighley); Tony Myler (Widnes), Ashton (Oldham); Mike O'Neill (Widnes), Noble (Bradford Northern), Goodway (Oldham), Fieldhouse (Warrington), Worrall (Oldham), Flanagan (Oldham)

Substitutes: Smith (Salford) for Fieldhouse after 60 minutes, Hulme (Widnes) not used

Scorers: tries—Clark (3), Fieldhouse, Duane; goals—Burke (2)

Referee: J. Holdsworth (England)

Attendance: 1,500

The International Season

The previous day, 15 January, at Apt the following sides had represented France and Great Britain Colts in a match drawn 12–12:

France Colts: Salgado (Pia); Gril (Carcassonne), Sokolow (Carcassonne), Castel (Albi), Lotrian (Châtillon); Lacourt (Toulouse), Entat (Avignon); Montgaillard (XIII Catalan), Bartello (Carcassonne), Mercadal (Limoux), Bosch (Villefranche), Lope (Lézignan), Cunac (Lescure)

Scorers: tries—Bosch, Gril, Lope; goal—Lacourt; drop goal—Lacourt

Great Britain Colts: Conway (Leeds); Atkinson (Oldham), Banks (Featherstone Rovers), Atherton (Leigh), Maher (Oldham); Jones (Castleford), Walsh (Hull KR); Hartley (Castleford), Hughes (Leigh), Forber (St Helens), Proctor (Hull), England (Castleford), Bell (Hull)

Substitutes: Williams (Wakefield Trinity) for Forber after 39 minutes, Platt (St Helens) for Walsh at half time

Scorers: tries—England (2); goals—Bell (3)

Referee: J. McDonald (England)

17. The Great Britain Colts drew with the French at Apt and beat them convincingly at Leigh. One of the outstanding British players in these games was the Castleford forward, Keith England, preparing here to resist the challenge of the French captain, Pierre Montgaillard, during the match at Apt. On the right of the picture is Mark Conway, who played a number of exceptional games for Leeds at half-back during the season.

The International Season

Carcassonne, 20 February
France 5   Great Britain 20

Carcassonne saw the restoration of the international careers of John Joyner and Len Casey. Joyner had been one of the few players to return from Australia in 1979 with his reputation enhanced, but he had not played for Great Britain since the Tests against New Zealand in 1980, injury and a long, unresolved dispute with his club scarcely helping his career. Casey, though, was much the more contentious choice. He too had last played against New Zealand but now at 33 must have been surprised to find himself recalled.

The reasons given by Myler and Gemmell for his selection were logical enough. Britain were fielding a young, largely untried pack, and it was necessary, they felt, to include one old war horse, a player with experience of the battle. Casey certainly had that, having played in France, Australia and New Zealand, but many critics were disappointed that Myler and Gemmell had not made a complete break with the past.

Casey was also made captain, and it was discouraging—though perhaps hardly surprising, since it was unlikely that Casey had been brought in to keep the peace—to find the captain leading the assault when an early bout of knuckle fighting broke out. Casey was involved in another outbreak of violence soon afterwards, but after fifteen minutes the British—Casey included—won much admiration for the control that they showed under considerable provocation.

Had Don Wilson, the New Zealand referee taking charge of his first international, indeed his first match in Europe, sent a couple of players to the sin bin at the start of the game, much of the subsequent trouble might have been avoided. But the New Zealand referee made the extraordinary admission afterwards that he did not know the sin bin was at his disposal. In consequence, much of the violence went unchecked. Mr Wilson was criticized for his handling of this game and was berated even more vigorously after the return match at Hull; certainly the fussiness and dangerous leniency that he showed were an unsatisfactory mix. More was to be heard of Mr Wilson.

Fortunately, the unsavoury aspects of the game were less prominent than the appealing passages, and interwoven were moments of individual and collective excellence. The French handled at times with breathtaking flair; it was fortunate for the British that similar certainty was not shown in their finishing. Instead the French on a number of occasions reached sight of the

18. Joel Roosebrouck of Villeneuve, the French captain, had to limp through much of the international between Great Britain and France at Hull, but as always he exerted considerable influence on the game. Roosebrouck had announced his retirement from international rugby the previous season, but the way he played against Australia and Great Britain in 1982–83 suggested that he still had a lot to offer his country.

The International Season

British line and were then overtaken by carelessness, or they chose the wrong options.

The admirable Joel Roosebrouck, of all people, was guilty of one glaring miss when he knocked-on under the posts with a try there for the taking. On another occasion Guy Delaunay chose to turn the ball outside when his scrum-half, Grésèque, was running free inside him and almost certainly would have scored if he had been given the ball. Kaminski, too, appealed in vain for a pass from Cologni who ignored the pleas and opted, mistakenly, to try to score himself. The place kicking of Imbert was another bonus for Britain. He wasted four out of five kicks at goal.

The French were seen at their best either side of half-time, and Britain could be grateful that only once was the French approach play and finishing in total harmony. On this occasion the ball was switched so swiftly from right to left that a big overlap was created, and Didier Bernard was able to score simply in the corner. Britain held a lead of 13–3 at the interval, but it required some defending after half-time and Mick Burke and Des Drummond in particular produced a number of important tackles.

Andrew Gregory and Tony Myler formed the first club half-back partnership for Britain for thirteen years and brought a lot of creativity and energy to midfield; Joyner and Duane embarked on some dangerous runs; and there was much to admire in the pack, with Brian Noble having an outstanding match. Only one of Britain's tries, nevertheless, was the result of sustained teamwork. The other three were the outcome of individual enterprise from Lydon, Noble and Andy Goodway.

The first British try arrived early, after perfect dovetailing between Myler, Flanagan and Burke, the latter joining the attack from full-back with telling effect. Passes were timed with precision, and suddenly Joyner was free and sprinting for the line. Britain never quite achieved anything as effective again but, thanks to individual opportunism from Lydon and Noble, Britain had a comforting lead of 10 points at half-time.

Lydon's try resulted from a kick-ahead by Gregory. When Gregory kicked, the ball did not quite go where he intended. It struck Kaminski, ricocheted off him and into the path of Lydon, who kicked ahead. When he reached the ball a second time Lydon again kicked ahead and did so on this occasion with such control and with such perfect weight on the ball that by the time it reached the in-goal area it was coming gently to a halt. Lydon touched down joyfully. Then when Noble found himself in possession on the edge of the French '25' the hooker, in the absence of any real support, simply forged forward, probably in hope at first but with growing certainty as the French failed to lay hold of him. It was a fine piece of individual daring.

Joel Roosebrouck again showed his value to France, leading his country's assaults from the front. Had Roosebrouck been in Napoleon's army, he would have been a reluctant retreater from Moscow, but in spite of his inspiring leadership France were at their most profligate in the second half, and Britain's lead was preserved ... and then extended. In the closing stages Goodway, generating fierce pace from the edge of the French '25', burst clean through the French defence to score—a suitably vigorous end for Britain.

There was an unexpected bonus for Britain in this match. Burke's kicking was well below its best, and when the job passed to Lydon the youngster responded with commendable coolness on his first full international appearance. He took three kicks and was successful with each one.

France: Imbert (Le Pontet); Bernard (Carcassonne), Guigue (Avignon), Delaunay (XIII Catalan), Kaminski (Le Pontet); Laville (Villeneuve), Grésèque (XIII Catalan); Storer (St Gaudens), Macalli (Villeneuve), Chantal (Villeneuve), Ambert (Pia), G. Laforgue (XIII Catalan), Roosebrouck (Villeneuve)

Substitutes: Cologni (XIII Catalan) for Ambert after 49 minutes, Guiraud (Lézignan) for Grésèque after 76 minutes

Scorers: try—Bernard; goal—Imbert

Great Britain: Burke (Widnes); Drummond (Leigh), Joyner (Castleford), Duane (Warrington), Lydon (Widnes); Tony Myler (Widnes), Gregory (Widnes); Mike O'Neill (Widnes), Noble (Bradford Northern), Goodway (Oldham), Rathbone (Bradford Northern), Casey (Hull KR), Flanagan (Oldham)

Substitutes: Woods (Leigh) for Myler after 57 minutes, Smith (Featherstone Rovers) for Rathbone after 57 minutes

Scorers: tries—Joyner, Lydon, Noble, Goodway; goals—Burke, Lydon (3)

Referee: D. Wilson (New Zealand)

Attendance: 3,826

The International Season

The Boulevard, Hull, 6 March
Great Britain 17   France 5

The home dressing-room was a revealing place after this Test at the Boulevard. Great Britain had just beaten France for the second time in a fortnight, and there was not a smiling face to be seen. It was a joyless victory. But then what satisfaction could either side have taken in a contest devoid of grace, wit or skill? As those serious British faces showed, there was no pleasure to be derived from a contest that emphasized all the worst aspects of the sport and projected few of its attractions.

19. The New Zealand referee, Don Wilson, received considerable criticism for his handling of the international between Great Britain and France at the Boulevard. He was not, though, responsible for this unsightly brawl. There were few bystanders.

It was obvious from the start that considerable ill-feeling had been engendered in Carcassonne, and the bad blood soon spilled over. Mr Wilson was quick to make use of the sin bin this time. By the quarter-hour three players were spending time there, Jacques Guigue of France and Mike O'Neill and Brian Noble of Britain. There was, however, no cooling of tempers.

In the twentieth minute scarcely a player was not involved in a fight so

The International Season

vicious and intense that it seemed a matter more for the police than a referee, and Mr Wilson was unable to single out individuals for punishment. Frank Myler offered no defence of his team's behaviour or performance afterwards but said that it would have been impossible to have played fluent rugby with Mr Wilson in charge. Mr Wilson answered that charge by saying that whatever action he had taken, this was one of those matches that was destined to run a pre-determined course.

Mr Wilson did not have a good game. That mixture of fussiness and leniency that he had displayed in Carcassonne was even more pronounced this time, and a number of appalling acts of thuggery were allowed to go unpunished. But to blame Mr Wilson exclusively would be a nonsense. He was not, after all, responsible for aiming kicks or throwing punches.

Three years earlier, after a particularly unpleasant match at Narbonne between France and England, Bill Oxley, the chairman of the selectors, had called for an end to matches between the countries. The International Board were sufficiently concerned to seek assurances from France that there would be no repeat of the excesses which had besmirched a game that ended with the English referee, Billy Thompson, being pelted with beer cans thrown from the crowd. He required a police escort to the dressing-rooms, where he and the English officials, players and press were obliged to remain for more than an hour before it was thought safe for them to leave.

There were parallels with that squalid affair because Mr Oxley again was so concerned that at half-time he went to the referee's dressing-room to complain about the violent path that the game was following. 'That is something I have never done before,' said Mr Oxley, 'but I was afraid there was going to be a massacre.' Three years earlier Mr Oxley had said that it was not the fear of someone being injured that had worried him 'but the real fear that someone will get killed'. Objectivity can sometimes go haywire on these occasions, but Mr Oxley's concern sprang from valid fears.

Whereas at Carcassonne the good outweighed the bad, here the opposite was true, and it is doubtful if a single spectator among the crowd of 6,000 took away a memory of any lasting value. In their desire to use one another as human punch-bags, the players ignored practically every good habit. The scrums were as unsightly as slag heaps; teamwork was forgotten as forwards barged mindlessly into the opposition; organization was absent; dropped passes were depressingly commonplace.

From out of the confusion, however, Britain managed to fashion one try before half-time and two after it, while the French enjoyed a period midway through the second half that produced a try by Patrick Solal, who broke clear from 40 yards out and easily outpaced Keith Mumby in his dash to the line. Such enterprise was all too rare.

20. Ronnie Duane was one of the season's best young players. The Warrington centre has pace, strength, a lot of determination and a good attitude to the game. His try for Great Britain in the international against France at Hull was one of the brighter moments of a dismal game. On the right of the picture is the French captain, the great Joel Roosebrouck of Villeneuve.

Britain had opened the scoring as Ronnie Duane, the centre, moved upfield in support of a long, penetrating break by Tony Myler. The Widnes half-back, though, seemed to have spoiled his good work by clinging to the ball too long when support was available outside him. From the play-the-ball, however, Duane reached the try line. Keith Mumby, who had already landed a penalty, now added the goal points, and Britain led by seven points to nil at half-time.

That lead was quickly extended after the interval by Peter Smith, who replaced an ineffective Alan Rathbone and scored within two minutes of his arrival. Andrew Gregory made the important break, Terry Flanagan provided the crucial pass, and Smith galloped in under the posts.

Perhaps realizing that a semblance of co-operation was their only hope, the French began to throw the ball about, moved up in support and suddenly looked a vastly improved team. Vincent Baloup landed a penalty, Solal scored his good try and suddenly a deficit of seven points did not look like an insuperable barrier. However, while a more adventurous approach brought due reward, it was also responsible for Britain's victory.

Five minutes from time Baloup threw out a pass that was too ambitious. Gregory intercepted, ran through unhampered and scored under the posts. This was fitting recompense for Gregory, who had not had one of his best games, although he had always attempted to be constructive and, in spite of a sleepless night spent suffering from a stomach disorder, had risen above the grim general level.

Great Britain: Mumby (Bradford Northern); Drummond (Leigh), Joyner (Castleford), Duane (Warrington), Lydon (Widnes); Tony Myler (Widnes), Gregory (Widnes); Mike O'Neill (Widnes), Noble (Bradford Northern), Goodway (Oldham), Casey (Hull KR), Rathbone (Bradford Northern), Flanagan (Oldham)

Substitutes: Smith (Featherstone Rovers) for Rathbone after 45 minutes, Woods (Leigh) not used

Scorers: tries—Duane, Smith, Gregory; goals—Mumby (4)

France: Guigue (Avignon); Solal (Tonneins), F. Laforgue (XIII Catalan), Fourquet (Toulouse), Bernard (Carcassonne); Guiraud (Lézignan), Schiccitano (Carpentras); Chantal (Villeneuve), Macalli (Villeneuve), Storer (St Gaudens), Baloup (La Réole), G. Laforgue (XIII Catalan), Roosebrouck (Villeneuve)

Substitutes: Prunac (XIII Catalan) for Guigue after 54 minutes, Dauphin (Cavaillon) for F. Laforgue after 32 minutes

Scorers: try—Solal; goal—Baloup

Referee: D. Wilson (New Zealand)

Attendance: 6,055

The previous day, 5 March, at Hilton Park, Leigh, Great Britain Colts had beaten France Colts 24–10. They were represented by the following sides:

Great Britain Colts: Atherton (Leigh); Thornton (Hull KR), Eden (Wakefield Trinity), Atkinson (Oldham), Ingham (Leeds); Jones (Castleford), Conway (Leeds); Crooks (Hull), Hughes (Leigh), England (Castleford), Proctor (Hull), Platt (St Helens), Williams (Wakefield Trinity)

Substitutes: Tosney (Hunslet) for Atkinson, Beal (Hull KR) for Proctor, Dannatt (Hull) for Williams

Scorers: tries—Eden, Jones, Atkinson, Atherton, England, Ingham; goals—Crooks (3)

France Colts: Salgado (Pia); Perez (St Estève), Roses (Pia), Alberola (Lézignan), Gril (Carcassonne); Lacourt (Toulouse), Rouqueirol (Avignon); Montgaillard (XIII Catalan), Bartello (Carcassonne), Mercadal (Limoux), Lope (Lézignan), Bosch (Villefranche), Cunac (Lescure)

Substitutes: Homs (Carcassonne) for Bartello, Baloup (La Réole) for Lacourt, Castel (Albi) not used

Scorers: tries—Bosch, Montgaillard; goals—Lacourt (3)

Referee: R. Belle (France)

Attendance: 1,024

Perhaps the most significant postscript to these games was provided by the singular Mr Wilson. Had he been unduly sensitive, the New Zealand referee probably would have felt deeply hurt by the amount of criticism levelled at him at Carcassonne and Hull. Mr Wilson, however, extrovert, talkative, gregarious, was able to give as good as he received, and before returning to New Zealand he fired a few verbal salvos himself. They were close enough to the truth to warrant a hearing.

After the match in Carcassonne Mr Wilson was scathingly critical of French and British slowness at the play-the-balls. 'Conditions were ideal, but I thought the match was played at half-pace. Unless Britain and France speed up considerably, they will never match Australia,' he said. Australian inventiveness and speed at the play-the-balls in the Ashes series had offered, indeed, a glaring contrast to British sluggishness; and Mr Wilson maintained that many of the players who had taken part in this international would be excluded from Sydney first-grade football because of their slowness.

Mr Wilson's next volley, delivered after the game at Hull, was directed to some extent at the players but chiefly at Frank Myler. Mr Wilson said that the

British players were deficient in basic techniques, and he made particular reference to the scrummages and to tackling. 'Some of the forwards [in the scrums] did not know where to put their feet, and many members of the side did not know how to turn in the tackle and release the ball.'

Mr Wilson went on to say that unless the side was coached properly, the public would not see open rugby. 'The Great Britain side were very badly coached. It is the worst coaching I have come across. I believe that Frank Myler should get a coaching manual like the one written by Ray French and study it. It was the worst game I have refereed and the players were the worst behaved.' And with that Mr Wilson caught his plane home.

Myler, a man slow to lose his temper, was not inclined to join in the public debate, although his private views on Mr Wilson's refereeing had been couched in spicy language. At least the Rugby League authorities were satisfied with the way in which Myler and Gemmell had tackled their jobs. Gemmell was appointed manager for the tour of Australia in 1984, and Myler, in a significant new departure, was offered the Great Britain coach's job full-time. He was not long in deciding to accept it.

3

THE JOHN PLAYER TROPHY, THE WEBSTER'S YORKSHIRE CUP AND THE FORSHAWS LANCASHIRE CUP

THE JOHN PLAYER TROPHY

Wigan's victory over Leeds in the final of the lucrative John Player Trophy at Elland Road in January was evidence of the Lancashire club's returning influence. One of the most illustrious of all Rugby League clubs had gone through some bad years, discovering in 1980 that not even their prestige, power and traditions provided immunity against relegation.

It was always likely that their chances of returning to the surface would be much better than those of the *Titanic*, and after only one season they were refloated in first-division waters. The experience, apart from the slight humiliation of it, probably did them no irreparable harm. It was evident, nevertheless, that Wigan would require a period of convalescence before returning to full health.

Their prime objective on returning to the first division was to consolidate their position. This, under the stewardship of Maurice Bamford, they achieved, although respectability seemed to be not enough to satisfy the Wigan board, and Bamford departed, to be replaced by Alex Murphy.

Wigan's followers tend to be cautious. They will use their lungs with the gusto of bellows when they feel the cause justifies it, but even the arrival of Murphy was not enough to convince many of them that a renaissance was in the offing. Even the extrovert Murphy echoed that caution. A number of times

The John Player Trophy

throughout the season he insisted: 'We are not a great side ... but we are capable of becoming one.'

Yet while Wigan were not what they once were, it was clear that a Lancashire club to rival the support, clamour and vibrancy of Humberside was emerging. It was for this reason that their John Player triumph was a popular one. Most followers of Rugby League would be prepared to accept that a powerful Wigan side is good not for the town alone but for the game as a whole.

Wigan's victory in the first round must have given them particular cause for satisfaction. They beat Castleford 16–10 at Wheldon Road, where three years before they had been defeated in the same competition. They were so bad on that occasion that at the club's next board meeting the then coach and assistant coach, Vince Karalius and Peter Smethurst, successfully offered their resignations. Wigan's decline at that time was gathering momentum. Now, at the same venue, they boldly proclaimed a new, burgeoning spirit.

Castleford were unlucky to lose the dexterous Barry Johnson after only ten minutes with a dislocated shoulder, and his absence inevitably reduced the efficiency of the Castleford pack. Nevertheless, in spite of this misfortune Castleford reduced Wigan's commanding half-time lead of 13–0 to 13–10 but then found that their reserves were exhausted; it was Wigan who finished the stronger side, Colin Whitfield scoring a decisive try nine minutes from the end.

Wigan, never a club reluctant in the past to import outstanding talent from overseas, were helped significantly towards this win by the contributions of two New Zealand players, Danny Campbell, a fearless, hard-running prop, and the recently acquired Graeme West, a tall, second-row forward. Both scored fine tries during Wigan's profitable first half, in which Barry Williams, linking vigorously from full-back, also touched down excitingly. Castleford's retaliation after the interval was admirable, with their wingers, Barry Higgins and Terry Richardson, scoring tries in either corner, but it ran out of momentum before it caused Wigan too much discomfort.

West played an even more significant part in Wigan's win over St Helens in the next round at Central Park, although this time he did not score a try himself. Wigan must have felt that the £60,000 they had paid to secure the New Zealander's services had been shrewd business when, in the first twenty minutes of the match, West used his height to shovel out passes over the heads of the opposition, first to Dennis Ramsdale and then to David Stephenson, both of whom scored.

Before half-time Brian Juliff had scored a try after combining excitingly with Stephenson, and St Helens needed to give rather more than they had to offer to rescue the contest. A late flurry of activity brought their right-winger, Barry Ledger, a try; with five minutes remaining and four points the difference, St Helens had enough time, but not enough wit, to win the game.

The John Player Trophy

In the third round Wigan met surprisingly stern resistance from Salford, then placed second in the second division but a side of a somewhat flimsy nature. Not, though, on this occasion. Salford produced what was probably their most impressive defensive performance of the season in restricting Wigan to an uncomfortably close win 5–4, Wigan's loose forward, John Pendlebury, scoring the only try. If Salford in attack had shown ideas to compare only fractionally with their commitment in defence, they might well have achieved a memorable win.

The contest brought the Wigan coach Alex Murphy to such a state of agitation that the referee went to the dug-out and asked him if he would mind keeping his voice down ... or words to that effect. But Murphy was generous to Salford. 'I don't think we can possibly come up against a better defensive display than that,' he said. He was right.

Leeds, meanwhile, had taken a less arduous route to the semi-finals, removing two second-division sides, Bramley and York, before achieving a creditable away win at Barrow in the third round. Consistency was never Leeds's strongest quality in a fluctuating season, and in the first round a side showing more decisive finishing than Bramley might have taken advantage of a deal of careless defensive play by Leeds.

At home to York in the second round, they won with twenty-one points to spare but still made life unnecessarily hard for themselves. For the best part of half an hour only three points separated the sides and Leeds's 5–2 advantage would have been even slimmer if Terry Morgan had not squandered a simple penalty kick. The loss of a man can sometimes prove advantageous, however. Roy Dickinson was dismissed for an attempted assault on Geoff Pryce, and almost immediately Leeds improved ... not because Dickinson was no longer there but because they began to exploit their superior pace; and to throw the ball about more adventurously.

Four of their seven tries were scored by the Smiths, the youthful Andy on the left wing collecting three of them, the veteran Alan on the right gathering the other one. In this his last season before leaving to run a bar in Benidorm, Les Dyl tended to produce his old, blistering speed infrequently. But the 45-yard dash that brought him a try in this game was a moment to savour. Andy Smith, young enough not to have to worry yet about conserving energy, produced that sort of pace consistently, and his speed was a prime ingredient of Leeds's victory.

An even younger member of the staff helped to play a sizeable part in taking Leeds through to the semi-finals at the expense of Barrow. Mark Conway, a scrum-half sufficiently gifted to win some high praise from the Australian tourists, showed his sense of opportunism and presence of mind when he worked a try 10 yards from the Barrow line and, in a closely contested game, landed two good goals. Steve Herbert had given Barrow an early lead, and it

The John Player Trophy

was not until ten minutes from time, when Ian Wilkinson scored a try, that Leeds could feel reasonably secure.

The semi-finals were sharply contrasting affairs. Leeds beat Widnes 8–2 in a depressingly bad-tempered game at Huddersfield on 28 December, while Wigan defeated Warrington 15–14 in a fluctuating and exciting encounter at St Helens on 1 January. All was acrimony after the match at Fartown. David Ward, the Leeds hooker and captain, claimed that Widnes were the 'dirtiest team I have seen this season'. But then Leeds were not blameless either, although a penalty count of 20–11 against Widnes was a reasonably accurate indication of culpability.

Kevin Dick, Leeds's international scrum-half, had returned from holiday just before this game only to discover that Conway had retained his position, no great surprise after his energetic performance at Barrow. Robin Dewhurst, the Leeds coach, was justified in keeping faith with Conway, too, the young half-back landing all his side's points from penalties and showing many of the game's brighter ideas. It was almost inevitable that the violence would claim at least one victim, and a broken jaw ensured that there would be no place at Elland Road for Kevin Rayne, whose twin brother, Keith, was also excluded from the final because of injury.

Wigan played some excellent football in beating Warrington at Knowsley Road. They experienced a nervous opening, in which defensive carelessness allowed Ronnie Duane and Carl Webb to score tries, and suffered an anxious ending, with Warrington chipping away steadily at Wigan's interval lead of 15–6 until only a point separated the sides. That was how it remained. Warrington's coach, Kevin Ashcroft, claimed that a knock-on, unseen by the referee, had cost Warrington a try and the match, but Wigan's football, in between their uncertain periods, had been of high quality.

The chief feature of their play was the unfailing support that was given to the man with the ball and a refusal to allow the ball to 'die'. This determination to sustain moves for as long as possible produced a number of thrilling handling movements and three good tries from David Stephenson, Henderson Gill and Jeff Clare. Colin Whitfield played a significant part, too, reading his distances and angles accurately and landing three excellent goals—in contrast to the normally unerring Steve Hesford, who fluffed four out of five kicks.

The John Player Trophy Final, Elland Road, Leeds, 22 January
Wigan 15   Leeds 4

It was curious that, with the exception of a match played for the Hospitals Trust Cup at Dalymount Park in Dublin in 1935, Wigan and Leeds had never before met in the final of a cup competition. That the sides had managed to avoid one another for so long gave the occasion added piquancy, and a crowd of just under 20,000, on an unusually mild and pleasant January day, fully justified the decision to take the game to Elland Road, Leeds United's fine stadium, which had staged so successfully the replay of the Challenge Cup final the previous season.

The match did not betray its impressive setting, nor did it fall short of expectations. It was not a classic contest, but it contained enough good football, incident and endeavour to satisfy the most demanding of spectators. For the Leeds followers, of course, the afternoon was a disappointment, but the more generous-minded among them would accept that Leeds tried all they could to win the game. Their efforts were not quite sufficient to carry this day, however.

Leeds must have found the first half demoralizing. They put Wigan under sustained pressure; were especially enterprising at half-back, where Kevin Dick (reclaiming the scrum-half position from a slightly unfortunate Conway) and John Holmes initiated a succession of attacks; and threw the ball about at times with great assurance. Yet at the interval Leeds led only 4–3. Crucially, that extra yard of pace that might have brought a try was missing.

Holmes continued to ply a succession of choice and varied passes for fifteen minutes after half-time, but gradually his and his side's confidence began to evaporate as the points failed to materialize. Tony Burke strove hard to reach the line and was held just short of it; Les Dyl went over but was turned on to his back before he could ground the ball. Wigan had yet to match some of Leeds's better attacking moves, but their defence refused to yield. Having absorbed for an hour all Leeds's thrusts, Wigan were now in a position to launch their successful counter-offensive.

In the fiftieth minute Alex Murphy made what could have proved a risky substitution when he took off Graeme West for Brian Case, recently signed by Wigan and a player who had experienced little competitive football for seven months because of a lengthy and irreconcilable dispute with Warrington. The switch worked more smoothly than Murphy could have expected, Case

21. Henderson Gill, the Wigan left winger, was adept at accepting half-chances, and his opportunism was seen at its best in the John Player Trophy final against Leeds at Elland Road. He was slightly fortunate in having an inexperienced winger marking him, but his try was accepted with characteristic strength. He went over the line so hard that he had to retire soon afterwards with an injured shoulder.

bringing even greater drive to the Wigan pack and helping Nicky Kiss to win five of the last six scrums, a crucial piece of hooking which ensured that a tiring Leeds were kept pinned frustratingly in their own half.

It was Gill's opportunism, nevertheless, which produced the hard currency of points. Gill has that priceless asset of taking full advantage of limited opportunity. He was given only one clear chance in this game, and he accepted it, crashing over the line so hard that he injured his shoulder seriously enough to end his participation in the match four minutes later. Perhaps a more

The John Player Trophy

experienced player than Mark Campbell, deputizing for one of the most experienced players of all, Alan Smith, might have moved across more quickly to cover the danger, but when the muscular, fast and determined Gill is given a chance as inviting as this, he is not one to waste it.

Colin Whitfield, who had opened the scoring with a dropped goal in the seventh minute, added the goal points with a splendid kick from the touchline, and Kevin Dick's two penalties of the first half had now been overhauled. The ominous confidence now coursing through the Wigan side suggested that Leeds would do very well indeed to recover. All the effort that Danny Campbell and Mick Scott, Nicky Kiss, Glyn Shaw and John Pendlebury had poured into their afternoon's work was beginning to reap dividends.

The introduction of Brian Juliff for the injured Gill did not cause Wigan to reorganize. The former Welsh Rugby Union player had spent much of his time at Wakefield Trinity on the left wing before he moved into the forwards, so he was no stranger to the wing position. It was his straying into midfield five minutes from time, however, that put a summary end to Leeds's hopes, Juliff bursting jubilantly through a tired defence to score his side's second try. Whitfield added the goal points, and Wigan were beyond catching.

Wigan will look back on that afternoon's work with deep satisfaction, and justifiably. They have played better football before and since but they will rarely have worked harder, concentrated more or showed a keener sense of opportunism. It was a mature performance from a young side, and that, for a club trying to recover some of the old glory, was perhaps most satisfying of all. It was a pity that the 17-year-old amateur Jeff Clare had to miss it. He had played his part in helping Wigan to reach the final but failed to appear at Elland Road because of a fractured leg.

There was a significant postscript to a rewarding afternoon. From a crowd of 19,553 (paying competition record receipts of £49,027) the police found it necessary to haul away one drunkard, not because he was causing bother but because he was considered too inebriated for his own good. Meanwhile at the Baseball Ground at Derby, the Leeds United supporters were causing £20,000 of damage in a mindless display of vandalism.

Wigan: Williams; Ramsdale, Stephenson, Whitfield, Gill; Foy, Fairhurst; Shaw, Kiss, Danny Campbell, West, Scott, Pendlebury

Substitutes: Case for West after 50 minutes, Juliff for Gill after 61 minutes

Scorers: tries—Gill, Juliff; goals—Whitfield (5); drop goal—Whitfield

Leeds: Hague; Mark Campbell, Wilkinson, Dyl, Andrew Smith; Holmes, Dick; Dickinson, Ward, Burke, Sykes, Wayne Heron, David Heron

Substitutes: Heslewood, Conway not used

Scorer: goals—Dick (2)

Referee: R. Campbell (Widnes)

Attendance: 19,553

THE WEBSTER'S YORKSHIRE CUP

Few people seriously expected Bradford Northern to beat Hull in the final of the Webster's Yorkshire Cup at Headingley. Even Peter Fox, Northern's coach, not a man renowned for his self-effacement, must have experienced some misgivings as he prepared his players for Bradford's twelfth appearance in the final of this competition. While he had difficulty finding a side at all, Hull could afford to number Steve Norton among their substitutes.

Norton had been one of the most influential figures in so many of Hull's triumphs the previous season, and was still regarded as one of the best loose forwards in the world. If Hull could afford to start the match without such a talented performer, what hope had Northern? Bradford had won ten of their previous matches in the final, but it is doubtful if Fox derived much comfort from that encouraging piece of history.

Arthur Bunting, Hull's team manager, nevertheless went to some pains on the eve of the game to impress upon his players the considerable qualities of the opposition. He was wise to do so. In a match that Bunting afterwards described accurately as 'good, hard and clean' Northern played as well as could reasonably have been expected of them—even by the demanding Fox. They were behind by only a point at the interval but ran out of energy in the second half. Their defeat in the end was emphatic enough, although a margin of 18–7 flattered Hull slightly and did less than justice to the amount of effort that Bradford put into the game.

In reaching the final Northern had removed the other Humberside club, Hull Kingston Rovers, in the first round. This was a close and exciting game, distinguished by an outstanding try by Bradford's brave, energetic full-back,

The Webster's Yorkshire Cup

Keith Mumby, who ran 70 yards and hauled himself out of two tackles before touching down. But at the end the overriding feeling on both sides was probably one of relief that the game had been completed without any repetition of the bitterness that had disfigured their last meeting in the Premiership Trophy the previous May.

That game had given Rugby League one of its most unsavoury episodes of the 1981–82 season. In the fifty-sixth minute Jeff Grayshon, Northern's captain, was sent off, and the rest of his side—or what remained of it—followed him, claiming later that they were not receiving adequate protection from an over-tolerant referee. Five players had been dismissed in the first half. Grayshon was the sixth to be banished, and the misguided action of his colleagues in trooping after him caused the club to be severely disciplined. Bradford were refused admission to the following season's Challenge Cup, John Player Trophy and Premiership Trophy, a severe punishment that was later suspended for three years.

It was unfortunate that after so much acrimony the sides should meet again so soon but, mercifully, the enduring memories this time were not of malice and conflict but of the vigour of a weakened Bradford side, their recovery from arrears of 14–5 to win 15–14 and Mumby's excellent try.

Northern had only three points to spare against York in the second round, rather more against Featherstone Rovers in the semi-final. They won this match 11–0, but in an otherwise clean game their prop, Mick Atherton, was sent off, along with Steve Hankins of Rovers. This merely added to Peter Fox's selection problems later. It was Atherton's misfortune that the disciplinary committee should meet on the Thursday before the final. Atherton was suspended for only one match, but that was enough to deprive him of an appearance in the season's first major cup final.

Hull were making relatively untroubled progress meanwhile, parsimoniously conceding eight points in the three games to the final but collecting some injuries. Strangely, in view of their rewards elsewhere, Hull had tried unsuccessfully for four years to reach the second round of this competition, but now Huddersfield at the Boulevard seemed unlikely to extend that unhappy sequence and indeed presented the most modest of challenges. The handling of both sides was not helped by incessant rain, but if Hull's efficiency was impaired, they were still able to score eight tries, three of them by Kevin Harkin.

Hull's most impressive match of the campaign came the following Wednesday at Headingley, where they removed Leeds so emphatically that the eventual outcome of the tournament appeared pre-ordained. Leeds were already emerging as one of the season's most powerful sides, with three successive wins in the Slalom Lager Championship and an emphatic victory at

The Webster's Yorkshire Cup

Castleford in the first round of the Yorkshire Cup to their credit. Their form on this occasion was again good but nothing like good enough to disturb Hull.

In attack Leeds were so effectively shackled that they could conjure up not a single point, even from the accurate right boot of Kevin Dick; and defensively they were severely stretched by the weight, persistence and variety of Hull's attacks. Kevin Harkin, such an influential scrum-half against Huddersfield, was again irrepressible; David Topliss was an ebullient partner at stand-off. The ceaseless promptings of this pair found a ready response from the three-quarters and forwards, and Leeds were overwhelmed in every department. But Hull were to pay a price even in such excellence, losing their open-side prop, Keith Tindall, with a badly broken left leg, the result of an awkward tackle.

Hull's unfortunate opponents in the semi-final were Keighley, then struggling to haul themselves away from the bottom of the second division. An unequal contest was perhaps inevitable, but Keighley did manage to score three points where Leeds had failed to score any, while the dedication of their tackling restricted Hull to a modest twenty-three points. Hull, possibly unable to forget that they were superior beings, took some tortuous routes towards their opponents' try line when simplicity would probably have served them better. But Hull were in the Yorkshire Cup final for the first time for thirteen years and no one was complaining very loudly.

The Yorkshire Cup Final
Headingley, Leeds, 2 October
Hull 18   Bradford Northern 7

Hull had had their problems on the way to the final. Their most unfortunate casualty, of course, was Tindall with that shattered leg. But Norton had suffered from a persistent muscle strain; Gary Kemble, their fine, long-striding New Zealand full-back, had his return to the Boulevard delayed by a groin injury; Paul Rose, signed early in the season from Hull KR, was suffering from damaged ribs. The club also had problems at half-back and hooker, the latter resolved by the signing of the heavy-footed but experienced Keith Bridges ... from Bradford of all places.

They were still, nevertheless, able to field a formidably powerful side in the final. Not so Bradford. They had been beset by problems from the start of the season and were unable to disguise their weaknesses. At stand-off and left wing

22. Steve Norton has sometimes failed to do himself justice on major occasions, but not this time. He was forward substitute in the Yorkshire Cup final against Bradford Northern, replacing Mick Crane in the fifty-sixth minute. His influence was soon felt, however, and he played a major part in Paul Rose's second try.

they were forced to use inexperienced youngsters in Keith Whiteman and Steve Pullen. Alan Redfearn, such a valuable member of the side, was missing from scrum-half; the elusive and talented Ellery Hanley was unavailable.

Not that there was much weakness evident up to half-time. With Keith Mumby, unfailingly reliable, and Jeff Grayshon, until he suffered a late loss of temper, setting outstanding examples at full-back and open-side prop, Northern enjoyed a successful first half. They went six points in arrears when Paul Rose and Paul Prendiville scored tries after moves of ominous assurance, but retaliated splendidly through Whiteman, following up in support of a break by Gary Hale which took him clean through Hull's defences. Dean Carroll, who had earlier landed a dropped goal, improved the try, and at the interval only a dropped goal by Lee Crooks separated the sides.

What perhaps undermined Northern was the sight of Norton peeling off his tracksuit top and trotting to and fro along the touchline as he prepared to enter the conflict. Mick Crane at loose forward had done nothing noticeably wrong but was about to be replaced. It was little wonder that Bradford's spirit, and probably their belief that the match could be won, began to drain away. Norton had not been on the field ten minutes when he was heavily involved in the move which gave Rose his second try. Northern began to subside.

Crooks improved that try with a kick wide from the right and then landed a penalty when Grayshon, now showing obvious signs of evaporating temper, fouled Kevin Harkin. There was still time for Steve Evans to score a try, his sixth in six games, in the right corner.

That was a good moment for Evans who, in the eight months since his expensive move from Post Office Road to Airlie Street, had gathered a Challenge Cup winners' medal and a county cup winners' medal. Evans, better-known as a stand-off or centre, played on the right wing in this final. Severe competition for places had forced him into this position, but when asked afterwards if he was enjoying playing in a relatively strange position he replied that he was simply grateful to be in the side. From a player who had cost Hull £70,000 that was a nice touch of humility.

Hull: Kemble; Evans, Day, Leuluai, Prendiville; Topliss, Harkin; Skerrett, Bridges, Stone, Rose, Crooks, Crane

Substitutes: Norton for Crane after 56 minutes, Banks not used

Scorers: tries—Rose (2), Prendiville, Evans; goals—Crooks (2); drop goals—Crooks (2)

Bradford Northern: Mumby; Barends, Gant, Parker, Pullen; Whiteman, Carroll; Grayshon, Noble, Van Bellen, Idle, Jasiewicz, Hale

Substitutes: Smith for Pullen after 74 minutes, Sanderson for Van Bellen after 74 minutes

Scorers: try—Whiteman; goal—Carroll; drop goals—Carroll (2)

Referee: S. Wall (Leigh)

Attendance: 11,755

THE FORSHAWS LANCASHIRE CUP

The geographical absurdity of a club from London and another from Cumbria contesting the final of the Forshaws Lancashire Cup might well have materialized. Fulham, in their third season of existence, and Carlisle, in only their second, reached the semi-finals of the competition but were then removed by two longer-standing members of the establishment, Warrington and St Helens. For variety's sake and in the interests of the sport in these developing areas of the game, it might have been beneficial if Fulham and/or Carlisle had reached the final, though of course Warrington and St Helens, rightly, were not concerned with such considerations.

The first round provided a largely predictable set of results. All the second-division clubs drawn against opponents from the first division lost, so that Blackpool, Whitehaven, Rochdale, Huyton and Salford quietly made their exits. Indeed, only one side from the lower division reached the second round, John Crossley scoring three tries in Fulham's comfortable victory over Swinton. Much the most impressive result of the round was achieved at Naughton Park, where a try five minutes from time by Peter Gorley gave St Helens a merited win 14–12 over Widnes.

Things are very often not what they appear to be in Rugby League, and in the days before this match Widnes gloomily reported that their talented scrum-half, Andrew Gregory, was to enter hospital, possibly to undergo a cartilage operation. It was not certain how long he would be absent from the game, but there was the possibility that he would be unavailable for selection for the first Test between Great Britain and Australia at Hull on 30 October.

A couple of days later, coming on as substitute early in the second half, Gregory appeared to have won the game for Widnes when he flitted over for a try. Widnes had won this competition in 1974, 1975 and 1976, and again in 1978 and 1979, and now appeared to be well on their way again. Even Gregory's endeavours, however, were insufficient. St Helens, under Billy Benyon, were already showing a determination that had not always been apparent the previous season. Commendably, they chipped away at Widnes's lead and finally overhauled it.

The quarter-finals produced two excellent victories, all the more meritorious for being achieved away from home. Leigh, the holders, were beaten 13–12 by Carlisle at Hilton Park, and Fulham won with such conviction against Wigan at Central Park that their relegation from the first division the previous season

23. Bob Eccles for once is preoccupied with defensive duties as he attempts to stop the dangerous St Helens loose-forward, Harry Pinner, in the Lancashire Cup final. Eccles finished the season with 37 tries to his credit, a remarkable effort for a second-row forward and for a side struggling in the relegation zone for much of the season. He did, of course, collect his inevitable try for Warrington in this game.

seemed all the more unfortunate. Carlisle's win was due in part to the individual enterprise of Sanderson and Youngman, who collected three tries between them; Fulham's was the result of a superbly disciplined performance all round but with particularly impressive displays from their props, Tony Gourley and Harry Beverley.

St Helens meanwhile were fashioning their second narrow away win at Craven Park, Barrow, while Warrington had only two points to spare against a steadily improving Oldham side at Wilderspool. This brought St Helens up against Carlisle and Warrington against Fulham in the semi-finals; it also provoked one of the season's early disagreements. 'RL storm,' shouted one local newspaper headline. It was not quite that serious, but it was heated enough.

It was possible to sympathize with both sides. The previous season Warrington had had their main stand destroyed by fire; one of the consequences of that misfortune was that the club lost the use of their floodlights. Warrington, who had home advantage, asked for the start to be brought forward to 4.30 p.m. Fulham objected on the not unreasonable grounds that this early start would scarcely suit those Fulham supporters travelling from London to the game.

The authorities favoured Fulham and ordered the game to be played at Wigan. Angry that they had now lost home advantage, Warrington lodged a complaint. 'We were drawn at home, and that is where we intend to hold the tie,' said one of their officials. Fulham retorted that they would have been happy to accept the ruling whether it had been in their favour or not, so why couldn't Warrington? Warrington's appeal was rejected.

Warrington probably went into the semi-final smarting from a sense of injustice. If they did, it worked to their advantage. Fulham, too predictable and much less organized than they had been against Wigan, discovered too late the tactics that might have won them a coveted place in the final; Hussein M'Barki's splendidly individualistic try also came too late. Warrington's defence betrayed few of the vulnerabilities that Wigan had displayed in the quarter-finals, and in attack they were able to find two inspirational moments, in the first half when Ken Kelly made a decisive run through a broken field and in the second when his namesake, Mike, completed a brilliant move involving John Fieldhouse and Bob Eccles.

If the competition was to be given a surprise twist, there was now only Carlisle left to do it. Carlisle had had an encouragingly successful first season in Rugby League, securing promotion as the runners-up in the second division. Later, in their second season, they were to be beset by problems so serious that their very existence was threatened, and they suffered a succession of crushing defeats. Defeat from the start of the season was a familiarity to them, but in those early weeks, more often than not, they were beaten by narrow margins. A draw 7–7 at Knowsley Road showed that the side possessed potential. Carlisle even led at the interval, with one of their New Zealand imports, Clayton Friend, running 25 yards to score an excellent solo try under the posts. Their player-coach, Mick Morgan, was an admirable organizer and a calming influence, and in the second half St Helens were restricted to just the two points that earned them a replay at Brunton Park.

There St Helens were much more direct and positive and deserved their 9–5 win, a score which none the less reflected credit on Carlisle. Dennis Litherland scored the only try of a first half in which Dean Bell of Carlisle and Chris Arkwright of St Helens were sent off for fighting. Graham Liptrot monopolized the scrums, and drop goals from Harry Pinner and Neil Holding helped St Helens maintain control. Carlisle's deficit nevertheless was reduced to only four points early in the second half, when Graham Evans touched down and Andy Newton added the goal points, but thereafter they were heavily committed to defence, and a succession of superb tackles by Friend repeatedly thwarted St Helens.

The Lancashire Cup Final
Wigan, 23 October
Warrington 16   St Helens 0

For Billy Benyon, the St Helens coach, defeat in the final must have rankled. He had been sacked seven months earlier by Warrington, a dismissal that seemed especially harsh in view of the success that the club had enjoyed under his stewardship. Benyon received a lot of sympathy—not least from an industrial tribunal that upheld his claim that he had been dismissed unfairly—but Warrington in the final always looked likely to deny Benyon the satisfaction of a victory against his old club.

An uncompromisingly solid performance deservedly brought them the prize, the score of 16–0 accurately reflecting Warrington's pragmatism and St Helens's lack of scoring opportunities. St Helens were fortunate to concede only 16 points. Steve Hesford, whose accurate place kicking has won many a match for Warrington, missed seven out of nine kicks at goal, two of them striking a post—an unusually high degree of error for him.

St Helens had not won the Lancashire Cup since 1968, and it was clear by half-time that they were not going to win it this year either. When they are in the mood, Warrington are resilient enough in defence to absorb heavy pressure and sufficiently enterprising in attack to trouble the best of opponents. Most of Warrington's season was preoccupied with a struggle against relegation, but on this occasion there were few flaws. Certainly St Helens failed to find any.

The press came in for some ribald comment when they made Steve Hesford the man of the match, many spectators failing to understand how a man who had missed seven of his nine kicks at goal could possibly justify such an

24. Steve Hesford had a curious sort of match in the final of the Lancashire Cup for Warrington against St Helens. The full-back, normally the safest of place kickers, missed seven out of nine kicks at goal but was still voted the man of the match. Quite a number of spectators did not think this funny, but Hesford's contribution to Warrington's 16–0 win was undeniable.

accolade. There appeared to be other players with stronger claims to the award—in an excellent pack, John Fieldhouse and Bob Eccles especially—but in spite of his wayward kicking Hesford did play a significant part in his team's victory.

In the first half Hesford followed up his own high kick, caught it in spite of the attentions of a knot of St Helens players and immediately threw out a fast, accurate pass to the right wing. Paul Fellows took the ball at full stretch and scored in the corner. Then in the second half, after St Helens had thundered away in vain for ten minutes at the Warrington line, Hesford caught a rebound off a St Helens player and sent Mike Kelly over in the left corner.

St Helens's growing frustration manifested itself in the worst way when Graham Liptrot was sent off for a dreadful foul on his opposing hooker, Carl Webb, who had been brought into the side as a replacement for the injured Roger O'Mahoney. That lack of discipline—something of which Warrington that day were rarely guilty—made St Helens's prospects, already gloomy, practically hopeless; and in a final phase of growing Warrington confidence Eccles became the first forward in the history of the club to score tries in six successive games. His try was followed by a sweeping movement in which the admirable Fieldhouse combined with Paul Cullen to send Ken Kelly in under the posts.

Warrington: Hesford; Fellows, Duane, Bevan, Mike Kelly; Cullen, Ken Kelly; Courtney, Webb, Cooke, Eccles, Fieldhouse, Gregory

Substitutes: Chisnall for Cooke at half-time, Finnegan not used

Scorers: tries—Fellows, Mike Kelly, Eccles, Ken Kelly; goals—Hesford (2)

St Helens: Parkes; Ledger, Arkwright, Haggerty, Litherland; Peters, Holding; James, Liptrot, Bottell, Moorby, Gorley, Pinner

Substitutes: Mathias for Bottell after 55 minutes, Smith for Parkes after 70 minutes

Referee: J. Holdsworth (Leeds)

Attendance: 6,462

4

THE STATE EXPRESS CHALLENGE CUP

The 1983 State Express Challenge Cup final provided one of the biggest upheavals of form the competition has known. It brought together Hull, winners of the Slalom Lager Championship and the Yorkshire Cup and by far the best supported club in the Rugby Football League, and Featherstone Rovers, who needed attendances of 4,000 to balance their books but were struggling to exist on average crowds of 2,500. Featherstone consists chiefly of one street, Station Street, and has been described as a set of traffic lights on the road from Wakefield to Pontefract. The population of Featherstone is 14,000; the population of Hull more than 300,000. When two teams meet on a rugby field, respective population figures cease to have much meaning, but on this occasion they seemed to represent accurately the scale of the inequality of the sides. Featherstone won 14–12.

It was reasonable and logical to assume that Featherstone had little chance of winning. They had finished the season in better health than they had enjoyed throughout it, but the salient fact was that they had escaped relegation to the second division by only a point, and that thanks to Hull beating Barrow on the last day of the league season. On one embarrassing occasion in November they had conceded forty-five points to Wigan without reply at Central Park. For a club that prided itself on its resilience, that was a difficult result to swallow.

The arrival of Allan Agar was the significant event for Featherstone. Although he still lived locally, after leaving the club in 1969 he had been with Dewsbury, New Hunslet, Hull Kingston Rovers and, latterly, Carlisle. He was young, independent, modern-thinking, quiet but strong-willed. Keith Goulding, who had spent two previous periods with Featherstone at Post Office Road, was his chief rival for the job, which had become vacant when Vince Farrar was sacked. Goulding was asked if he would be prepared to act as assistant to Agar if he was not given the post. At first Goulding refused but then changed his mind. By the end of the season the partnership was working smoothly. As the final showed, Rovers were a much better organized side than they had been for a long time and, thanks to Goulding's influence, a much fitter team. It was impossible to foresee, nevertheless, that they would play as well as they did at Wembley.

It was in the quarter-finals, when Gilbert twice showed the St Helens defence the cleanest pair of heels, that Featherstone realistically emerged as serious challengers for the Cup. As they were to do in the semi-final against Bradford, Featherstone punished a side intent on playing cautious rugby. Even on their own ground at Knowsley Road, St Helens displayed little of the assurance which had taken them to a splendid win over Leeds in the second round. They were slow, predictable and too often opted for the central route through the Featherstone defence.

Rovers were far more adventurous, and they profited accordingly. Their attacking play was so good in the early phase of the game that it invited comparison with the Australians', and there could be no higher compliment than that. Gilbert showed considerable pace to score Rovers' first try, and when Marsden went over in the right corner after only eleven minutes Featherstone led 8–0. Midway through the second half, however, it was St Helens who seemed likelier to reach Wembley. Pinner and Haggerty scored tries; Griffiths landed both goals; and as the game entered the final minutes St Helens led 10–8. Again, though, Featherstone found the pace which had so troubled their opponents in the opening minutes, and a sweeping move ended with Gilbert scoring his second try.

This match was one of a sequence of improbabilities. To begin with, Widnes had been expected to beat Leeds at home at Naughton Park. They were no longer the power of old, but as the Cup approached they were showing form impressive enough to make them the favourites to reach Wembley for a third successive year. Leeds, though still top of the league at this point, were vulnerable and were also suffering from injury serious enough to deprive them of half a pack. Yet they produced one of their most convincing displays of the season, showing an all-round solidity that must have bemused their coach, Robin Dewhurst.

The Leeds props, Sykes and Burke, were ceaselessly combative, their forward rushes so fierce and decisive that their colleagues would have been shamed not to follow their example. It was, nevertheless, an impish piece of opportunism by Conway just after the interval that inspired Leeds, the scrum-half intercepting Mike O'Neill's pass on the half-way line. Immediately he was clear of all would-be pursuers.

O'Loughlin's try brought the score to 6–7, and at that stage Leeds must have remembered anxiously the previous season's semi-final against the same opponents. On that occasion, with only seconds remaining and Leeds in the lead, Adams had hoisted a kick which had bounced back fortuitously off the crossbar and into the grateful hands of O'Loughlin, who had plunged over the line for the decisive try. Adams attempted the tactic again, but this time Leeds prevailed and Wayne Heron ended all their anxieties with a late try.

Dewhurst had said beforehand that the side that won this game would win the Cup. It was not an outrageous claim, and after the performance that Leeds gave he could justly feel that his side was capable of reaching the final. The next round dashed any such hopes. Now it was St Helens who emerged as major contenders for the prize after beating Leeds in a game passionate and exciting enough to bear comparison with the unforgettable meeting of the sides in the 1978 final.

St Helens, disturbingly, had not won at Headingley for ten matches, but as a counterbalance to that Leeds were without their hooker, Ward, who had been suspended for two games. It was to prove a crucial absence. His replacement, Sowden, was unable to control his opposite hooker, Liptrot, in either scrum or loose, and from a greater share of possession the St Helens forwards, the faster and more mobile set, inflicted considerable damage.

A broken leg four minutes after half-time brought a sad and painful end to the season for Gill, the Leeds full-back, whose reputation was steadily growing as defender, attacker and place kicker. Soon after his departure Leeds reduced their arrears to only two points when Dick scored a clever, opportunist try, but two late tries by Haggerty gave St Helens a cushion of ten points at the end. They were now given a home draw against Featherstone in the quarter-finals and must have felt confident, probably certain, that they would be appearing in the semi-finals. Gilbert and company had different ideas.

Before that splendid display against St Helens, Featherstone had removed Batley at home and Salford away—a commendable performance this, since Salford themselves had enjoyed an encouraging win against Leigh in the first round. The heavy conditions were best suited to a functional game, and Featherstone, with Smith selfless as always, provided it.

Salford twice worked the ball wide in a spell of five minutes in the first half and scored tries through Fielding and Aspey. Curiously, they then began to channel their attacks down the middle, a mistake against such a powerful pack as Featherstone's. Barker restored Featherstone's lead just before half-time when, direct from a scrum, he sprinted 35 yards for a try, his second of the half; and the best moment in the second half came when Hudson wrong-footed the Salford defence to score from 25 yards.

There had, meanwhile, been no shortage of unexpected results elsewhere, the most outrageous being provided by Hunslet in the first round. The only point in their favour against Hull Kingston Rovers, it seemed, was ground advantage, but although they conceded three tries to one, they deserved their

12–11 victory. They could, though, have been deprived of a memorable win in an extraordinary finish.

When Hartley scored a try in the last seconds, and Fairbairn added the goal points, Hunslet were left holding a lead of 12–11. This was not as breathless as it might seem, however, because the electronic scoreboard at Elland Road was already indicating full-time. All that was required was for Fitzsimons to restart the game and the hooter would have sounded. To his chagrin, and to the anguish of the home supporters, Fitzsimons, who had done so much to give Hunslet victory with three goals and three dropped goals, now kicked the ball full into touch. That gave Fairbairn a penalty from the centre spot and the opportunity to win the match. The script, however, was too good to ruin, and Fairbairn's kick dropped short.

Hunslet caused the first division further embarrassment in the second round. The vanquished this time were not nearly as illustrious, but a 17–8 win over Halifax was gratifying enough. King, with tries in first half and second, scored crucial points, but once again the inspiration behind so much of Hunslet's play was John Wolford, their captain and loose forward and a player whose skills had enriched the game during ten years at Bramley and spells at Bradford, Dewsbury and now Hunslet.

Wolford intended to retire at the end of the season. His spirit was as willing as ever, his passion for the game as keen, but the legs were not as strong as they were. Wembley would have been a fitting stage for Wolford to end his career. There was scarcely anyone playing with more intelligence, more subtlety or with a greater feel for the game's artistries. He was a craftsman, and a versatile one at that, having familiarized himself with most positions throughout his long career. It was good that so much talent was suddenly on display before sizeable audiences again—14,000 when Hunslet met Castleford in the third round at Elland Road.

That, though, was the end for Hunslet and for Wolford, but not without another admirable performance. Paul Daley, the Hunslet coach, appraised this game laconically and realistically. 'If we stand back and let them play, they'll score a bucketful,' he said. In fact, they scored only thirteen points, three of them, to their relief, two minutes from time. Hunslet indeed led twice, first at 3–2, when Smith drove in hard for a good try, and then at 6–5, when Fitzsimons dropped a goal from 20 yards. Fitzsimons's kicking had been a crucial ingredient in Hunslet's victories in the earlier rounds, but this time he missed with three penalties. Only when Hyde scored his try in the seventy-eighth minute, however, could Castleford feel assured of their place in the semi-finals.

Hull's most difficult match by far on their way to the semi-finals was their away game with Warrington at Wilderspool in the quarter-finals. Their first two matches had been simple enough. Blackpool Borough had brought commendable spirit—and two late tries—to their defeat 11–19 at Borough Park, but Hull had practically insured themselves against defeat by scoring five tries in a comparatively compressed spell of twenty-five minutes. Their match in the next round against Wakefield Trinity followed a similar course, with Hull establishing a handsome lead and Wakefield earning commendable but late and largely irrelevant points.

Bridges and Stone both scored tries, their first in more than two years, an indication of the ease of Hull's task. The one anxiety for Hull's followers was the way in which the side's concentration wavered over the final period, when Fletcher and Rotherforth scored tries. It was not, though, a trait that they were to reveal very often.

Warrington, although they spent most of the season in the relegation area, were not a side to be underestimated. They had beaten Hull 18–16 in a league match in early February at Wilderspool, a game which had amply demonstrated their capabilities. This time they lost 4–10 after an untidy, ill-tempered and controversial contest but one which also lacked nothing in excitement. At the end the police were hard-pressed to keep the Warrington supporters from attacking the departing, jubilant Hull followers. There were some minor skirmishes, and the scenes were more consistent with a soccer ground than a Rugby League stadium.

What most angered Warrington and their followers was the refusal by Billy Thompson, the referee, to allow a 'try' by Ford, who had collected an intelligent kick by Cullen and sprinted to the posts. The referee ruled that Ford was off-side. The decision was certainly marginal enough to incense the Warrington crowd. Had that decision gone in Warrington's favour, Hull might have lost. As it was, they did not ensure victory until injury time, when Warrington, forced to abandon all caution, lost possession close to their own line and Edmonds was permitted one of the easiest tries he will ever enjoy.

Thus the competition moved to the semi-final stage. Featherstone Rovers were drawn against Bradford Northern at Headingley on 26 March, and Hull were drawn to play Castleford a week later, also in Leeds but at the Elland Road stadium, on Easter Saturday, 2 April.

The State Express Challenge Cup

The Challenge Cup Semi-final
Headingley, Leeds, 26 March
Featherstone Rovers 11   Bradford Northern 6

Bradford Northern, who had reached the semi-finals by dint of three unremarkable but solidly efficient displays against York, Fulham and Workington Town away, were almost paralysed by caution in their semi-final against Featherstone Rovers. And they suffered the consequences of their excessive wariness. A Bradford Northern follower sat disconsolately afterwards, staring into space and asking of no one in particular, 'Who'd have believed that that was the same side that beat Warrington last Sunday?' Under Peter Fox, Northern had gained a reputation for dour efficiency. They were not the most admired side, and this display provided a reason why.

Northern's tactics were starkly fundamental: drive hard down the middle, pass only when safe to do so, and do not open out play until the opponents' line is firmly in view. The plan miscarried, but there was at least one glorious exception to Northern's persistent sterility, a try by Hanley, who covered practically the length of the pitch in an improbable run to his opponents' line. It was the kind of try which deserved, really, to win a game.

There was little doubt that Featherstone's tackling was at fault. For a considerable length of his run Hanley, close to the touch line, had little more than a foot of room in which to work; and yet he preserved his balance and his pace as he handed-off two would-be tacklers. He had collected the ball close to his own line from Redfearn, eased his way past Gilbert, resisted the attentions of Kellett and Barker and foiled the final attempt of Quinn to stop him.

Hanley, with a neatly timed pass to the charging Van Bellen, had engineered an earlier try by Bradford in the seventeenth minute, and at the interval Northern led 6–3, but the moments of inspiration were confined to the first half. In the second Featherstone concentrated on working the ball wider, and their policy proved successful, with tries scored in either corner. It was when they went into arrears that Bradford exposed their own limitations and those of the plan that had been rigidly imposed upon them.

In beating St Helens to reach the semi-finals, Featherstone had produced some thrilling and decisive attacking moves. This victory, too, had its moments in attack, but it was a win due largely to solid defence and a pragmatic acceptance of the few chances to arrive in attack.

Like Malcolm Reilly of Castleford, Allan Agar, the Featherstone coach, had

25. There is no more honest forward in the game than Peter Smith of Featherstone Rovers. Loyal, admirably consistent, he played a major part in Featherstone's victory over Bradford Northern in the Challenge Cup semi-final in spite of not being fully fit.

not been satisfied with his side's form before the semi-final. Agar had joined in mid-season a club facing an anxious struggle to avoid relegation, and in the week of the semi-final he had some harsh things to say about his side's performance in the league against Hull Kingston Rovers the previous Sunday. The attitude of some players, he said, had been 'appalling'. They had played without pride and had let themselves and their supporters down.

It was, though, a satisfied Agar who outlined to the press afterwards the methods which had brought about Bradford's downfall in the second half. And he could have few complaints either about the way in which his players had followed his instructions to work the ball wider and try to get round the back of the Bradford defence or about their dedication.

Of the Featherstone side which had lost in the Cup semi-final to Leeds in 1978, only Gilbert, Gibbins and Smith remained, and all three, perhaps not wishing to relive the disappointment of that occasion, made significant contributions to victory. Gilbert, so dangerous against St Helens in the quarter-final, scored a try, while Gibbins and Smith toiled selflessly in the pack. Smith's was an especially commendable performance, since a debilitating stomach disorder had left him feeling less than fully fit.

Redfearn was a good scrum-half for Northern, but Rovers were particularly well served at half-back, with the young Banks making a number of damaging runs and Hudson showing a remarkable appetite for work. There was, too, an intelligent, industrious display from Rovers' right-winger, Marsden—a contrast indeed with the Northern wings, Smith and Whiteman, neither of whom saw much of the ball.

The gaps were so slow to appear, the early pace of the match so funereal, that Marsden's opening try in the eleventh minute came with unexpected simplicity. Marsden, a former full-back, showed an appetite for the unorthodox in this game—he was not, for example, afraid to go roving—but his try was straightforward enough, the winger bursting on to Hankins's pass to score from close range.

Northern persisted in playing one-man rugby throughout, but there was nothing dull about either of their tries, Van Bellen charging through an inviting gap provided for him by the timing of Hanley's pass and Hanley himself then scoring that memorable try four minutes from the interval after Smith, perpetrating one of his few errors, had failed to hold a pass close to the Bradford line. Redfearn had gathered the loose ball and then sent Hanley on his long, successful run.

Bradford lost Idle and Rathbone in the second half, but their absences had little to do with Bradford's defeat. Five minutes after half-time Featherstone cruelly exposed the barrenness of Northern's tactics when Gilbert scored in the left corner after a move which saw the ball pass through eight pairs of hands.

Grayshon, Bradford's open-side prop, likes to hold the ball out to opponents, tempting them to take it from him, and for a big man his passes have a delicate touch, but any subtle moments from Grayshon were little more than light asides in the dull, heavy script which had been written for Northern. When Hudson, after more good work from Marsden, scored Rovers' third try ten minutes from time it was too late for Northern to break free of the chains in which they had draped themselves.

Featherstone Rovers: Barker; Marsden, Quinn, Gilbert, Kellett; Banks, Hudson; Siddall, Handscombe, Gibbins, Hobbs, Hankins, Peter Smith

Substitutes: Bell for Siddall after 76 minutes, Pickerill not used

Scorers: tries—Marsden, Gilbert, Hudson; goal—Quinn

The State Express Challenge Cup

Bradford Northern: Mumby; David Smith, Hanley, Davies, Whiteman; Hale, Redfearn; Grayshon, Noble, Van Bellen, Jackson, Idle, Rathbone

Substitutes: Jasiewicz for Idle after 29 minutes, Carroll for Rathbone after 60 minutes

Scorers: tries—Van Bellen, Hanley

Referee: J. Holdsworth (Leeds)

Attendance: 10,676

**The Challenge Cup Semi-final
Elland Road, Leeds, 2 April
Hull 14   Castleford 7**

Two days after losing to them in the semi-final, Castleford beat Hull 21–16 in a league match at home at Wheldon Road, scoring five tries to two. Their form on Easter Monday, however, could have been nothing more than hollow compensation for their disappointing display at Elland Road on Easter Saturday. For their followers the experience was all too familiar; when it mattered most Castleford had failed to realize their capabilities.

It was not that they were lacking in effort. Shortly before the semi-finals, Castleford in a league game had conceded thirty-one points at home to Widnes, and Malcolm Reilly, their coach, had been unable to contain his annoyance. 'They must learn that they can't play just when they feel like it,' he said heatedly. After this expenditure of so much honest energy there could have been no justification for anger. He must, though, have felt frustration. Castleford were capable of far more daring than this as they had shown when, quite brilliantly, they had removed Wigan at Central Park in the first round, one of the best team displays of the whole competition.

Eight minutes after half-time England, the promising young second-row forward, resisted the attentions of three Hull defenders and forced his way under the posts for a try. Hyde was left with a simple kick at goal, and Castleford had taken the lead at 7–6. The hordes of black-and-white bedecked Hull followers, massed at the scoreboard end, were reduced to silence. Soon, though, the noise and the enthusiasm were restored. Castleford's supremacy was to prove transitory.

26. Steve Evans, the Hull centre, was one of the leading try scorers of the season. He had been signed the previous season for £70,000 from Featherstone Rovers but took some time to reveal his true potential. One of his greatest assets was his pace, demonstrated here in the Challenge Cup semi-final against Castleford at Elland Road, Leeds.

In the impressive setting of Elland Road, and in front of 26,000 spectators, Castleford were never quite at their ease. They appeared slightly overwhelmed by the occasion, and tried to hide their discomfort, it seemed, in a redoubling of physical output. That was fine, but there were few subtle touches to go with it; there was little evidence of cohesion and no signs of a game plan, and against a side as well equipped as Hull, energy alone was not enough.

Again, Castleford had no individual capable of taking hold of the match and shaping it to his own designs. On another occasion Ward, one of the outstanding forwards of the season, might have achieved this; so, too, might the clever, skilful Johnson, the smooth-moving Joyner or the swift and opportunistic Hyde. At the end of eighty minutes, however, Castleford had achieved little more than industrious anonymity.

The State Express Challenge Cup

Hull, on the other hand, discovered that mixture of collective unity and individual excellence that carries such important occasions as this. Since their irresistible rise from the second division in 1979, they had become increasingly familiar with grand occasions. They fitted into them as smoothly as a hand into a good glove.

They were sufficiently at their ease to fashion two tries in the first twenty-two minutes. The first, by O'Hara, was the result of smart approach play (and a fortuitous bounce off a Castleford player); the second was the product of Leuluai's sense of adventure. The first reaction to this splendid try was that it had been made possible by careless Castleford tackling; second opinion demanded that all the credit be given to Leuluai, who, just inside the Castleford half, beat one man, then another, and then, stepping bewilderingly from left foot to right, caught the Castleford full-back, Coen, hopelessly wrong-footed. Crooks was unable to add the goal points for either try, which was as well for Castleford, who could scarcely have relished a deficit of ten points so early in the match.

A penalty by Hyde reduced the arrears, and England's try and the goal for it put Castleford into profit. But there had been enough evidence in that first half to suggest that Hull were carrying the more dangerous weaponry. No Castleford forward, for example, could equal the defensive impregnability or courage of Skerrett, the hard, destructive running of Rose, the creative touches of Norton, fitful before half-time but utterly assured after it.

Castleford were unfortunate to lose Bob Beardmore and Higgins early in the first half, making life marginally less demanding for Harkin and Norton. These departures were partially counter-balanced, it seemed, in the forty-fifth minute, when the Hull bench decided that the influential Topliss had suffered as many knocks as he could stand and took him off. But although Castleford were to score their try almost immediately, the arrival of Day was to prove instrumental in their downfall. So too was the hooking skill of the wily Bridges, who, as one writer observed, 'does little more than trundle from one scrum to another these days' ... but with what effect!

The scrums overall finished only marginally in Bridges's favour, 12–11, but a sequence of six successive heels by him midway through the second half, all of them achieved in prime opposition territory, kept Castleford ensnared. Hull are not a side merely to tease opponents when they have them trapped; they punished them severely enough to ensure there would be no retaliation.

The first wound that Day inflicted upon Castleford was made with the cleanness and incisiveness of a scalpel. Day had intended to pass, changed his mind and sent a low, accurate kick threading its way through an inviting opening. A split-second later Evans touched down. The try was achieved so quickly, so efficiently and so simply that the consensus of opinion, in the press

27. One of the shrewdest entries Hull made into the transfer market was for three New Zealanders, Gary Kemble, James Leuluai and Dane O'Hara. Here O'Hara shows the decisiveness of his finishing to score Hull's first try in the Challenge Cup semi-final against Castleford at Elland Road, Leeds.

box at least, questioned whether Evans could have been on-side. Television's slow-motion replay dismissed that theory.

Having made a fine try, Day now scored one, eleven minutes from time. Bridges won another scrum; the ball was worked right, and Norton's pass to Day was concealed beautifully. Day curved away to the right and around the last remnants of Castleford's cover. Crooks's place kicking at this time—not simply in this match—had lost its accuracy, but he did land one excellent kick

The State Express Challenge Cup

from far out on the right, and Hull were through to their third Challenge Cup final in four seasons.

Hull: Kemble; O'Hara, Evans, Leuluai, Prendiville; Topliss, Harkin; Skerrett, Bridges, Stone, Rose, Crooks, Norton

Substitutes: Day for Topliss after 45 minutes, Crane for Crooks after 78 minutes

Scorers: tries—O'Hara, Leuluai, Evans, Day; goal—Crooks

Castleford: Coen; Richardson, Marchant, Hyde, Kear; Joyner, Robert Beardmore; Connell, Kevin Beardmore, Johnson, England, Ward, Higgins

Substitutes: James for Higgins after 22 minutes, Orum for Robert Beardmore after 27 minutes, Higgins for James after 65 minutes

Scorers: try—England; goals—Hyde (2)

Referee: W. H. Thompson (Huddersfield)

Attendance: 26,031

**The Challenge Cup Final
Wembley Stadium, 7 May
Featherstone Rovers 14   Hull 12**

There was no more disconsolate figure than David Topliss, the Hull captain, after his side had suffered this extraordinary defeat against Featherstone before a crowd of 85,000 at Wembley. Slumped in his seat in the South dressing-room, he was beyond consoling. Topliss had secured his winners' medal the previous season, but that triumph had come in a replay against Widnes at Elland Road. Three times now Topliss had played at Wembley, first with Wakefield Trinity in 1979, and each time he had been deprived of victory. It was little wonder that he looked desolated.

The bookmakers had stopped taking bets on Hull, and at odds of 1–4 on they were the strongest favourites within living memory to take the game's most

28. David Hobbs, Featherstone's second-row forward, had an outstanding game in the Challenge Cup final at Wembley against Hull, scoring both his side's tries and being awarded the Lance Todd Trophy. Featherstone's chairman, Bob Ashby, maintained that Hobbs was one of the most complete forwards in the game, and his performance in this match tended to support that view. Gary Siddall and Peter Smith obviously think highly of Hobbs too.

prized trophy. But the brilliant form that had carried them through the final weeks of the season with the remorselessness of a bush fire deserted them as if it had never existed. They were wracked by uncertainty and nerves, in stark contrast to a Featherstone side that was assured, purposeful, and clear-minded.

Hull must have wondered with some bitterness afterwards how they had

29. Keith Bridges, the Hull hooker, was twice helpless to prevent David Hobbs, the powerful Featherstone second-row forward, from scoring tries at Wembley. Hobbs's first try came in the seventh minute during Featherstone's first serious attack.

come to play with such fluency in the weeks before the final only to find, on the most important day of all, that their cohesion and confidence had evaporated. In place of the support play which had brought them so much success there was a desperate desire to resort to one-man rugby, the head-down-and-charge tactics which the Australians had so ruthlessly exposed, and to return to a dark age from which Hull, above all, had been trying to rescue the game.

Had the match been run under the auspices of the Jockey Club, an inquiry might have ensued. What on earth had happened for the favourite to fall so short of form? It would be scandalous, however, even to hint that Hull lost the Cup rather than that Featherstone won it. They were admirable, well organized and obviously thoroughly prepared by Allan Agar, their manager/coach, and his assistant, Keith Goulding. When Hull, after conceding five points early in the game, took a lead of 12–5 by the fifty-third minute, it seemed that they would win in spite of playing badly, that all the pre-match predictions would prove correct after all. But to make any such assumption was to denigrate Featherstone's resilience, self-belief and fitness.

The State Express Challenge Cup

Even Bob Ashby, the Featherstone chairman, conceded afterwards that deep down he found it hard to believe that Featherstone could defeat a side that he considered the 'best rugby team outside Australia'. What sustained his optimism was a belief that there was simply no forecasting which players might 'freeze'. This affliction invariably overcomes a number of players at Wembley and is as likely to strike the experienced player as the tyro. Mr Ashby must have been as surprised as anyone to see the paralysis take such a collective grip on Hull and bypass Featherstone.

Considering that Hull had played at Wembley in 1980 and again in 1982, their errors and their lack of cohesion were baffling. Nervousness was apparent even when the game had entered first-half injury time, with Day and Stone dropping important passes. At no time did Hull's play reveal their true capabilities; and only for two periods, in the first five minutes and early in the second half, did they look Featherstone's superiors.

It was always likely that Featherstone's chief strength would lie with their pack, and so it proved. Hobbs was a magnificent second-row forward and a thoroughly deserving recipient of the coveted Lance Todd Trophy, awarded to the game's outstanding player. He scored both his side's tries, ran powerfully, tackled ceaselessly, handled skilfully and generally justified the claim of his club's chairman that he was one of the most complete forwards in the game. The occasional laziness that Mr Ashby maintained was Hobbs's only flaw was not apparent on this occasion.

Hobbs was the outstanding member of an impressive pack. Handscombe was in pain from an early stage with a long-standing back injury but refused pain-killing injections at the interval and consistently outheeled the experienced Bridges at the scrums. Gibbins and Hankins were admirably purposeful props, and although Slatter inevitably had difficulty matching Hobbs's brilliance in the second row, he did enough to deserve his slightly unexpected appearance in the final. Smith, as always, was honesty epitomized, a player who would not know how to give less than his best.

Few attacking opportunities were given to the Featherstone three-quarters or full-back, but defensively they showed few flaws, and there was another ceaselessly industrious display from Hudson at scrum-half. The Featherstone followers, who can be uncompromisingly critical as well as fiercely loyal, had so hounded Hudson at one stage of his career that the club wondered if it might not be best if he pursued his football elsewhere. Hudson, to his credit, had opted to stay and had, according to Mr Ashby, done more than anyone to get the club to the final. Now he helped to ensure that they won it. Banks, at 17, was a precocious half-back partner.

It was distressing for Hull that after only nineteen minutes they should lose Harkin, carried off on a stretcher, severely concussed, after Hudson

30. Keith Bridges's lack of pace was compensated more often than not by his ability to win the ball in the scrums. In the Challenge Cup final at Wembley it proved a liability. Here David Hobbs leaves the Hull hooker heavy-footed and helpless as he races over for his second try.

31. Robin Whitfield, the young Widnes referee, was consistently one of the best officials in 1982–83. His handling of the Challenge Cup final may not have been perfect, but it was very good. Here, perfectly positioned, he awards Crooks an obstruction try after the Hull forward has been impeded by Hobbs. Although the Featherstone forward has that 'Oh no' look on his face, there was little doubt that Mr Whitfield was right.

32. Gary Kemble, the Hull and New Zealand full-back, was given few opportunities to show his attacking capabilities in the Challenge Cup final. Here he shows his long-striding, determined style, but with Hudson already tugging at his shorts and a Featherstone reception committee of Barker, Slatter and Smith waiting for him, he seems unlikely to make much yardage this time.

accidentally kicked him when challenging for a ball that had rebounded from the scrum. In Harkin's absence Hull tried Topliss, then Crane, at scrum-half, but Handscombe continued to monopolize the scrums. Even Featherstone were sympathetic afterwards that Hull had been deprived of such a specialist as Harkin, but Hull would have been deceiving themselves if they had offered his absence as an excuse for defeat.

The first half was not the perfect advertisement for Rugby League. Good football was at a premium, and there were a number of unsavoury incidents, the worst arriving close to the interval, when Rose, with a late, stiff-arm tackle on Gilbert, abruptly halted one of Featherstone's most promising moves in which Hudson and Smith had thrown out two of the half's most adventurous passes. That tackle saw Gilbert carried off and Rose sent off, the first man to be sent to the sin bin in a Wembley final. Rose could scarcely have complained if he had been dismissed for good.

Hudson was also sent to the sin bin in the second half for misuse of the boot, but this second period was intensely exciting, swinging first in Hull's favour and then decisively back to Featherstone. The quality of the football rarely rose above the cautious, but there were enough incidents to satisfy the most demanding appetite.

Featherstone had spent the first seven minutes absorbing a deal of Hull pressure, but the first time they went on the offensive they scored a try through Hobbs. From a differential penalty at a scrum Quinn found touch. Hudson took the tap penalty; Hobbs burst on to the ball and ran sharply past Leuluai for the right corner flag. A fellow forward embarked on a decoy run, which was not particularly subtle but was distracting enough to give Hobbs a valuable extra second, and he crashed through to touch down in the corner.

At half-time Featherstone led 5–0, with Quinn landing the first of his three penalties in the thirty-second minute. Kemble halted a dangerous break by Banks with a firm, well-timed tackle but then spoiled his good work by not allowing the stand-off to play-the-ball. Thirteen minutes after half time, however, the match seemed to be running its predestined course with Hull now 10–5 in the lead, the result of first an obstruction try by Crooks and then a score by Leuluai that at last showed Hull at their best.

The award of an obstruction try often needs a degree of courage, but Mr Whitfield was almost certainly in the right on this occasion. From close to the Featherstone line and in front of the posts Crooks, at a play-the-ball, tapped the kick to himself, put through a little kick and pursued it, only to be brought down by a tackle by Hobbs. Soon afterwards Hull produced by far their most confident and decisive handling move of the match, with Bridges, Crane, Topliss and Rose combining swiftly to open up a gap for Leuluai. For the first and only time in the match the New Zealand centre was able to run on to the ball at damaging pace. A quick change of direction took him inside and gave him a clear path to the posts. For the second time Crooks was left with a simple goal-kick from in front of the posts.

Hudson's foul on Topliss in the fifty-seventh minute cost the Rovers' captain ten minutes in the sin bin and his side another two points, with Crooks landing his third kick. A lead of seven points seemed sure to be enough for Hull, who were now expected to display their acknowledged superiority. They had emerged from a long period of self-doubt, it seemed, and would now remorselessly accumulate the points. So much for that particular theory. Featherstone had no intention of being its victims.

In the sixty-fourth minute Featherstone were awarded a penalty to the right of the posts. Smith, in the temporary absence of Hudson, directed Quinn to take the kick instead of seeking the more valuable reward of five points. It was a wise decision. Quinn landed the kick, and Featherstone were now within one score of their opponents. It was no surprise that Hobbs again provided it. This time Hobbs burst on to a fine pass from Hankins and ran irresistibly through a

33. Allan Agar proved himself to be one of the brightest young coaches in the game. He took over at Featherstone from Vince Farrar mid-way through the season and, without any new players, helped the club to stay clear of relegation and win the Challenge Cup. He prepared his team shrewdly and thoroughly for the final. His unconstrained delight is well justified.

big gap, brushing effortlessly past Leuluai and the slow-moving Bridges on the way. Quinn added the goal points, the score was 12–12, and a second successive Wembley cup final replay was possible.

    First Hobbs tried to pre-empt that eventuality when he took careful aim with a drop kick and sent the ball sailing high between the posts. He was

34. The 1983 Challenge Cup final between Hull and Featherstone provided one of the biggest upheavals of form for more than fifty years. Against all predictions and against all logic—but deservedly—the trophy, held here by Gary Siddall and Terry Hudson, went to Featherstone Rovers.

desperately unlucky: the ball struck a Hull hand on the way. In the final minute, however, Featherstone received their due reward when, at the intervention of a linesman, they were given a penalty for a butt by Stone on Smith. Quinn afterwards said that had he known how little time was left, his legs would have probably turned to rubber. There was no sign of that as, once again, he took careful aim and sent the ball unerringly between the posts.

Featherstone Rovers: Barker; Marsden, Quinn, Gilbert, Kellett; Banks, Hudson; Gibbins, Handscombe, Hankins, Hobbs, Slatter, Smith

Substitutes: Lyman for Gilbert after 39 minutes, Siddall for Slatter after 69 minutes

Scorers: tries—Hobbs (2); goals—Quinn (4)

The State Express Challenge Cup

Hull: Kemble; O'Hara, Evans, Leuluai, Prendiville; Topliss, Harkin; Skerrett, Bridges, Stone, Rose, Crooks, Norton

Substitutes: Day for Harkin after 19 minutes, Crane for Day at half-time

Scorers: tries—Crooks, Leuluai; goals—Crooks (3)

Referee: M. R. Whitfield (Widnes)

Attendance: 84,969

5

THE SLALOM LAGER CHAMPIONSHIP AND PREMIERSHIP TROPHY

THE SLALOM LAGER CHAMPIONSHIP

The Slalom Lager Championshp did not consistently achieve the highest standards. Leeds, except for brief interludes, led the race through autumn, winter and approaching spring. But they did not appear to possess the stamina and sinew that might have seen them through the last, crucial stages of the season. In the final weeks Hull Kingston Rovers and Wigan made claims to the title, but their challenges flared and then faded, which left Hull. And to them, beyond a shadow of doubt, the prize deservedly went.

Hull had to wait until the final day of the season to make certain of the crown, though their form during the run-in suggested that they would grasp it. In the end only Wigan could have deprived them, but to do so Wigan needed to beat Widnes at Naughton Park by the improbable margin of forty-six points, while Hull had to lose at home to Barrow. Neither outcome seemed likely, and neither transpired. Widnes, who had ended the season strongly, beat Wigan 21–17, and Hull overwhelmed Barrow 31–13. That left Hull with forty-seven points, four more than their Humberside rivals, Hull Kingston Rovers—whose superior points difference brought them second place—and Wigan.

There were a number of reasons why Hull merited the championship. Quite simply, they possessed an enviable number of good players and a knowledgeable coach to guide them. But character and attitude also played significant parts. Hull were most impressive when the pressure was at its most severe—during the last weeks of the season. As the challenges became more demanding, Hull's assurance expanded to meet them. There was no sign that

The Slalom Lager Championship

increasing pressure intimidated them. Instead, it seemed to draw from them individual and collective qualities that withered practically all opposition.

Quality in depth also proved of vital importance. No side in a sport as 'hurtling in conflict' as Rugby League can expect to survive a season without suffering injuries. How many injuries is largely a matter of luck. Hull suffered their share, but because they possessed so many good players the permanent loss of Keith Tindall and the absences at various times of such men as O'Hara and Leuluai, Topliss and Kemble, Skerrett and Stone proved distressing but not calamitous.

Between them the experienced Harrison and Sutton and the 25-year-old Edmonds—signed from their neighbours Hull Kingston Rovers for £10,000 in January—made sure that the front row suffered no serious loss of efficiency; Banks frequently came into the team at full-back or centre with total reliability; Day could be included at centre or stand-off and, as he showed in the Challenge Cup semi-final, could dictate the course of a game. At scrum-half Hull were almost embarrassingly well served. Harkin was most frequently in possession but the coach, Arthur Bunting, must at times have felt like tossing a coin to decide between him or Dean. In Wayne Proctor, who made a number of appearances in the second row and was frequently a substitute, Hull had a talented young forward.

Such strength could not have been envisaged eight years earlier, when the club was on the point of financial ruin, with support that had trickled, in one glum game with Huyton, to less than a thousand. That desperate situation was resolved by new blood in the boardroom, good husbandry and, later, some shrewd signings. When the trophies began increasingly to adorn the Boulevard sideboard, detractors would accuse Hull of buying success. But it would have been extremely difficult to accuse them of wasting money.

In 1979 Hull made their farewells to the cheerless seventies—and to the second division—in glittering fashion, winning all twenty-six league games and scoring more than 700 points in the process. That was the impressive beginning to a period of influence, power and success. Within four seasons Hull had made three appearances in the Challenge Cup final, had won the Yorkshire Cup and the John Player Trophy and had twice appeared in the Premiership Trophy final. Now, by winning the Slalom Lager Championship, they showed that they possessed durability, character, resilience, patience. League championships have less immediate appeal than cup competitions, but they are a truer guide of a team's strength.

The 1975 game with Huyton had been the nadir. Now, in this time of prosperity, crowds in excess of 10,000 were commonplace, and against Hull Kingston Rovers more than 20,000 spectators squeezed into the Boulevard. Such a profound change in Hull's fortunes could not have been wrought without vision and boldness ... and a willingness to write out some sizeable cheques. Hull's entries into the transfer market were invariably shrewd, but they were prepared to spend heavily if that would secure the best players available. They would have become the first club to spend more than £100,000 on a player if Leigh had been willing to part with their gifted stand-off, John Woods. Nothing, though, better illustrated the scope of their ambitions than the signing of their three New Zealand players, Kemble, O'Hara and Leuluai. After their 1980 tour to Great Britain the importation of New Zealand players became fashionable, but Hull were the club to set the trend.

They wanted to sign the jewel of that squad, Fred Ah Kuoi, but he opted for Australia and North Sydney. As compensation, Hull brought Kemble, O'Hara and Leuluai to Humberside at a quarter of the cost they would have paid for three British players of equivalent talent. And what might have been a gamble proved to be one of the most enterprising entries a British club has ever made into a foreign market.

Towards the end of the season Hull turned to France and Patrick Solal for a further strengthening of their squad. In the international between Great Britain and France at the Boulevard in March, Solal, the Tonneins winger, had scored a fine, powerful try, although Hull's interest in the player had been aroused in 1981 in the international at Marseilles, where Solal had inflicted enormous damage on Great Britain. It was not immediately apparent how Solal would fit into the side, but it must have been good for the Hull club to know he was there ... and at no cost other than his wages.

Possessing the most talented squad of players is useful, of course. It is still necessary, nevertheless, to keep individuals contented, to find the right blends, to maintain enthusiasm, to ride injury and to retain, over a long season and through a variety of discouraging conditions, ambition and efficiency. It is vital that when a side goes through its duller periods it should still be good enough to collect the points. Hull met all the requirements of champions. They were always heavily in contention for the title, and when the heat became fiercest they had the ambition and resources to carry them singlemindedly towards it.

With such a solid, dependable team manager as Arthur Bunting in control, Hull were never likely, nor were allowed, to lose control of their perspectives. A club of such virility and enterprise, bustle and activity, needed a man of Bunting's quiet detachment. Bunting had been a good scrum-half in days when good scrum-halves were plentiful and was one of those performers who tend to be taken for granted but are sorely missed when they are no longer available. Qualities which had made him such a respected player now made him equally respected as a coach. His was a quiet style of management, but his integrity, honesty and thorough knowledge of the game were more than enough to earn his players' respect.

The Slalom Lager Championship

Bunting had a lot of rich material with which to work, but since he had played a significant part in the gathering of that material no one could begrudge him his good fortune. The importance of teamwork in a team game needs no labouring, but obviously the more talented individuals there are within the team framework the better it must be.

Leeds's decline and eventual disintegration—they were beaten 51–2 by Leigh in their final league game—was not altogether surprising, since their coach, Robin Dewhurst, did not try to disguise his doubts about his side's strength. More than once during the season Dewhurst, a quiet man not given to public criticism of his side, expressed his surprise at finding his team occupying top place. This was not hard to understand, since Leeds were prone to the most alarming lapses. The first serious evidence of structural weakness came in their ninth game against Hull at the Boulevard. Before this game they had won eight successive league games, scoring 213 points, which even at that early stage was sixty-one points more than the next highest scoring club, Hull Kingston Rovers. But Hull showed no respect for these statistics. They won 35–5 with Crooks playing one of the games of his young life and scoring twenty-three points from three tries and seven goals.

A brief period of stability followed. Featherstone Rovers, Hull Kingston Rovers and St Helens were defeated, but then Leeds failed against Castleford almost as wretchedly as they had done against Hull, losing 32–5, a performance as 'dim as the Wheldon Road floodlights', the *Yorkshire Post* noted. Again Leeds set themselves back on course, and in spite of points dropped at home to Oldham (a game they drew) and to Featherstone (a match they lost) after twenty games—or two-thirds of the season—they were top with four points to spare. Seven defeats in their last ten games indicated how oppressively the problems came crowding in on them towards the end.

Specific misfortunes could be held responsible for undermining Leeds. They lost Pitchford with a broken arm early in the season—he was to break it again before the end—and Dickinson from January. Both the Raynes, Kevin and Keith, suffered serious injury, and the loss of the suspended Ward at an important stage of the season, though for only two games, was to prove crucial. These were, nevertheless, superficial reasons for Leeds's disappointing season. In truth, their squad was neither big enough nor good enough.

Leeds's excellent start, too, possibly induced some self-deception at the club. Dewhurst was not fooled by that string of wins and realized that there were weaknesses. Inevitably, though, while the side was winning, most people at the club, most significantly the board, were reasonably contented. Over the final weeks inherent weaknesses in the pack and a lack of pace in the backs became glaringly obvious. Holmes and Dick, both gifted but not the fleetest of half-backs, received less and less protection from a struggling pack.

The Slalom Lager Championship

Hull Kingston Rovers responded with more sensitivity than most to the lessons taught by the Australians. Since their chairman, Colin Hutton, was also the Great Britain manager at the time, this was perhaps to be expected. Rovers increased their training from two nights to three and adopted some of the methods and aids that were an accepted part of Australian training. But, good though they looked at times, Rovers ultimately paid the price of their erratic form over their first twenty games. In their last ten games they dropped only three points, although two of them were in what was arguably the most important league game of the season, the Humberside derby match at the Boulevard.

Before the start of the season Rovers paid Wakefield Trinity £60,000 for a 21-year-old second-row forward, Andrew Kelly. They recovered half that amount by selling Paul Rose to Hull but then must have watched in some dismay the extraordinary form that Rose displayed, while Kelly frequently struggled to justify his hefty transfer fee. Rovers also followed the fashion that Hull had set the previous season by signing two New Zealanders, both of whom proved to be sound investments: Gary Prohm, a left-winger who was also capable of playing in the forwards, and Gordon Smith, an industrious and creative scrum-half.

Watkinson, in his muscular, aggressive fashion, was a reliable pivot around which the pack revolved, contributing much more than an important presence at the scrums. The correct mix, though, seemed tantalizingly to elude Roger Millward, the coach. His problems in the forwards and the backs never quite resolved themselves, although in the search for the right combination promising young talent was unearthed in Garry Clark, an 18-year-old winger, in John Lydiat, whose sureness at full-back allowed Rovers the experiment of playing Fairbairn in the centre, and in Tracy Lazenby, a forward of considerable destructive and constructive potential.

If Wigan's followers had known before the start of the season that their club would finish third in the league and would win the John Player Trophy, they would probably have been well satisfied. The arrival of Alex Murphy from Leigh was always likely to have a galvanizing effect upon the club, but Wigan had not done nearly enough the previous season to be considered serious contenders for the title. In the event, therefore, Wigan exceeded expectations. They re-established themselves as a club of influence, a genuine rival, in terms of support and power, to the Humberside clubs. Yet in spite of all their progress it was possible to detect at the end disappointment among their followers, a sense of potential unfulfilled.

There were occasions when Wigan looked a genuinely exciting team: for an hour against Warrington in the John Player Trophy semi-final; when they beat Hull early in the season; and in running in forty-five points without reply against Featherstone Rovers, to give just three examples. But their success was founded chiefly on the necessary but duller virtues of hard work and application. They possessed some fine players but no truly great ones. Just one player of, say, the quality of Andrew Gregory or David Topliss might have made the difference for Wigan between being a good side and becoming champions. Henderson Gill was a splendid winger, a dangerous finisher, but most of the tries he scored in the season were hard-earned. A winger playing in a good side should expect a few simple touchdowns at least, the result hopefully of crossfield moves that stretch the opposition cover beyond recovery. But Gill rarely enjoyed such luxuries.

The signing of the New Zealand captain, Graeme West, brought variety to Wigan's play, for the tall forward was adept at keeping the ball alive. When West received the support he deserved Wigan could look a superior team. There were consistently fine performances, too, from another New Zealand forward, Danny Campbell, who at the start of the season seemed not to enjoy the complete faith of his coach but who had earned it by the end.

Shaw was another dedicated forward until he broke a leg at the Boulevard; there was no more enthusiastic hooker anywhere than Kiss, and a pack that also contained the selfless Scott and the intelligent Pendlebury could compare with the best sets of forwards, especially after the signing of Brian Case from Warrington. For all that, the forwards were frequently predictable, and behind the pack that dash of inspiration was often missing. Of the top five clubs Wigan scored fewest points and conceded fewest points—an accurate reflection of their efficiency.

These then were the clubs who were seriously to dispute the title. Leeds declined so badly towards the end that St Helens and Widnes finished above them, but at no stage of the season were Widnes ever serious candidates, while St Helens, although at one point only four points adrift of the leaders, never quite manoeuvred themselves into a position of real strength. On 22 March, the day on which the run-in began in earnest, the situation was this:

	P	W	D	L	F	A	Pts
Hull KR	25	18	0	7	414	215	36
Hull	23	17	1	5	413	223	35
Leeds	25	17	1	7	452	335	35
Wigan	23	16	2	5	388	178	34
St Helens	23	15	1	7	371	330	31
Widnes	24	14	2	8	443	295	30

From this point onwards Hull started to play with impressive skill, assurance and authority. On the morning of 22 March it was possible to make out a

The Slalom Lager Championship

particularly strong case for Wigan winning the championship. At 9.0 p.m. that same evening any such case would have required hasty revision after they had been overwhelmed by Hull at the Boulevard.

The main danger to Hull appeared to be their involvement in the Challenge Cup. Their semi-final with Castleford was looming, and there seemed to be a chance that Hull minds might not be fully concentrated. Leeds had suffered four successive defeats and, with these, a serious draining of their confidence. Recovery for them was unlikely, which seemed to leave Wigan and Hull Kingston Rovers advantageously placed. Unlike Hull, they could afford to direct all their attention to one prize.

Wigan suffered wretched misfortune in the opening minute of the Hull match, when they lost Shaw with a broken leg after a heavy but legal challenge by Edmonds. Hull could also consider themselves fortunate to finish with a full complement of players. Crooks was sent to the sin bin for ten minutes after an off-the-ball assault on Jimmy Fairhurst which, in less lenient times, would almost certainly have earned permanent dismissal. In such a charged atmosphere, and in so important a game, the loss of the experienced Shaw was demoralizing for Wigan. It is not possible to say how the match would have developed with him, but it was difficult to imagine that his presence would have made so much of a difference that Wigan could have won.

The following Sunday the three leading sides all won: Wigan by one anxious point, 27–26, at Barrow, who led 15–5 at one stage; Hull Kingston Rovers 23–17 against Castleford; and Hull 21–18 in a marvellous match against Widnes at Naughton Park. Hull's mid-week win against Wigan had taken them to the top of the league, a point ahead of Hull Kingston Rovers. This win kept them there, but though they were manifestly the superior side, they were to endure a nerve-wracked second half before collecting both points.

Hull had not won at Widnes for thirteen years but were comfortably in control when they led 18–6 five minutes after half-time. A first half of swift, fluent football from both sides had been followed by a second half slightly more cramped and more prone to error but of mounting tension. Two minutes from time Lydon scored a try, added the goal for it, and to Hull's consternation a lead of twelve points had dwindled to only one. A penalty from 35 yards by Crooks a minute from time was a great relief for them.

Hull Kingston Rovers meanwhile had slightly more to spare in their match against Castleford at Craven Park, a game which saw the return of Malcolm Reilly at loose forward for Castleford. Two tries by Kevin Beardmore (the Beardmore brothers were to score fifteen of Castleford's seventeen points between them) took Castleford into a useful lead, but then Rovers, their forwards running wide and punishingly, scored three tries in a spell of seven minutes, two of them by Hogan and the other by Prohm. A Rovers' lead of 16–10

The Slalom Lager Championship

was then reduced to a single point before Prohm scored his second try.

Wigan were helped by their opponents' misfortune at Craven Park, where Barrow had three men taken to hospital and finished the game with twelve men. Before being consumed by misfortune, however, Barrow had led 15–5, a position that Wigan might have found difficult to rectify if Barrow had not been so badly weakened. As it was, Wigan were able to pay off their arrears and to move, twenty minutes from time, into a lead of nine points. But it was to prove only just enough as Barrow made a spirited late rally.

The following Wednesday Hull Kingston Rovers played a Warrington side below strength and still seeking to avoid relegation, but there was, nevertheless, a determination and purpose about Rovers which suggested a healthy self-belief. It was extraordinary, in view of the discrepancy in quality between the sides, that Rovers should lead only 8–7 with twelve minutes remaining, but they scored another eight points in those remaining minutes, collected their two points and in so doing replaced Hull in top place.

On Good Friday Wigan, suffering no serious alarms, but showing no great inspiration, had beaten St Helens 13–6 before a crowd of 12,400 at Central Park. St Helens were too dependent on too few players (Arkwright and Pinner particularly), and although Wigan had to toil for their two points, they achieved them comfortably enough, with tries from Juliff, Case and West, who again demonstrated his enviable ability to keep attacks in motion. Leeds, meanwhile, had brought an end to a demoralizing run of defeats, but a point from a draw 5–5 against Bradford was not nearly enough for them at this crucial stage of the season. The leading three positions (Leeds were now four points adrift with four games left) were:

	P	W	D	L	F	A	Pts
Hull KR	27	20	0	7	453	239	40
Hull	25	19	1	5	457	247	39
Wigan	26	18	2	6	434	233	38

The next twist to the plot came on Easter Monday at Wheldon Road. Hull had removed Castleford in the semi-final of the Challenge Cup at Elland Road on Easter Saturday, but now found Malcolm Reilly's enigmatic side in greatly superior form only two days later. Hull had made six changes from their cup side, but with Norton and Kemble as the two substitutes they could scarcely claim that they were below strength. Both substitutes were quickly required, too, as Evans was carried off in the opening minutes and Crooks departed before half time.

Although Castleford had only five points to spare at the end, five tries to two was fair evidence of the disparity between the sides. There was not a great deal wrong with Hull—although Kemble, who had been suffering from influenza, failed to stop two tries that on another day he would almost certainly have prevented. Simply, Castleford struck close to their best form, and when they do so no side is safe against them. Castleford no doubt would have preferred to produce this form two days earlier, but the result of a 21–16 victory was to ensure even greater interest in the next major confrontation, the game between Hull and Hull Kingston Rovers four days later.

In between times, Wigan just failed to move into top place when they defeated Warrington 15–5 at Central Park. Had they won by fourteen clear points they would have done so, but that objective eluded them. Warrington, with Dave Chisnall slipping out a stream of choice passes, were threatening for fifteen minutes, but tries by Stephenson either side of the interval set Wigan on course for two points which helped to keep the issue simmering. When Hull and Hull Kingston Rovers met two days later interest was intense; a capacity crowd of 20,570 at the Boulevard was the highest since the formation of two divisions in 1973.

It is doubtful, given all the circumstances, if there was a more completely convincing performance all season than Hull's splendid victory by 21–3. Hull Kingston Rovers ran with strength and determination during the first twenty minutes but simply made no progress against the certainty of Hull's defences. When Hull themselves turned their attention to attack Rovers had no deterrent to the pace, thrust and imagination, the sheer sweep, of Hull's forays.

Sour undercurrents ran throughout the match, and in the fifty-fifth minute the two full-backs, Kemble and Lydiat, were sent off for exchanging blows, and Holdstock, the Rovers prop, spent time in the sin bin, yet the lasting memories would be not of the game's violent passages but of its purple ones. Hull looked a formidably accomplished team, superbly served throughout the side by players performing at the height of their powers.

There were five tries. Only one of them, Leuluai's, owed anything to fortune, Prendiville's kick downfield bouncing luckily off the crossbar to the Kiwi centre. Prendiville's try in the first half was the outstanding one, the result of glorious running by Leuluai, who then was able to slip out an unexpected pass after colliding with his opposite centre. A quick sidestep and Prendiville had cut at speed inside Lydiat, leaving the full-back helpless. Rovers had nothing to offer in reply to football of that quality.

Rovers seemed so deflated by this defeat that on the following Sunday they were unable to beat a Warrington side which contained ten reserves. This match brought Rovers their only drawn game of the season, but that was not nearly good enough. Their ambition, it was apparent, had evaporated. Hull, meanwhile, were defeating Carlisle—comfortably, though more modestly than

The Slalom Lager Championship

might have been expected of a side which had conceded sixty-six points to Castleford on the night that Hull were crushing Rovers—and Wigan were taking two points off Oldham in a hard, sapping match in vile conditions at Central Park.

The matter now rested between Hull, left with an away match against Leeds and a home game with Barrow, and Wigan, who had to visit Featherstone and Widnes. Wigan's match with Featherstone on the Wednesday started at 6.30 p.m., which meant that the result had reached Headingley long before the end of Leeds's game with Hull. Surprisingly, Wigan could manage nothing better than a draw—a result that had not entered into most people's calculations—and that only after a belated retaliation and a penalty from long range by Whitfield.

Hull, however, showed no such inhibitions against Leeds. Their form, especially in the first half, was an extension of their play against Hull Kingston Rovers. Leeds had been driven mercilessly out of the contest after only fifteen minutes, Evans, Topliss and O'Hara running in tries. Leeds, their confidence severely undermined, were never likely to recover from such a ferocious onslaught. Hull, with every department of the team working with precision and efficiency, reduced their output in the second half to a single penalty, and Leeds were given some encouragement as the pressure on them eased. But Hull did not relax too much. Leeds were allowed a try—by Mitchell, playing in his first full game—and a goal (from Conway) but no more.

Only a statistical nicety now stood between Hull and the championship. Wigan could still win the title if they defeated Widnes at Naughton Park by forty-six clear points and if Hull lost at home to Barrow. But Widnes, even in their least guarded moments, were not prone to conceding games by such margins, while Hull were in no mood to lose to any side, let alone one destined for the second division. In the event, the arguments were settled emphatically in Hull's favour. They beat Barrow 31–13, while Widnes defeated Wigan 21–17. Barrow went down, and Hull, after the twists, turns and the mathematical calculations of the final weeks, had four points to spare at the end.

Although Barrow looked a shade too good for relegation, Hull's win was free of alarm or difficulty. Barrow were fiercely physical at times, perhaps chiefly out of desperation, but they were limited. Hull would have had genuine cause for concern if they had been confronted by thirteen players of the quality of David Cairns, but the scrum-half was one of the few consistent sources of danger to the home side.

Cairns ran 40 yards to score a fine try in the second half, and Wall also scored two tries, reward for an enterprising display in the loose by the hooker. But these scores were little more than pin-pricks of irritation to Hull. They ran and handled with an assurance that suggested that all the hard labour was behind

35. After Hull had won the Slalom Lager Championship title, beating Barrow at the Boulevard, they were led in the Maori war dance, the Haka, by their New Zealanders, Gary Kemble, James Leuluai and Dane O'Hara, three splendid players who had contributed hugely to Hull's success throughout the season. It was fitting that each of them should score a try in the second half of this match.

them. A crowd of 17,100 was in no mood to pay much attention to the occasional flaw.

In the first half there was the rare sight of Skerrett scoring a try and the much more familiar ones of Topliss, after working a glorious run-around with Evans, and Prendiville racing over. Crane scored a clever try, too, and in the second half Hull's three New Zealand players each scored tries. Kemble, O'Hara and Leuluai had played an enormous part in helping to make Hull such a successful club; it was fitting that three players who had been such a credit to themselves, their country, Hull and British Rugby League should have such an important, final say in the championship. After the Championship Trophy had been presented to the Hull captain, Topliss, the Hull players needed little urging to join Kemble, O'Hara and Leuluai in the Haka, the Maori dance so beloved of New Zealand teams.

The Slalom Lager Championship

Division 1

	P	W	L	D	F	A	Pts
Hull	30	23	6	1	572	293	47
Hull Kingston Rovers	30	21	8	1	496	276	43
Wigan	30	20	7	3	482	270	43
St Helens	30	19	10	1	516	395	39
Widnes	30	18	10	2	534	357	38
Leeds	30	18	10	2	480	443	38
Castleford	30	18	11	1	629	458	37
Oldham	30	15	13	2	346	320	32
Bradford Northern	30	14	14	2	381	314	30
Leigh	30	13	14	3	488	374	29
Warrington	30	13	15	2	423	410	28
Featherstone Rovers	30	10	16	4	350	447	24
Barrow	30	11	18	1	472	505	23
Workington Town	30	6	22	2	318	696	14
Halifax	30	5	24	1	221	651	11
Carlisle	30	2	28	—	252	751	4

Of the four sides who were promoted in 1982, three returned to the second division, maintaining a pattern that has become only too familiar over the years. Oldham were the exception. Under the guidance of Frank Myler, a young, imaginative side finished eighth, a position for which most people at the club would have settled at the start of the season. But long before the season's end it was apparent that there would be no salvation for Carlisle, Halifax or Workington Town.

All three clubs had their problems, and Carlisle at one stage seemed unlikely to complete their fixtures. Halifax lost their coach, Ken Roberts, as early as September after four heavy defeats. Roberts was one of those fortunate people who was not in the sport for the money, and he was bitterly critical of his players on his resignation. 'I can excuse a lack of ability and I can excuse mistakes, but I cannot forgive players for going out with the attitude that they can't win,' he said.

Colin Dixon, the former Halifax and Salford forward, took over. He was not a man to accept non-triers either. Halifax did improve but only marginally, and five wins and a draw was not nearly enough to preserve their first-division status. Workington Town had fired their coach, Tommy Bishop, at the end of the previous season and had turned then to Ike Southward, one of the best wingers the club had ever had. It was never intended that Southward should act as anything other than a caretaker, and in early March Dave Cox was enticed from Sydney to take charge. No sooner had he arrived in England, however, than he had to return to Australia where his wife had suffered a stroke. Once again, Town had to enlist Southward.

From the end of October these three clubs occupied the bottom positions, and so most interest in this area centred on the fourth relegation place, which threatened at various times to claim Bradford Northern, Featherstone Rovers, Warrington and Barrow. In the end Barrow were the victims. It was a little hard to accept that a side with players of the quality of Steve Tickle and Ian Ball, Derek Hadley, Mel Mason and David Cairns, a team capable of bold, attractive rugby, deserved to be condemned to the second division. Once again, the wisdom of promoting four sides and relegating four sides was in question.

There was no question, though, about Fulham's right to return to the first division, from which they had been relegated in their second season in the game. Because of problems with their Craven Cottage pitch, Fulham had to play two of their final 'home' league games at Widnes after their request for an extension to the season had been rather pettily rejected. Fortunately for their supporters, the ground was playable for the game with York which Fulham won 21–13, a victory which ensured they would return to the first division as champions.

Fulham were the outstanding side of the second division. Reggie Bowden, their player-coach, quashed theories that he might take charge of the vacant coach's job at his old club, Widnes, where Doug Laughton had resigned owing to the increasing pressures of his business. Bowden showed his faith in Fulham by signing a new three-year contract, and there was no question that the cheerful, likeable Bowden had good material with which to work. Fulham were still relying on some of the players who had helped win promotion in the club's first season of existence—Bowden himself, Harry Beverley, David Eckersley, Tony Gourley—but some excellent young players were also developing in Peter Souto, a signing from Welsh Rugby Union, Hussein M'Barki, a former Moroccan Rugby Union captain, who had been playing Rugby Union in France with Cahors, and Steve Bayliss, for whom Fulham paid St Helens £30,000, one of the season's most expensive entries into a depressed transfer market.

Wakefield Trinity pursued Fulham over the full course but were always likely to have to settle for second place. Salford finished third and reclaimed the first-division status they had lost two seasons earlier, but although they, like Fulham, had a number of emerging youngsters, such as Ronnie Smith and

36. Fulham won the second-division championship with three points to spare from Wakefield Trinity. One of the principal contributors to their campaign was Hussein M'Barki, the former Moroccan Rugby Union captain who had been playing Rugby Union in France with Cahors. Since joining the London club he had steadily made himself into one of the most exciting wingers in the game. He scored 23 tries in the season.

Gerard Byrne, some alarming fluctuations in form did not inspire confidence for their first-division safety.

The fourth promotion place went to Whitehaven, which meant that Cumbria would have one first-division club after all. Whitehaven resisted late challenges from Swinton, Hunslet and Bramley, but the side providing the most interesting finish to the season was Cardiff City. Since their formation their attendances had declined steadily, and inevitably there were doubts about their ability to survive. But by the end of their second season the Welsh club had made modest but steady progress, ready to make a serious attempt to gain entry to the first division.

Division 2

	P	W	L	D	F	A	Pts
Fulham	32	27	4	1	699	294	55
Wakefield Trinity	32	25	5	2	672	381	52
Salford	32	24	8	—	686	363	48
Whitehaven	32	20	9	3	464	298	43
Bramley	32	20	11	1	560	369	41
Hunslet	32	17	10	5	553	448	39
Swinton	32	19	12	1	549	454	39
Cardiff City	32	17	13	2	572	444	36
Keighley	32	15	12	5	470	423	35
York	32	15	17	—	516	455	30
Blackpool Borough	32	13	18	1	381	433	27
Huddersfield	32	13	18	1	397	524	27
Rochdale Hornets	32	10	17	5	361	469	25
Dewsbury	32	8	23	1	325	507	17
Batley	32	6	25	1	305	719	13
Huyton	32	6	26	—	250	687	12
Doncaster	32	2	29	1	307	799	5

THE PREMIERSHIP TROPHY

The Slalom Lager Premiership Trophy has been criticized as a superfluous, contrived end to the season, but healthy crowds, consistently entertaining games and a memorable final between Hull and Widnes at Leeds provided

The Premiership Trophy

powerful arguments in its favour. Widnes retained the trophy by winning 22–10 and in so doing looked to have a bright future. Widnes had lost their coach, Doug Laughton, before the end of the season but, rather than hastily appoint a successor, the club had allowed control of the team to pass to two members of the coaching staff, Harry Dawson and Colin Tyrer. The quality of Widnes's performance in the final was the testimony of how well the pair had run affairs in Laughton's absence.

In a game of exceptionally high quality one performance surpassed all. Tony Myler, the 21-year-old stand-off, was the orchestrator of Widnes's victory. He scored one try and fashioned the other three. One of the great skills of Rugby League is to run into the right places. Unerringly, Myler did so and with enough power and assurance to cause Hull persistent consternation. Man-of-the-match awards have become devalued in Rugby League because there are too many of them. The Lance Todd and Harry Sunderland Trophies, however, are still coveted awards, and the votes for them are usually close. In selecting Myler for the Sunderland award, however, a sizeable press corps could not find even one player to rival him.

Of the eight teams (those finishing in the top eight places of the first division) to contest the trophy, Oldham were the surprise package. They had been promoted the previous season, and under the guidance of Frank Myler and his assistant, Peter Smethurst (who was to leave Oldham to take charge at Leigh and then return to Oldham again), had emerged as a side of promise with some especially good, young forwards in Flanagan, Worrall and Goodway.

Two of their best performances had been given in league games against Hull. At home they were unfortunate to be beaten 5–2 but then became the only side to win at the Boulevard in the league when they defeated Hull 8–2. They were unable, however, to produce a repeat of that performance in the first round of the Premiership, although again they caused Hull considerable trouble, and this in spite of the absence of Flanagan and Worrall. They led 9–2, were overhauled and then seemingly left behind, but they disturbed Hull by scoring ten points in the final four minutes, reducing the score from 24–11 to 24–21. Hull could not have taken any more of that particular form of retaliation.

Much the most unexpected result was provided by Leeds. The previous weekend they had conceded fifty-two points to Leigh at Hilton Park in a league game. It seemed reasonably safe to assume that such a defeat would have left them demoralized and in no mood to resist Wigan at Central Park. To their credit, they tackled wholeheartedly, showing a determination that had been all but absent the previous Sunday, and their victory, 12–9, was the more meritorious for being achieved after conceding five points in the first four minutes. Eleven of Leeds's twelve points came from Conway with a try and four goals. One of Wigan's few consolations in an error-strewn game was the form of the 20-year-old forward, Brian Dunn, whose appearances for the club had been limited but promising.

David Hall, meanwhile, was scoring four tries for Hull Kingston Rovers—a record for the competition—in a convincing 35–14 victory over Castleford at Craven Park, while Widnes were beating St Helens 11–7 at Knowlsey Road, recovering splendidly from a deficit of seven points. Much of Widnes's inspiration stemmed from a try by Lydon that involved him running 80 yards after taking Gregory's pass close to his own '25'. Rovers, for their part, were in one of those moods in which they look as accomplished as any side in the game, and Castleford were unable to cope with a team in which all the parts were working with the precision of an expensive watch. Hull Kingston Rovers though, and not for the first time, were soon to appreciate how elusive consistency can be.

As the competition moved into the semi-final stage, Hull Kingston Rovers were drawn at home against Widnes, and Hull were to play Leeds at the Boulevard. Both matches were to take place over the spring Bank Holiday week-end.

**The Premiership Trophy Semi-Final
Craven Park, Hull, 30 April
Hull Kingston Rovers 10   Widnes 21**

For half an hour in the first semi-final at Craven Park, Hull Kingston Rovers bore some comparison with the side which had crushed Castleford the previous week. They took an 8–0 lead, but then fell away alarmingly. They were beaten 2–1 at the scrums, but their troubles ran deeper than a lack of possession. Where their handling seven days earlier had been so assured, it was now vulnerable, nervous; and whereas against Castleford the whole side had functioned at a high level of efficiency, now there were only one or two individuals trying to provide the inspiration.

Against Castleford Hartley had been at his best, a rare experience for him in a season which at one stage had drained his confidence dry. Here, though, he was outplayed by Tony Myler who scored three tries in a powerful display. After an opening which brought tries for Prohm and Clark, Rovers had perhaps only Hogan to compare with the Widnes stand-off, and that was not nearly enough to win them an important cup-tie.

The Premiership Trophy

Widnes had the misfortune, too, to lose Gregory for the second half. The Widnes scrum-half is prone to dispute referees' decisions, a problem which could have proved costly in this match. That weakness, however, was redressed in singular fashion. In an incident off the ball Holdstock gave Gregory a fierce and painful blow in the mouth, an assault which deserved much more than a simple penalty. (The Disciplinary Committee thought so too, for Holdstock, from television evidence, was given a suspended six-match ban.) Nevertheless, this forced Gregory to keep his mouth shut, and although he did not reappear after half-time, he helped the Widnes recovery by cleverly engineering their first try.

Fairbairn extended his side's half-time lead of 8–7 with a penalty soon after the interval, but from then on Widnes first assumed and then maintained control. Myler had scored the first of his tries before half-time; he now scored his second as a result of Fairbairn's inability to cope with a high kick from Adams into the in-goal area. The full-back flapped helplessly at the ball, which bounced away from him; although Rovers claimed that Myler failed to touch down, the referee, Stan Wall, was close enough to be in no doubt.

Myler's third try owed something to poor Rovers tackling but much also to assertive running and a sense of opportunism, and he beat three Rovers defenders on his way to the line. Finally, Adams again kicked ahead, the ball bounced off a post and the loose forward, following up, caught the ball and touched down. Adams had done this kind of thing before. He claimed that it was something he practised. Was he joking? It was hard now to be sure.

Hull Kingston Rovers: Fairbairn; Clark, Mike Smith, Hall, Prohm; Hartley, Gordon Smith; Holdstock, Watkinson, White, Kelly, Hogan, Lazenby

Substitutes: Robinson for Hall at half-time, Burton for Kelly after 61 minutes

Scorers: tries—Prohm, Clark; goals—Fairbairn (2)

Widnes: Burke; Linton, Lydon, Hughes, Basnett; Tony Myler, Gregory; Mike O'Neill, Elwell, Tamati, Gorley, Prescott, Adams

Substitutes: Hulme for Gregory at half-time, Whitfield for Tamati after 50 minutes

Scorers: tries—Myler (3), Adams; goals—Lydon (4); drop goal—Elwell

Referee: S. Wall (Leigh)

Attendance: 7,196

37. This sprint start by David Topliss took the Hull captain away from the challenge of Eric Hughes and on to his twenty-fourth try of the season in the Premiership Trophy final against Widnes. Hull have had great value from their stand-off since his move from Wakefield, and Topliss felt he had played as well in this season as at any stage in his career.

**The Premiership Trophy Semi-Final
The Boulevard, HULL, 1 May
Hull 19   Leeds 5**

This second semi-final at the Boulevard was played in conditions which in January would have been considered miserable enough. For May they were scarcely credible, as the pitch quickly turned into a morass. By the end of a

The Premiership Trophy

match which, in view of the conditions, was a credit to both sides, identification of players had to be achieved by shape and size (although an ancient-looking scrum cap was a help in spotting Edmonds). Hull, less than a week away from the Challenge Cup final at Wembley, would probably have opted for a less demanding contest but their win was convincing enough.

Leeds could have had no great relish for this encounter. In three previous meetings against Hull in the season they had conceded seventy-five points and scored only ten in reply. There never seemed much possibility that Leeds would be recompensed for those thrashings, but they performed with a lot of spirit, even though it was evident long before half-time which side was going through to the final.

This match admirably illustrated the strength of the Hull squad. Four of their tries came from players who failed to win a place in the Cup final side, although Patrick Solal, the Frenchman, was cup-tied and could not have played anyway. But there were especially fine performances from Edmonds and Banks, both of whom scored tries, and from Dean and Solal, who showed the strength of his finishing just before the interval, when he dragged Andrew Smith over the try line with him.

Holmes, who was injured in that incident, failed to appear for the second half, and Leeds, already in a difficult position, lost much of their direction and organization. Sykes and Burke, their props, continued to slog spiritedly through the mud, but Hull's defence was sound. The ebullient Topliss, too, thrived even more now that Holmes was missing, and there were a number of fine moves from Hull in attack, none better than the one inspired by Crane, Norton's substitute, that brought Banks his try ten minutes from time.

Misguidedly, Leeds persisted in trying to find routes down the middle during the second half, and they simply were not there. Much greater enterprise had been shown early in the first half, when David Heron had thrown the ball wide to Heselwood. The centre had had to juggle with the ball above his head, had somehow kept control and had then burst powerfully to the line. Conway added the goal and that brought the scores to 5–5, Wileman (with a try) and Crooks (with the goal) having given Hull the lead.

Hull: Banks; Solal, Evans, Day, O'Hara; Topliss, Dean; Edmonds, Wileman, Stone, Skerrett, Crooks, Norton

Substitutes: Crane for Crooks after 59 minutes, Harkin for Topliss after 71 minutes

Scorers: tries—Solal, Skerrett, Edmonds, Wileman, Banks; goals—Crooks, Evans

The Premiership Trophy

Leeds: Hague; Mitchell, Heselwood, Wilkinson, Andrew Smith; Holmes, Conway; Sykes, Sowden, Burke, Keith Rayne, Squire, David Heron

Substitutes: Dick for Holmes at half-time, Armitage for Squire after 53 minutes

Scorers: try—Heselwood; goal—Conway

Referee: W. H. Thompson (Huddersfield)

Attendance: 11,581

**The Premiership Trophy Final
Headingley, Leeds, 14 May
Widnes 22   Hull 10**

If Widnes had not won the final at Headingley, it would have been the first time in nine seasons that they had failed to capture at least one of the game's major trophies. This was one tournament, however, for which Widnes had a particular liking, having beaten Bradford Northern in 1980 and Hull in 1982. It was soon evident that Widnes had no intention of letting the trophy go.

Here was a fitting climax, a game more exciting, more committed and faster, than the 17,813 spectators could really have expected at the end of a long, tiring campaign. The first hour was marvellous, and though afterwards, with Widnes in control and Hull drained of energy, the excitement subsided, it was a game which saw Rugby League at its best. It produced, too, that exceptional performance from Tony Myler, quite one of the outstanding displays of the season.

Hull played some excellent football in the first half and showed few signs of neurosis after their defeat against Featherstone Rovers in the Challenge Cup final the previous Saturday. Crucially, though, in the second half they tired visibly. Bridges had been one of the side's weaknesses at Wembley, and his vulnerability in defence was again apparent. Other experienced players, such as Stone and Norton had to struggle to make any impact.

Widnes were not lacking experienced players either, but the peaks of their performance were the displays of Myler and Gregory, Lydon, Basnett and Mike O'Neill, maturing young players likely to be strong candidates for a future Great Britain side. There was also much promise from Ralph Linton on the right

The Premiership Trophy

wing and, especially, from Fred Whitfield in the second row. It was impossible to look at these riches and not be excited by them.

At half-time, after forty stirring, fluctuating minutes, the sides were locked at 10–10, a faithful indication of the closeness of the contest. Hull were clearly determined to make reparation for their calamitous performance at Wembley, and with Kemble, Topliss and Dean, and Leuluai particularly sharp, they had the better of the first half-hour. But Myler was dangerous every time he received the ball; Gregory was a superb half-back partner; and with both half-back partnerships working so effectively the flow was ceaseless, the pace exhausting.

By half-time Topliss and O'Hara had scored tries for Hull and Myler and Basnett tries for Widnes and there was still, at that stage, equality between the goalkickers, with Crooks and Lydon kicking two apiece. But Hull's stamina began to evaporate in the second half; Widnes grew in confidence, and Myler started to wreak even more havoc. Injury reduced his effectiveness over the final fifteen minutes, but by then he had made tries for Basnett and Gregory, and Hull were beyond redemption. Three further goals from Lydon were embellishments.

So ended, in the most optimistic fashion, a season for Widnes that had been one of change and readjustment, a search for a new identity. It was difficult to see how, after this display, they could fail to challenge for all the trophies available in the 1983–84 season. As for Hull, the new season would tell whether they had been overcome by nothing more serious than tiredness.

Widnes: Burke; Linton, Lydon, Hughes, Basnett; Tony Myler, Gregory; Mike O'Neill, Elwell, Gorley, Whitfield, Prescott, Adams

Substitutes: Steve O'Neill for Whitfield after 67 minutes, Hulme for Gregory after 73 minutes

Scorers: tries—Myler, Basnett (2), Gregory; goals—Lydon (5)

Hull: Kemble; O'Hara, Day, Leuluai, Evans; Topliss, Dean; Skerrett, Bridges, Stone, Rose, Crooks, Norton

Substitutes: Crane for Norton after 54 minutes, Solal for Day after 57 minutes

Scorers: tries—Topliss, O'Hara; goals—Crooks (2)

Referee: G. F. Lindop (Wakefield)

Attendance: 17,813

38. Tony Myler, the 21-year-old stand-off, gave one of the season's outstanding individual performances for Widnes in the final of the Premiership Trophy against Hull. He scored a try, played a part in his side's other three and secured the vote of every press man for the Harry Sunderland man-of-the match Trophy.

6

REFLECTIONS

A mood of pessimism settled on the British game after the departure of the 1982 Australians. The tourists had exposed the sterility of domestic playing standards, the lack of fitness, of dedication and of ideas. The profundity of Frank Stanton's methods of coaching were a denunciation of the shallow, predictable approach to the game of so many British coaches. It would have been hard to watch the Australians and not conclude that the British game was in need of overhaul. Test matches between Australia and Great Britain should transcend all in Rugby League. Instead, because of the disparity in playing standards between the two sides, they were becoming an embarrassment almost.

Time will tell if the 1982–83 season was not one of lost opportunity. The game had been forced to take a hard look at itself, but by the end of the season it was difficult to detect the concerted drive so patently required if British standards were to match Australia's. The Rugby League Council, the game's governing body, could on occasions act surprisingly adventurously and altruistically, as they showed in their support for the admission to the league of the newly formed Maidstone club, Kent Invicta. David Oxley, the League's secretary-general, described this as a 'brave decision', but, confronted with other issues of importance, the Council could be depressingly parochial, entrenched, inflexible.

Again, time will tell if the responses to the lessons of the Australian tour have amounted to much more than an awareness of things wrong, token gestures made in acknowledgement of the problems. One of those responses was to appoint Frank Myler full-time Great Britain coach and to give him and Dick Gemmell, the Great Britain manager, exclusive responsibility for choosing the British side. After the embarrassing tangles in which the selectors had found themselves during the Ashes series, these were positive moves.

There were just enough indications in the international against France at

Reflections

Carcassonne (though, it must be admitted, scarcely any in the return match at Hull) that Great Britain were emerging from the darkness. An Under-24 match and two full internationals were not sufficient evidence to judge the success of Myler's and Gemmell's stewardship but one sensed the kindling of a new spirit. Disturbingly, there were few signs of renewal at club level. A stranger watching the Premiership Trophy final between Widnes and Hull at Leeds might have asked, with justification, what could possibly be wrong with a sport which can produce skill and entertainment of that standard? But in a sense the Premiership final was a condemnation of current standards. It illustrated the exalted levels to which the game can aspire but which in 1982–83 it so often failed to reach.

No one absorbed the lessons of the Australian tour more thoroughly than Phil Larder, the game's new National Director of Coaching. The Australians had as profound an effect upon Larder as the 1953 Hungarian soccer side had upon the young Ron Greenwood, later to become manager of West Ham United and England. A measure of the greatness of the Australians was that they could make someone change the way he thought about the game, even one such as Larder who had played professionally for fourteen years. Energetic, enthusiastic and with a sense of mission, Larder threw himself with renewed vigour into formulating a coaching scheme that he believed would be the salvation of the game. He was soon to discover that not everyone shared his reforming zeal.

In February a conference of club coaches was held at Rugby League headquarters. Its importance needed no stressing. Here was a response by the clubs to the Australian tour, yet of the league's thirty-three clubs fourteen failed to send a representative. Five of the absentees (all from the second division) wrote to say that they could not attend. The rest did not even bother to apologize: among them were such influential clubs as Bradford Northern, Leigh, Warrington, Widnes and Wigan. Such apathy, indifference or even opposition to this meeting was an example of Rugby League at its most obtuse.

There are some coaches in the game, some of whom have been outstanding players in their time, who clearly think that there is little new to learn. It was not difficult to detect among some of the old, hardened, former professionals a dismissive attitude towards the new ideas which were being propounded and for the men propounding them. Larder was well aware that a lot of old, reactionary views would need to be displaced if his National Coaching Scheme was to win the support it deserved. Yet no one attending this meeting could have failed to benefit from it.

Larder was privileged to spend a great deal of time with the 1982 Australians and had thus been able to make a detailed study of Stanton's methods. Those methods were outlined to the conference, and perhaps for the first time the amount of thought, planning and detail that the Australian coach had poured into his work began to be understood and appreciated. One of the qualities which made Stanton so exceptional was his restless search for perfection—in sharp contrast to those British coaches who obviously felt that nothing was to be gained from attending the meeting.

As a result of his researches Larder made a number of recommendations, of which the three major ones were:

- more people must be encouraged to play Rugby League;
- coaching must improve at all levels;
- the fitness, dedication and commitment of professional players must improve.

Larder concluded that the reasons for the higher standard of football in Sydney and Brisbane were that players arriving at clubs there were more skilful, dedicated, fitter and committed than players joining professional clubs in Britain. This, he maintained, was the result of superior coaching at school and junior levels. He said:

> In Australia all coaches have to go through their National Coaching Scheme. In 1960 Peter Corcoran, the director of coaching, after having studied Rugby League in Great Britain and France, Rugby Union in New Zealand, athletics training and the motivational and coaching techniques of American grid-iron football, related all his knowledge to Australian Rugby League. He produced a coaching manual and a coaching scheme which were rubber-stamped by the Australian Rugby League and which were enforced by the Sydney clubs. Only qualified coaches gained appointments.

On the fitness of players Larder had this to say:

> There is little doubt that the Australian Rugby League player is fitter and more dedicated than his English counterpart. Yet the Australian clubs train no more than three evenings a week and the players are not full-time professionals. Higher fitness standards are demanded by the clubs. During pre-season, which usually lasts six weeks, the players are tested and given intense, individual training schedules. They are expected to train at least five times a week, which means them doing sessions on their own similar to those performed by athletes. Such training requires a change in attitudes, a little organization, but no additional finance. It is essential that the professional clubs in this country follow suit and the younger players are encouraged, indeed made, to intensify their work.

At the same meeting Rod McKenzie, senior physical education lecturer at

Reflections

Carnegie College, Leeds, had some revealing things to say about the fitness of the British players who had attended the previous year's 'summer camps'. He also had some worthwhile recommendations to make as a result of his researches. Three camps had been held, the first two over three days, the third over two days. The fitness tests revealed 'in the main, that the fitness levels of the players was low with some players, forwards and backs, carrying substantial percentages of subcutaneous fat'.

More encouragingly, McKenzie found that the players worked hard in pre-season training and that their fitness levels showed a 'marked improvement'. He pointed out, too, that for the type of training that had been envisaged four to six weeks were required for each stage but the timescales to which the British squad were working did not permit this. Among his recommendations McKenzie suggested that players should be made more aware of their fitness needs by the following methods: conferences of coaches; players' seminars; use of written material for coaches and players; closer analysis of the work rates required in individual positions; the development of Rugby League fitness norms; the availability for coaches of advice on training facilities.

The third act in this conference was provided by the coaches themselves. They were divided into three groups and were asked to produce solutions to three questions: How should the Rugby League respond to the Australians' tour? What preparations should be made for the 1984 tour of Australia? And how should clubs respond to the lessons taught by the Australians?

The response of the coaches was to provide what might well be a blueprint for the future of the British game. They felt that:

- there was an urgent need for the use of coaching education material, written and on video (it was recognized that Australia and, to a lesser extent, New Zealand had taken advantage of research into fitness science and it was essential that British coaches should be kept fully informed of modern trends);
- there was a need to establish the game at lower levels, with emphasis placed on basic skills;
- the Great Britain management team of coach and manager should have sole powers of selection;
- the Great Britain management team of coach and manager should consult club coaches for regular guides to form and for character assessment;
- the age limit for Under-24 internationals should be reduced to Under-21;
- coaching courses should be introduced for promising young players, especially those thought capable of becoming international players;
- the structure of club football below first-team level should be reviewed;
- some form of international exchange should be arranged so that British

players could sample Australian training methods and club football and vice versa;
- there was a need to encourage more discipline, commitment and improved attitudes from young players;
- the League should be constantly vigilant in punishing foul play, especially the sort of play which eliminates the talents of the ball player;
- the League should be divided into three divisions (not a unanimous proposal).

In fairness to the absentee coaches, conferences had been held before, recommendations made ... and no action taken. This time a number of these recommendations were adopted. Rod McKenzie became available full-time to give clubs advice on all matters concerning fitness; more video and coaching material became available; the Great Britain coaching job became a full-time appointment; and the management team of Frank Myler and Dick Gemmell was made solely responsible for choosing the national side; the drive to encourage the game at lower levels did take place.

In schools, colleges and universities and at other levels of the amateur game Rugby League is expanding but there remains, nevertheless, a lack of initiative on the part of the professional clubs. There seems to be reluctance, inability even, to see beyond the immediate requirements of their own team, although two clubs who can be excused such criticism are Hull and Hull Kingston Rovers, both of whom have shown an encouraging appreciation of the need to foster young players.

Hull and Hull KR were the first of the professional clubs to introduce 'mini-footy', a game that has long proved popular and highly successful in Australia. The primary aim of this game is to give enjoyment to younger players—both the Hull and the Hull KR initiatives are aimed at children under 10—but it is also a discipline which encourages good habits, basic skills and natural ability, and it can be played with advantage by youngsters of various ages. Hull began with forty boys, split into four teams of ten, who were then placed under the expert supervision of Ken Windley and Ron Hood, two coaches, and a former Hull stand-off, Terry Devonshire. At Craven Park, Gary Prohm and Phil Hogan were deputed to look after the first batch of youngsters. This is the kind of direction that the professional clubs generally should be giving to young players. It is all too rare.

Larder's philosophy for improving standards is based on a belief that as many young players as possible should be encouraged to play the game. Quantity is essential. From quantity will come higher quality, he believes. The Humberside clubs' encouragement of 'mini-footy' is an endorsement of that philosophy. It also shows that the Hull clubs are aware of their responsibilities.

Reflections

Hull's coach, Arthur Bunting, said: 'I feel that senior clubs do have a responsibility to the game and its future. It is very important to get as many youngsters as possible playing the game as early as possible. This game gives them that chance.' Larder was appointed to his post in April 1982, and before the end of the 1982–83 season he had become responsible for coaching at all levels of the game, professional and amateur.

A belief that had gathered strength during the season was that Rugby League might best be served if the professional and amateur sides of the game were run from one headquarters. Since its formation in 1973 the British Amateur Rugby League Association has made exceptional progress. It has set a target of presiding over a truly national sport by 1995—the hundredth anniversary of the game's break with Rugby Union. In 1973 this might have been seen as a pious ambition. By 1983 it was well set for achievement. There had been signs, nevertheless, that all within the amateur game was not at ease. Were too many factions pulling in too many different directions?

With justification BARLA can claim that they had rescued a dying amateur game in 1973. Since then they have been fiercely proud of their progress and of the respect they have won. The clinical standards of amateurism required by BARLA, especially of their representative teams, are more severe than those demanded by the high temple of amateurism, the Rugby Union. The Sports Council has recognized their progress by making them a foremost organization for grant aid. Not unnaturally, BARLA are determined to preserve their authority and the considerable independence they possess.

One of the game's most encouraging areas of growth was in upper schools and colleges, a vacuum until the formation of the British Upper Schools and Colleges Amateur Rugby League Association (BUSCARLA). Founded by Martyn Sadler, a lecturer at Sheffield Polytechnic, and Steve Alderson, a teacher at Wheelwright College, Dewsbury, and later given tremendous vitality by the energetic Peter Deakin, a Brighouse policeman and former professional with Oldham who acted as its development officer, BUSCARLA grew with remarkable rapidity in its first two seasons of life.

It expanded with sufficient pace to cause alarm to the Rugby Union authorities. Rugby Union, which had long enjoyed an unchallenged position in many educational establishments, found that it had a serious rival. Schools and colleges which at one time would not have dreamed of playing Rugby League embraced it. In its first season of existence BUSCARLA entered twenty-one teams in a cup competition run by *Open Rugby* magazine. In its second season that number had doubled—with, significantly, nine entries from Humberside where the previous season there had been none. Sadler, Alderson and Deakin were confident that the number would double again as the Association entered its third season of existence.

Central to the philosophy of these three zealots is a belief that Rugby League is a product which needs to be sold. It is no use sitting and waiting for the sport to come to you. Deakin maintains that there is little difference between selling Rugby League and a packet of soap powder—it is necessary to knock on doors and convince potential customers that the product is worthwhile. It is this combination of the drive of the salesman and the vision of the missionary that has helped BUSCARLA to grow so rapidly. Its future progress will be watched with interest. It is fostering the game among players within a vital age group, who might well become the sport's future coaches, administrators and apologists.

An argument aired a number of times throughout the season was that the sport should return to a single division of thirty-three clubs. A counter-argument to this was that there should be three divisions instead of two. Two-divisional Rugby League had been one of the recommendations of the Caine report—a commissioned investigation into the state of the game in 1971—and it had been adopted for the start of the 1973–74 season. Then, as now, teams at the top of the first division could attract healthy crowds; teams at the bottom of the second division were barely able to eke out a living.

Surprisingly, there was considerable popular support for a return to a single division. One of its most persistent advocates was Jack Grindrod, the chairman of the Rugby League Council and also the chairman of Rochdale Hornets. Before the end of the season his club was involved in discussions about a possible merger with the town's soccer club, and it was not surprising, as Hornets' attendances dwindled below 500, that Mr Grindrod, in common with many other harassed club chairmen, should be desperate to adopt any scheme that might generate more revenue.

Mr Grindrod argued that if there were one division, smaller clubs such as Rochdale would be better off because they would able to play against Hull, Leeds, Widnes and Wigan. Nor would the benefits be only financial. Playing against better opposition, the argument ran, would help to raise the playing standards of the less fortunate. The opposite view was that the gulf in standards between such clubs as Hull and Rochdale would be so embarrassingly wide that spectators simply would not bother to watch contests that were likely to be meaninglessly one-sided.

Mr Grindrod, however, was in no doubt how important it was to return to one division. The game's survival, no less, depended upon it. Mr Grindrod would have found sympathy for his claim that the game was being held to ransom by too many old players who were far past their best (Frank Stanton, too, believed this to be one reason why the sport was being stifled) and that clubs in the second division were having to dispense with players because they could not afford to run an 'A' team. He would, however, have found less support for his assertion that 'If we return to one division, it will give the smaller clubs the advantage of better gates when they meet the Hulls, Widnes, Wigans and Warringtons.'

A more persuasive argument possibly—certainly a more revolutionary one—was that the league should be divided into three divisions. Cautious support was given to this idea by the conference of coaches in February, while Ray French, the Cowley schoolmaster, former international and television commentator, made out an interesting case for such a structure in his weekly column in the *Rugby Leaguer*. The nub of his argument was that three divisions would foster much greater competition, an essential ingredient of the game, and would encourage the development of younger players.

French advocated three divisions with thirteen, ten and ten teams respectively. He envisaged six first-division games each week-end with one team resting, five in the second division and five in the third. The first division would thus be placing its emphasis—as in Sydney—on quality rather than quantity and, hopefully, engendering the sort of intense competition which produces Test players.

The second division, under French's scheme, would be one filled with many well supported teams 'who would meet with success. Good up-and-coming sides would have time to develop and build a side for promotion.' The third division would not be totally professional but would comprise sides of several professionals complemented by good amateurs 'eager to make names for themselves'. Such a league, he argued, could perform a similar function to the 'country leagues around Sydney where the players are mainly young'. No Rugby League system had ever proved perfect, French concluded, but if the three-divisional idea were not to win support, he hoped the administrators would examine the inadequacies of the present system.

From 1980 Rugby League had pursued a policy of expansion. Fulham had joined the league that year and twelve months later Cardiff City and Carlisle were admitted. These were limited by positive moves, attempts to make the sport truly national. Season 1983–84 would see another new arrival, Kent Invicta, playing at the home of Maidstone United, the non-league soccer club, but the buoyancy, the optimism, of previous years had shrivelled. It was evident in 1982–83 that most clubs were in serious financial distress. The previous summer Blackpool Borough had belatedly been rescued from the

Reflections

grasp of the Receiver. Now sounds of real misery were heard from Halifax and Huddersfield, Doncaster, Dewsbury, Bramley and especially Carlisle. It was a surprise that the season ended with all clubs still alive.

That Carlisle managed to remain in existence was perhaps most remarkable of all. Their difficulties in a season which saw them finish bottom of the first division after being promoted in their first season of life offered the Rugby League some salutary lessons. As one official put it: 'The Carlisle board seemed to view the Rugby League club like a publican might view a juke box. Install it. Watch it twinkle. Enjoy the music but take it out the moment it shows signs of losing money.'

The first public evidence that all was not well at Brunton Park came in December, when the managing director, Colin Hutchinson, sent a letter to all first- and second-division clubs calling for radical changes in the contracts system after five players, valued at £40,000, had walked out on the club. Hutchinson's proposals were designed to protect clubs against this sort of action. 'The idea,' he wrote, 'is to protect clubs from stay-away players but it could also give players the opportunity to take clubs to tribunals for breach of rules and to appeal against unreasonble transfer fees.'

A month later Carlisle announced that eighteen of their players were for sale. The only players the club was not prepared to sell were the player-coach, Mick Morgan, and three New Zealanders, Clayton Friend and the brothers Ian and Dean Bell. The crisis quickly gathered pace. Two weeks later it seemed probable rather than possible that the club would fold; Hutchinson gloomily forecast that Carlisle would go out of business 'within the next few days' unless a consortium could be formed to take over the company and its debts. The chances of survival were estimated at no higher than fifty–fifty.

Carlisle received no sympathy from the Rugby League headquarters. When their financial affairs were examined it was felt that at least twenty-five clubs would willingly have changed places with them. 'Carlisle's financial situation is not as serious as that of some other clubs,' said David Oxley, the League's secretary-general, 'and they have been asked to show the same resilience and determination as other club directors in these stringent times. We spelled out strongly to Carlisle that, when they were admitted to the league, they gave certain assurances that they intended to give the venture a lengthy trial.'

The response of the Carlisle board to this stricture was to resign almost en bloc, reinforcing an impression that had been gathering strength that the directors at Brunton Park, mostly non-Rugby League men, were keen to cut their losses and make a swift exit. There was little sign of commitment to a cause which had been embraced with such enthusiasm less than two years earlier. The postponed matches began to accumulate as Carlisle's fate remained unsure; their three New Zealand players returned home disillusioned, as likely as not, with their first experience of British Rugby League. But after a meeting of creditors and shareholders Carlisle remained in existence and, in spite of dispiriting difficulties and unrelieved defeat, completed their fixtures, an achievement for which the two remaining directors, George Graham and Geoff Holmes, deserved considerable credit.

Another of the league's newest clubs, Cardiff City, struggled along throughout the season on home attendances that rarely rose above a thousand. Fulham, in spite of winning promotion from the second division for the second time in their three years of existence, were supported by crowds much smaller than those in their first season. Nevertheless, interest in joining the league was expressed from Bristol to Sheffield. In the event, a firm application came only from Maidstone, though Hull made application on behalf of Hull White Star, while Hull Kingston Rovers, not wishing to be overshadowed by their ambitious neighbours, attempted to get Kingston Raiders into the league. These last two applications were not accepted by the Rugby League Council. Though the clubs concerned would disagree, they were seen as self-interested gambits rather than as steps in the game's general development. Maidstone's application was successful.

Rugby League's cemetery of deceased clubs is sizeable enough to remind newcomers of the difficulties of staying alive in a sport that has found difficulty in extending its boundaries. Yet Kent Invicta were far too promising to reject. The club proffered the chance—which Fulham had not done—of establishing the game in the south. One of Kent Invicta's ambitions was to have the majority of their players living and working in the area.

The club appeared to have much to offer and the two prime movers of the venture, Jim Thompson, the chairman (and almost exclusive owner) of Maidstone United football club, and Paul Faires, a young businessman who had taken a late but seemingly addictive liking to the sport, presented an impressive case to a special meeting of clubs at Leeds. Thompson and Faires could scarcely have expected to be given such gruelling questioning, but they emerged from their interrogation impressively. The meeting was satisfied with the thoroughness with which Maidstone presented their case and voted them into existence by a massive majority—twenty-six against three.

One of the most persuasive aspects of Maidstone's case was that concept of having the side populated with players living and working in the area. Increasingly criticism of the Fulham experiment was to be heard: the charge was that while they had brought professional Rugby League to London, they had not done a great deal to promote the game in the south. Kent Invicta now seemed to offer the chance of encouraging the sport to take hold, in new territory, at the grass roots.

Reflections

The most controversial decision taken by the International Board at their annual meeting at the Walton Hall country club at Wakefield in November was to reaffirm the existing ban which prevented players from moving between British and Australian Rugby League. The meeting took place during the middle of the Australian tour; the skills and brilliance of the tourists, then the chief object of attention in the game, had the effect of making the decision seem all the more shortsighted and reactionary.

Most of the New Zealanders who had entered the British game in recent seasons had done so with considerable success. Hull had benefited enormously from the signings of Kemble, Leuluai and O'Hara. Hull Kingston Rovers had reason to be well satisfied with the contributions of Gordon Smith and Prohm. Wigan's play had been given an extra dimension by West. Friend and the Bell brothers had, before financial crisis overtook the club, been three of Carlisle's best players. What was the game losing by sealing off such a potentially rich seam as Australia? The legislation had been brought in, in the first instance, to protect the interests of both countries, but in a game that was having to fight to sustain its appeal there was a strong case to be made for rescinding it.

Whether such a ban would have stood up in a court of law is debatable. It smacked of the 'restraint of trade' syndrome which some years earlier had proved so costly to the cricket authorities in their fight with Kerry Packer, the Australian television magnate. The Professional Players Association (PPA) was vehemently opposed to the ban and was prepared to take the matter to court if necessary. It argued that the authorities' fear that there would be an exodus of leading players to Australia was groundless.

The PPA advised its members that any player given the opportunity to join an Australian club should take up the option and ignore the ban. It had sought legal advice and clearly felt that it was on safe ground. A confrontation was not necessary, however. By the end of the season there were distinct signs of a shift of position by the authorities and clear evidence to suggest that the ban would be lifted. The authorities did not appear to believe passionately enough in this cause to want to fight it in the courts.

Other changes were made whose worth was still to be judged. The value of the try was increased from three to four points, and the ball was to be released to the opposition after the sixth tackle without forming a scrum. This significant change was endorsed by Britain, but it was agreed that countries could adopt it at whatever level they wished and report on the success or otherwise of their experiments at the next board meeting in Auckland. Australia, New Zealand and Papua, however, adopted it immediately, and the early indications were that it had added even more pace to the already breathless Australasian game. At a meeting in March 1983 Britain agreed to adopt the new rule for first-team games from the beginning of the 1983–84 season.

A change in the scrummaging rules held out hopes of improving what had long been one of the game's greyest areas. The non-offending team at the scrum were now to be awarded the loose head and the put-in, while the scrum-half, holding the ball at its two points, would feed the scrum by rolling the ball along the ground. This was much closer to Rugby Union's concept of scrummaging—which has so much to teach Rugby League. One senior referee, Gerry Kershaw, was so disturbed by Rugby League's scrums that he advocated that the referee should feed the scrum rather than the scrum-half. His novel plan won little support, but his argument that Rugby League would not become a national, marketable item while the scrums remained such a mess was valid enough.

Judgement has yet to be passed on these changes, but it is to be hoped that they will be received with less hostility than the sin bin. This measure had been available under international rules to British referees for some time but had never been used. Julien Rascagnères, the French referee, employed it during the Ashes series with Australia, and initial reactions to it were favourable. It seemed to offer a worthwhile way of allowing players who had not necessarily deserved dismissal to recover lost tempers and a useful means of punishing players for persistent technical offences.

By the end of the season, though, the sin bin was being roundly condemned, although whether this was the fault of the sin bin itself or the manner in which referees were using it was debatable. It had undeniable faults. In far too many instances players were being sent to the sin bin who should have been dismissed for good. The introduction of the sin bin initially brought about a drop in the number of players appearing before the disciplinary committee and a corresponding decrease in the number of suspensions. But at a time when discipline needed tightening the unmistakable feeling was that players who deserved punishment were escaping much too lightly.

The system, nevertheless, merited the chance of being made to work, and proposals for the new season offered hope of curing some of the anomalies. Under a system of penalty points five minutes in the sin bin would mean one black mark, ten minutes two black marks. A player collecting six marks would automatically be suspended for one game.

Nothing reflected more accurately the financial distress of the game in 1982–83 than the transfer market. The previous season had suggested that the first £100,000 transfer was imminent. But the recession was soon to bite hard; the bottom fell out of the market, and players of quality became available at jumble-sale prices (a help, of course, to a newcomer such as Kent Invicta, who could hope to build a side for less than half the sum they first thought of). Carlisle were to cite the depressed state of the market as one of the reasons for their financial crisis, and certainly the money circulating within the game all but dried up. Much the costliest transfer between English clubs was that of Andrew Kelly, who moved from Wakefield Trinity to Hull Kingston Rovers for £60,000. In contrast, Featherstone Rovers were able to sign Tim Slatter from the same club for £2,000, perhaps one of the season's best examples of the bargains to be had.

Season 1982–83 began and ended with the threat of players' strikes. The first one, brought about by a dispute over insurance payments, jeopardized the whole of the programme of 26 September. The latter was much more localized and involved Bramley players, angered at being told they would have to take a sizeable reduction in wages. Both issues were resolved without resort to a strike, but they were two more signs of unrest in a season of unease.

Insurance schemes, wages, contracts, strikes. Was it not time for an archaically constructed game to initiate a thorough investigation into its affairs? The Caine report had served, if with qualified success, just such a purpose in 1971. Twelve years later, was the sport not again in need of thorough self-examination? Throughout the season one was to hear from various quarters divers reasons for the game's problems. Bad coaching, lack of dedication by the players, too many old men in the game, lack of fitness, greed, mismanagement, illegal payments....

Roy Waudby, of Hull, one of the most progressive of the game's chairmen, was particularly disturbed by the 15 per cent gate levy placed on first-division clubs. This fund was helping to keep second-division clubs in existence but was, claimed Mr Waudby, draining the first-division clubs of vital finance. That, though, was but one of Mr Waudby's concerns. He, too, thought the time was ripe for reform but was not convinced that it would happen. 'It seems to me that there are a lot of old people managing the game,' he said. 'I am not criticizing them, but I think the structure of the Rugby League Council and everything else needs a dramatic change. And, sadly, I'm doubtful that the will for change is there.' (It is worth noting that at the Rugby Football League's AGM in June 1983 it was agreed to entrust the day-to-day business of the League to a nine-man management committee.)

That would be a realistic but slightly pessimistic note on which to end. In spite of everything, there is still cause for optimism. Sponsorship is not necessarily the yardstick by which a game's health is measured, but it can act as a guide. Rugby League has steadily attracted increasing sums of sponsors' money, and just after the end of the season another deal worth £100,000 was

Reflections

announced. The money had been put up by Modern Maintenance Products of Harrogate, who had decided that two-thirds would be spent on ground maintenance at professional clubs and one-third on support for the Great Britain tour of Australia and New Zealand in 1984.

Amounts such as this would not be poured by hard-headed businessmen into an undeserving cause and Rugby League is certainly not that. It can be the most exciting, skilful of games and, at its best, provides an unrivalled spectacle. The Australians emphasized these truths vividly in what, after all, was their season. They set the standards, exhilarating ones. But as the Australians departed the field, trailing their clouds of glory, we knew that the old domestic game would never seem quite the same again.

Afterword

The 1982–83 season will be remembered for the brilliance of Frank Stanton's Australians. They outplayed Great Britain in all three Tests, and their victories called for a thorough examination of playing standards in this country. Unfortunately, many critics attributed the Test defeats to poor selection, over-emphasis on fitness training or a lack of commitment by many players. However, to take so complacent a view is to underestimate the vast gulf that now exists between the playing skills of Australian and British Rugby League.

Even the greatest teams have their poor days, games when key performers relax or team combinations falter. The Australians were no exception. They were human. Yet they played fifteen games in Britain and seven matches in France during their ten-week European tour, and their record of twenty-two games played, twenty-two games won, 714 points for, 100 against, 166 tries for and only nine against could not have been more emphatic.

I expected the tourists perhaps to be fitter than British players (the standard of fitness of many of our professionals is appalling), more powerful and faster. I was aware that each Sydney Grade One game is recorded and studied by coaches, so I expected them to be more tactically aware, but I still expected British players to be more skilful.

What a shock. The tourists were far in advance of the British in every aspect of the game, and the more their performances are studied, the greater the difference is seen to be.

The Australians are the best side in the world. They play six-tackle Rugby League as it was meant to be played. Their players possess all the basic skills and perform them at remarkable speed. Tackling in Rugby League has always been one of the game's strengths, especially when compared with Rugby Union. Yet the Australians made the British tackling appear feeble. Australia's tackling was exemplary. The first tackler went in hard and low; the second man smothered the ball.

This method is surely far more efficient than British smother-tackling, which can, as the Australians proved, be so easily broken. But it was the speed

Afterword

with which the Australians moved up that was so difficult to combat. All the team, when defending, sprinted quickly at the opposition, offering Britain's so-called ball players no chance to show their skills. Anyone who is given the opportunity should study the video of the 1982 Australia–New Zealand Test series. At least New Zealand made attempts to emulate the Australians. The defensive formation, strength of tackle, cover defence, willingness to be involved and speed at which the defence moves up are some of the factors that make Rugby League in the southern hemisphere greatly superior to the modern British game. In attack, too, speed, direct running and support play are the most important factors in the Australians' game. The ball player has disappeared. The Australians, thankfully, have dispensed with those team tactics which revolve around one ball player who usually dictates everything from first man. What is more boring than such a player—usually an 'old head'—slowing down the game and trying to prise open a defence in the middle of the pack with no intention of playing the ball quickly wide and introducing the three-quarters into the game?

The Australians involve all thirteen players. They move the ball as quickly as possible across the field to a player running hard and direct, and they support him. They play the ball correctly and at speed. The acting half-back passes efficiently from the ground without picking the ball up and without taking time-wasting steps. The players position themselves much wider apart and pass the ball like lightning, often while standing still.

Such methods are far more efficient than the British style, which has too many players in the line standing too close together, all moving forward with the ball. Such tactics against fast, alert, well organized defences are worthless. In Australian Rugby League all the players are involved. All of them attack. The ball is moved from one touchline to another in seconds, often through only four pairs of hands. The wingers are scoring tries again. Surely, Frank Stanton's method of Rugby League could be Britain's salvation: breed them young, play them young and pick footballers who can tackle rather than tacklers who cannot play football.

I offer three of the more obvious reasons for Australian supremacy. Their players are more skilful; they are fitter, faster and more powerful; and the players and teams play a more efficient style of rugby. All three are the result of coaching. The greatest single factor in Australia's supremacy at international and club level has been the success of their excellent National Coaching Scheme since the 1960s. They were not too proud to learn from us. Let us hope that in the 1980s we shall not be too proud to learn from them.

Phil Larder
National Director of Coaching

Appendix 1

THE AUSTRALIAN TOUR

THE AUSTRALIANS IN BRITAIN

Craven Park, Hull, 10 October: Hull KR 10   Australians 30

Hull KR: Fairbairn; Hubbard, Mike Smith, Robinson, Clark; Hartley, Walsh; Holdstock, Watkinson, Crooks, Burton, Kelly, Prohm

Substitutes: Lowe for Holdstock after 22 minutes, Laws not used

Scorers: tries—Hartley, Prohm; goals—Fairbairn (2)

Australians: Brentnall; Ribot, Meninga, Rogers, Grothe; Kenny, Sterling; Young, Krilich, Morris, Boyd, Reddy, Price

Substitutes: Lewis for Ribot after 65 minutes, Muggleton for Morris after 65 minutes

Scorers: tries—Sterling (2), Young, Rogers, Lewis, Meninga; goals—Meninga (6)

Referee: G. F. Lindop (Wakefield)

Attendance: 10,742

Central Park, Wigan, 13 October: Wigan 9   Australians 13

Wigan: Williams; Ramsdale, Stephenson, Whitfield, Gill; Foy, Stephens; Bamber, Kiss, Shaw, Juliff, Scott, Pendlebury

Substitutes: Campbell for Bamber after 51 minutes, Fairhurst for Foy after 67 minutes

Scorers: try—Gill; goals—Whitfield (3)

Australians: Schubert; Anderson, Ella, Miles, Boustead; Lewis, Mortimer; McKinnon, Brown, Hancock, McCabe, Muggleton, Pearce

Substitutes: Rogers for Anderson after 57 minutes, Price for Muggleton after 57 minutes

Scorers: tries—McCabe, Muggleton, Boustead; goals—Ella (2)

The Australian Tour

Referee: D. G. Kershaw (Easingwold)

Attendance: 12,158

Craven Park, Barrow, 15 October: Barrow 2   Australians 29

Barrow: Tickle; Bentley, O'Regan, McConnell, James; Mason, Cairns; Gee, Wall, Flynn, Gillespie, Szymala, Hadley

Substitutes: Herbert for Gillespie after 60 minutes, Whittle not used

Scorer: goal—Tickle

Australians: Schubert; Anderson, Ella, Miles, Ribot; Lewis, Murray; Hancock, Conescu, Morris, Boyd, Reddy, Pearce

Substitutes: Brown for Hancock after 20 minutes, Rogers for Boyd after 71 minutes

Scorers: tries—Schubert (2), Conescu, Murray, Pearce, Ella, Rogers; goals—Lewis (3), Rogers

Referee: D. W. Fox (Wakefield)

Attendance: 6,282

Knowsley Road, St Helens, 17 October: St Helens 0   Australians 32

St Helens: Griffiths; Ledger, Arkwright, Fairclough, Litherland; Peters, Holding; James, Glover, Gelling, Forber, Mathias, Platt

Substitutes: Smith for Griffiths after 54 minutes, Brownbill for Gelling after 70 minutes

Australians: Brentnall; Boustead, Meninga, Rogers, Grothe; Kenny, Sterling; Young, Krilich, Boyd, Pearce, Muggleton, Price

Substitutes: Morris for Price after 25 minutes, Lewis for Boyd after 75 minutes

Scorers: tries—Boustead (2), Grothe (2), Boyd (2), Rogers, Sterling; goals—Meninga (4)

Referee: M. R. Whitfield (Widnes)

Attendance: 8,190

Headingley, Leeds, 20 October: Leeds 4   Australians 31

Leeds: Hague; Alan Smith, Wilkinson, Dyl, Andrew Smith; Holmes, Conway; Dickinson, Ward, Burke, Keith Rayne, Wayne Heron, David Heron

Substitutes: Massa for Alan Smith after 68 minutes, Sykes for Rayne after 68 minutes

Scorer: goals—Conway (2)

Appendix 1

Australians: Brentnall; Boustead, Meninga, Rogers, Grothe; Kenny, Sterling; Young, Krilich, Boyd, McCabe, Muggleton, Pearce

Substitutes: Morris for Boyd after 53 minutes, Ella for Sterling after 65 minutes

Scorers: tries—Meninga (2), Boustead, Rogers, Grothe, Ella (2); goals—Meninga (5)

Referee: W. H. Thompson (Huddersfield)

Attendance: 11,511

Ninian Park, Cardiff, 24 October: Wales 7 Australia 37

Wales: Hopkins (Workington Town); Camilleri (Widnes), Fenwick (Cardiff City), Bevan (Warrington), Prendiville (Hull); Hallett (Cardiff City), Williams (Cardiff City); Shaw (Wigan), Parry (Blackpool Borough), David (Cardiff City), Herdman (Fulham), Juliff (Wigan), Ringer (Cardiff City)

Substitutes: McJennett (Salford) for David after 70 minutes, Wilson (Swinton) not used

Scorers: try—Williams; goals—Hopkins, Fenwick

Australia: Ella (Parramatta, Sydney); Anderson (Canterbury-Bankstown, Sydney), Lewis (Fortitude Valley, Brisbane), Miles (Wynnum-Manly, Brisbane), Ribot (Manly, Sydney); Murray (Fortitude Valley, Brisbane), Mortimer (Canterbury-Bankstown, Sydney); McKinnon (North Sydney), Brown (Manly, Sydney), Morris (Wynnum-Manly, Brisbane), McCabe (Manly, Sydney), Reddy (St George, Sydney), Schubert (Eastern Suburbs, Sydney)

Substitutes: Conescu (Northern Suburbs, Brisbane) for Morris after 59 minutes, Boustead (Eastern Suburbs, Sydney) for Ella after 70 minutes

Scorers: tries—Ella (4), Murray, Ribot (2), Lewis, McKinnon; goals—Lewis (4), McKinnon

Referee: D. G. Kershaw (England)

Attendance: 5,617

Boothferry Park, Hull, 30 October: Great Britain 4 Australia 40

Great Britain: Fairbairn (Hull KR); Drummond (Leigh), Hughes (Widnes), Dyl (Leeds), Evans (Hull); Woods (Leigh), Nash (Salford) captain; Grayshon (Bradford Northern), Ward (Leeds), Skerrett (Hull), Gorley (Widnes), Crooks (Hull), Norton (Hull)

Substitutes: David Heron (Leeds) for Crooks after 47 minutes, Kelly (Warrington) not used

Scorer: goals—Crooks (2)

The Australian Tour

Australia: Brentnall (Canterbury-Bankstown, Sydney); Boustead (Eastern Suburbs, Sydney), Meninga (Southern Suburbs, Brisbane), Rogers (St George, Sydney), Grothe (Parramatta, Sydney); Kenny (Parramatta, Sydney), Sterling (Parramatta, Sydney); Young (St George, Sydney), Krilich (Manly, Sydney) captain, Boyd (Manly, Sydney), Pearce (Balmain, Sydney), Reddy (St George, Sydney), Price (Parramatta, Sydney)

Substitutes: Ella (Parramatta, Sydney), Muggleton (Parramatta, Sydney) not used

Scorers: tries—Meninga, Boyd, Grothe, Price, Boustead, Kenny, Pearce, Reddy; goals—Meninga (8)

Referee: J. Rascagnères (France)

Attendance: 26,771

Hilton Park, Leigh, 3 November: Leigh 4   Australians 44

Leigh: Hogan; Drummond, Henderson, Donlan, Worgan; Woods, Green; Wilkinson, Tabern, Pyke, Chisnall, Clarkson, Potter

Substitutes: Hunter for Chisnall after 58 minutes, Tomlinson for Hogan after 69 minutes

Scorer: goals—Woods (2)

Australians: Ella; Anderson, Meninga, Miles, Ribot; Lewis, Mortimer; McKinnon, Brown, Morris, McCabe, Muggleton, Schubert

Substitutes: Murray, Conescu not used

Scorers: tries—Ribot (3), Anderson (3), McCabe (3), Lewis, Muggleton (2); goals—Meninga (3), Lewis

Referee: T. J. Court (Leeds)

Attendance: 7,680

Odsal Stadium, Bradford, 7 November: Bradford Northern 6   Australians 13

Bradford Northern: Green; Barends, Mumby, Davies, Pullen; Kells, Redfearn; Grayshon, Noble, Van Bellen, Idle, Jasiewicz, Rathbone

Substitutes: Parrott for Jasiewicz, after 60 minutes, Carroll for Kells after 69 minutes

Scorer: goals—Mumby (3)

Australians: Brentnall; Anderson, Miles, Rogers, Grothe; Kenny, Murray; Young, Conescu, Hancock, Reddy, McCabe, Price

Substitutes: Brown for Conescu after 60 minutes, Boustead not used

Appendix 1

Scorers: tries—McCabe, Brentall, Miles; goals—Rogers (2)

Referee: T. M. Beaumont (Huddersfield)

Attendance: 10,506

Brunton Park, Carlisle, 9 November: Cumbria 2   Australians 41

Cumbria: Hopkins (Workington Town); Mackie (Whitehaven), Bell (Carlisle), McConnell (Barrow), Moore (Barrow); Mason (Barrow), Cairns (Barrow); Herbert (Barrow), McCurrie (Oldham), Flynn (Barrow), Pattinson (Workington Town), Gorley (St Helens), Hadley (Barrow)

Substitutes: Beck (Workington Town) for Mason at half-time, Hartley (Workington Town) for Pattinson after 65 minutes

Scorer: goal—Hopkins

Australians: Brentnall; Boustead, Meninga, Ella, Ribot; Lewis, Sterling; McKinnon, Krilich, Hancock, Muggleton, Schubert, Pearce

Substitutes: Rogers for Sterling at half-time, Price for Krilich after 65 minutes

Scorers: tries—Ribot (2), McKinnon, Sterling, Rogers, Ella, Meninga, Boustead, Pearce; goals—Meninga (7)

Referee: S. Wall (Leigh)

Attendance: 5,748

Craven Cottage, Fulham, 14 November: Fulham 5   Australians 22

Fulham: Eckersley; Cambriani, Allen, Diamond, M'Barki; Crossley, Bowden; Beverley, Dalgreen, Gourley, Herdman, Souto, Doherty

Substitutes: Tuffs for Doherty after 30 minutes, Lester not used

Scorers: try—M'Barki; goal—Diamond

Australians: Ella; Anderson, Miles, Lewis, Ribot; Murray, Mortimer; McKinnon, Brown, Boyd, McCabe, Muggleton, Schubert

Substitutes: Conescu for Brown after 76 minutes, Kenny not used

Scorers: tries—Murray, Ella, McCabe, Muggleton, Ribot, McKinnon; goals—Lewis, Ella

Referee: W. H. Thompson (Huddersfield)

Attendance: 10,432

The Australian Tour

The Boulevard, Hull, 16 November: Hull 7   Australians 13

Hull: Kemble; O'Hara, Evans, Leuluai, Prendiville; Topliss, Dean; Harrison, Bridges, Rose, Proctor, Crooks, Crane

Substitutes: Banks for Leuluai after 55 minutes, Sutton for Harrison after 76 minutes

Scorers: try—Topliss; goals—Crooks (2)

Australians: Brentnall; Boustead, Meninga, Rogers, Grothe; Kenny, Sterling; Young, Krilich, Boyd, Pearce, Reddy, Price

Substitutes: Lewis for Brentnall after 71 minutes, Brown not used

Scorers: tries—Grothe (2), Boustead; goals—Meninga (2)

Referee: J. Holdsworth (Leeds)

Attendance: 16,049

Central Park, Wigan, 20 November: Great Britain 6   Australia 27

Great Britain: Mumby (Bradford Northern); Drummond (Leigh), Smith (Hull KR), Stephenson (Wigan), Gill (Wigan); Holmes (Leeds), Ken Kelly (Warrington); Grayshon (Bradford Northern) captain, Dalgreen (Fulham), Skerrett (Hull), Eccles (Warrington), Burton (Hull KR), David Heron (Leeds)

Substitutes: Woods (Leigh) for Holmes after 61 minutes, Rathbone (Bradford Northern) for Burton after 74 minutes

Scorer: goals—Mumby (3)

Australia: Brentnall (Canterbury-Bankstown, Sydney); Boustead (Eastern Suburbs, Sydney), Meninga (Southern Suburbs, Brisbane), Rogers (St George, Sydney), Grothe (Parramatta, Sydney); Kenny (Parramatta, Sydney), Sterling (Parramatta, Sydney); Young (St George, Sydney), Krilich (Manly, Sydney) captain, Boyd (Manly, Sydney), Pearce (Balmain, Sydney), Reddy (St George, Sydney), Price (Parramatta, Sydney)

Substitutes: Lewis (Fortitude Valley, Brisbane) for Grothe at half-time, Brown (Manly, Sydney) for Reddy after 69 minutes

Scorers: tries—Price, Sterling, Grothe, Meninga, Rogers; goals—Meninga (6)

Referee: J. Rascagnères (France)

Attendance: 23,216

Naughton Park, Widnes, 23 November: Widnes 6   Australia 19

Widnes: Burke; Basnett, Lydon, O'Loughlin, Camilleri; Gregory, Hulme; Tamati, Elwell, Steve O'Neill, Newton, Prescott, Tony Myler

Appendix 1

Substitutes: John Myler for Lydon after 65 minutes, Lockwood not used

Scorer: goals—Burke (3)

Australians: Ella; Anderson, Meninga, Rogers, Ribot; Lewis, Mortimer; Young, Brown, Morris, Boyd, McCabe, Schubert

Substitutes: Muggleton for Young after 45 minutes, Murray for Lewis after 70 minutes

Scorers: tries—Mortimer (2), McCabe, Ribot, Rogers; goals—Meninga (2)

Referee: J. McDonald (Wigan)

Attendance: 9,790

Headingley, Leeds, 28 November: Great Britain 8 Australia 32

Great Britain: Fairbairn (Hull KR); Drummond (Leigh), Mike Smith (Hull KR), Stephenson (Wigan), Evans (Hull); Topliss (Hull) captain, Gregory (Widnes); Mike O'Neill (Widnes), Noble (Bradford Northern), Rose (Hull), Peter Smith (Featherstone Rovers), Crooks (Hull), Crane (Hull)

Substitutes: Courtney (Warrington) for O'Neill after 70 minutes, Woods (Leigh) not used

Scorers: try—Evans; goals—Crooks (2); drop goal—Crooks

Australia: Brentnall (Canterbury-Bankstown, Sydney); Boustead (Eastern Suburbs, Sydney), Meninga (Southern Suburbs, Brisbane), Rogers (St George, Sydney), Ribot (Manly, Sydney); Kenny (Parramatta, Sydney), Sterling (Parramatta, Sydney); Boyd (Manly, Sydney), Krilich (Manly, Sydney) captain, Morris (Wynnum-Manly, Brisbane), McCabe (Manly, Sydney), Reddy (St George, Sydney) Pearce (Balmain, Sydney)

Substitutes: Lewis (Fortitude Valley, Brisbane) for Ribot after 54 minutes, Brown (Manly, Sydney) for Boyd after 70 minutes

Scorers: tries—Ribot, Krilich, Boustead, Rogers, Pearce, Kenny; goals—Meninga (7)

Referee: J. Rascagnères (France)

Attendance: 17,318

THE AUSTRALIANS IN FRANCE

Roanne, 1 December: Roanne 0 Australians 65

Roanne: Gaye; Atkinson, Bartoli, Pages, Amrani; Reygasse, Dauphin; Fournioux, Cagnac, Marty, Placid, Gonzales, Lafargue

Substitutes: Jacqueletto, Sanantonio

The Australian Tour

Australians: Anderson; Grothe, Miles, Ella, Ribot; Murray, Mortimer; McKinnon, Conescu, Morris, Muggleton, Hancock, Schubert

Substitutes: Lewis, Brown

Scorers: tries—Grothe (5), Ribot (3), Anderson (2), Ella, Murray, Mortimer, Muggleton, Schubert; goals—Ribot (10)

Referee: R. Belle

Attendance: 1,506

Avignon, 5 December: France 4   Australia 15

France: Perez (Toulouse); Solal (Tonneins), Guigue (Avignon), Delaunay (XIII Catalan), Fourcade (Le Barcarès); Guiraud (Lézignan), Grésèque (XIII Catalan); Daniel (Pia), Macalli (Villeneuve), Chantal (Villeneuve), Ambert (Pia), G. Laforgue (XIII Catalan), Roosebrouck (Villeneuve) captain

Substitutes: Caravaca (Limoux) for Ambert after 71 minutes, Laumond (Villefranche) for Fourcade after 73 minutes

Scorer: goals—Perez (2)

Australia: Brentnall (Canterbury-Bankstown, Sydney); Boustead (Eastern Suburbs, Sydney), Rogers (St George, Sydney), Kenny (Parramatta, Sydney), Meninga (Southern Suburbs, Brisbane); Lewis (Fortitude Valley, Brisbane), Sterling (Parramatta, Sydney); Young (St George, Sydney), Krilich (Manly, Sydney) captain, Morris (Wynnum-Manly, Brisbane), McCabe (Manly, Sydney), Boyd (Manly, Sydney), Pearce (Balmain, Sydney)

Substitutes: Grothe (Parramatta, Sydney), for Lewis after 27 minutes, Brown (Manly, Sydney) for McCabe after 60 minutes

Scorers: tries—Grothe (2), Pearce; goals—Meninga (3)

Referee: M.R. Whitfield (Great Britain)

Attendance (estimated): 8,000

Villeneuve-sur-Lot, 7 December: Aquitaine Select 2   Australians 67

Aquitaine Select: Vrech (Villeneuve); Jean-Noel Tremouille (Tonneins), Torres (Tonneins), Laville (Villeneuve), Montaud (Villeneuve); Delgal (Villeneuve), Dumas (St Gaudens); Zalduendo (Villeneuve), Covolan (La Réole), Aillères (Toulouse), Verdes (Villeneuve), Jean-Pierre Tremouille (Tonneins), Baloup (La Réole)

Scorer: goal—Dumas

Australians: Anderson; Ribot, Ella, Miles, Grothe; Murray, Mortimer; McKinnon, Brown, Hancock, Conescu, Muggleton, Schubert

Appendix 1

Scorers: tries—Ella (7), Ribot (4), Mortimer (3), Grothe (2), Muggleton; goals—Ribot (4), Grothe, Murray, Mortimer, Conescu

Referee: H. Martinez

Attendance: Not announced

Stade de Minimes, Toulouse, 9 December: France Under-24 3 Australians 42

France Under-24: Wosniack (Villefranche); Jacquoletto (Roanne), Maury (Cahors), Fourquet (Toulouse), Palisses (St Estève); Perez (Toulouse), Dauphin (Cavaillon); Durand (Albi), Gomez (Pia), Verdières (St Estève), Carpène (Toulouse), Balez (Albi), Bret (XIII Catalan)

Scorer: try—Maury

Australians: Anderson; Ribot, Ella, Miles, Grothe; Murray, Mortimer; McKinnon, Brown, Hancock, Conescu, Muggleton, Schubert

Scorers: tries—Anderson (3), Ella (2), Mortimer (3), Miles, Grothe; goals—Ribot (6)

Referee: A. Cerda

Attendance: 2,026

Stade Gilbert Brutus, Perpignan, 12 December: Catalans de France 2 Australians 53

Catalans de France: Alibert (St Estève); Rodriguez (Pia), Palisses (St Estève), Delaunay (XIII Catalan), Fourcade (Le Barcarès); Naudo (XIII Catalan), Pla (Pia); Daniel (Pia), Gomez (Pia), Valls (Le Barcarès), Perez (XIII Catalan), Ambert (Pia), G. Laforgue (XIII Catalan)

Substitutes: Baco (XIII Catalan), Arasa (XIII Catalan)

Scorer: goal—Naudo

Australians: Brentnall; Boustead, Muggleton, Meninga, Ribot; Ella, Sterling; Boyd, Krilich, Hancock, McCabe, Reddy, Pearce

Substitutes: Kenny, McKinnon

Scorers: tries—Ella (3), Sterling (3), Ribot (3), Meninga (2), Muggleton (2); goals—Meninga (7)

Referee: J. Rascagnères

Attendance (estimated): 10,000

The Australian Tour

Pamiers, 12 December: Selection Midi-Pyrénées-Rouergue 0   Australians 26

Selection Midi-Pyrénées-Rouergue: Meneghin (Toulouse); Lacombe (Albi), Lapeyre (St Gaudens), Baccou (Toulouse), Lacroix (St Gaudens); J. Estadieu (St Gaudens), Dumas (St Gaudens); Stein (Albi), Sampaio (Villefranche), Durand (Albi), Balez (Albi), Meurin (Albi), Aillères (Toulouse)

Substitutes: Casenave (Pamiers), C. Estadieu (St Gaudens)

Australians: Anderson; Grothe, Miles, Rogers, Ribot; Kenny, Murray; McKinnon, Conescu, Hancock, McCabe, Muggleton, Schubert

Substitutes: Mortimer, Brown

Scorers: tries—Grothe (2), Kenny (2), Rogers, Conescu; goals—Rogers (4)

Referee: C. Alba

Attendance: 1,072

Narbonne, 18 December: France 9   Australia 23

France: Guigue (Avignon); Solal (Tonneins), Delaunay (XIII Catalan), Laumond (Villefranche), Kaminski (Le Pontet); Guiraud (Lézignan), Grésèque (XIII Catalan); Zalduendo (Villeneuve), Macalli (Villeneuve), Chantal (Villeneuve), Cologni (XIII Catalan), G. Laforgue (XIII Catalan), Roosebrouck (Villeneuve) captain

Substitutes: Caravaca (Limoux) for Cologni after 63 minutes, Laville (Villeneuve) for Laumond after 66 minutes

Scorers: try—Grésèque; goals—Kaminski (3)

Australia: Brentnall (Canterbury-Bankstown, Sydney); Boustead (Eastern Suburbs, Sydney), Rogers (St George, Sydney), Meninga (Southern Suburbs, Brisbane), Grothe (Parramatta, Sydney); Kenny (Parramatta, Sydney), Sterling (Parramatta, Sydney); Young (St George, Sydney), Krilich (Manly, Sydney) captain, Boyd (Manly, Sydney), McCabe (Manly, Sydney), Reddy (St George, Sydney), Pearce (Balmain, Sydney),

Substitutes: Ella (Parramatta, Sydney), Brown (Manly, Sydney)

Scorers: tries—Grothe (2), Meninga, Reddy, Kenny; goals—Meninga (4)

Referee: M.R. Whitfield (Great Britain)

Attendance (estimated):   7,000

Appendix 2

THE WEBSTER'S YORKSHIRE CUP

1st round		*2nd round*		*Semi-finals*		*Final*	
Halifax	4	Keighley	16				
Keighley	14			Keighley	3		
Dewsbury	11	Dewsbury	3				
Doncaster	2					Hull	18
Castleford	10	Leeds	0				
Leeds	33			Hull	23		
Hull	36	Hull	20				
Huddersfield	5						
Hunslet	7	Featherstone R.	21				
Featherstone R.	19			Featherstone R.	0		
Bramley	15	Bramley	8				
Wakefield T.	13					Bradford N.	7
Bradford N.	15	Bradford N.	8				
Hull KR	14			Bradford N.	11		
York	38	York	5				
Batley	7						

Appendix 3

THE FORSHAWS LANCASHIRE CUP

1st round		2nd round		Semi-finals		Final	
Warrington	43	Warrington	16				
Huyton	5			Warrington	17		
Blackpool B.	10	Oldham	14				
Oldham	27					Warrington	16
Wigan	18	Wigan	4				
Salford	13			Fulham	8		
Fulham	20	Fulham	15				
Swinton	8						
Workington T.	12	Barrow	6				
Barrow	20			St Helens	7		
Widnes	12	St Helens	9				
St Helens	14					St Helens	0
Leigh	32	Leigh	12				
Rochdale H.	20			Carlisle	7		
Carlisle	16	Carlisle	13	(replay: 9–5)			
Whitehaven	8						

Appendix 4

THE JOHN PLAYER TROPHY

Preliminary round			*1st round*			*2nd round*		
			Cardiff C.	7		Rochdale H.	5	
			Rochdale H.	11		Barrow	27	
			Dewsbury	11				
			Barrow	28		Leeds	31	
			Leeds	17		York	10	
			Bramley	7				
Huyton	9		York	18		Carlisle	2	
Workington T.	19		Workington T.	15		Widnes	10	
			Carlisle	26				
			Doncaster	17		Bradford N.	12	
			Widnes	17		Hull	12	
			Wakefield T.	12		(replay: 10–8)		
			Keighley	0		Warrington	36	
			Bradford N.	18		Blackpool B.	15	
			Featherstone R.	14		Hull KR	36	
			Hull	18		Leigh	7	
			Warrington	19		Salford	21	
			Halifax	8		Huddersfield	19	
			Blackpool B.	6		Wigan	9	
			Batley	5		St Helens	5	
			Hull KR	42				
			Whitehaven	3				
			Leigh	13				
			Oldham	12				
			Salford	23				
			Hunslet	11				
			Swinton	13				
			Huddersfield	22				
			Castleford	10				
			Wigan	16				
			St Helens	17				
			Fulham	5				

The John Player Trophy

3rd round		Semi-finals		Final	
Barrow	8				
Leeds	13	Leeds	8		
Widnes	16			Leeds	4
Bradford N.	10	Widnes	2		
Warrington	11				
Hull KR	10	Warrington	14		
Salford	4			Wigan	15
Wigan	5	Wigan	15		

Appendix 5

THE STATE EXPRESS CHALLENGE CUP

Preliminary round			1st round			2nd round	
			Widnes	6		Leeds	13
			Leeds	12			
			St Helens	52		St Helens	23
			Carlisle	0			
			Salford	12		Salford	11
			Leigh	5			
			Featherstone R.	21		Featherstone R.	17
			Batley	5			
			Oldham	5		Workington T.	14
			Workington T.	8			
			Swinton	21		Swinton	9
			Doncaster	13			
			Rochdale H.	4		Fulham	4
			Fulham	24			
			Bradford N.	23		Bradford N.	11
			York	5			
			Hunslet	12		Hunslet	17
			Hull KR	11			
			Huddersfield	5		Halifax	8
			Halifax	13			
			Barrow	18		Barrow	9
			Whitehaven	6			
Wigan	14		Wigan	7		Castleford	14
Cardiff C.	4		Castleford	17			
			Warrington	41		Warrington	34
			Bramley	3			
			Dewsbury	7		Huyton	2
			Huyton	13			
			Blackpool B.	11		Hull	32
			Hull	19			
			Wakefield T.	27		Wakefield T.	15
			Keighley	5			

The State Express Challenge Cup

3rd round   *Semi-finals*   *Final*

St Helens   10
                            Featherstone R. 11
Featherstone R.   11
                                                       Featherstone R. 14
Workington T.   0
                            Bradford N.   6
Bradford N.   17

Hunslet   8
                            Castleford   7
Castleford   13
                                                       Hull   12
Warrington   4
                            Hull   14
Hull   10

203

Appendix 6

THE SLALOM LAGER CHAMPIONSHIP FINAL LEAGUE TABLES

Division 1

	P	W	L	D	F	A	Pts
Hull	30	23	6	1	572	293	47
Hull KR	30	21	8	1	496	276	43
Wigan	30	20	7	3	482	270	43
St Helens	30	19	10	1	516	395	39
Widnes	30	18	10	2	534	357	38
Leeds	30	18	10	2	480	443	38
Castleford	30	18	11	1	629	458	37
Oldham	30	15	13	2	346	320	32
Bradford N.	30	14	14	2	381	314	30
Leigh	30	13	14	3	488	374	29
Warrington	30	13	15	2	423	410	28
Featherstone R.	30	10	16	4	350	447	24
Barrow	30	11	18	1	472	505	23
Workington T.	30	6	22	2	318	696	14
Halifax	30	5	24	1	221	651	11
Carlisle	30	2	28	—	252	751	4

Final League Tables
Division 2

	P	W	L	D	F	A	Pts
Fulham	32	27	4	1	699	294	55
Wakefield T.	32	25	5	2	672	381	52
Salford	32	24	8	—	686	363	48
Whitehaven	32	20	9	3	464	298	43
Bramley	32	20	11	1	560	369	41
Hunslet	32	17	10	5	553	448	39
Swinton	32	19	12	1	549	454	39
Cardiff C.	32	17	13	2	572	444	36
Keighley	32	15	12	5	470	423	35
York	32	15	17	—	516	455	30
Blackpool B.	32	13	18	1	381	433	27
Huddersfield	32	13	18	1	397	524	27
Rochdale H.	32	10	17	5	361	469	25
Dewsbury	32	8	23	1	325	507	17
Batley	32	6	25	1	305	719	13
Huyton	32	6	26	—	250	687	12
Doncaster	32	2	29	1	307	799	5

Appendix 7

THE SLALOM LAGER PREMIERSHIP TROPHY

1st round

Hull	24
Oldham	21
Wigan	9
Leeds	12
Hull KR	35
Castleford	14
St Helens	7
Widnes	11

Semi-finals

Hull	19
Leeds	5
Hull KR	10
Widnes	21

Final

Hull	10
Widnes	22

Appendix 8

LEADING SCORERS

Tries

Eccles (Warrington)	37
Evans (Hull)	28
Crossley (Fulham)	27
David (Cardiff C.)	26
Topliss (Hull)	24
M'Barki (Fulham)	23
Hyde (Castleford)	22
McDermott (York)	22
Leuluai (Hull)	21
Ford (Warrington)	20
Clark (Hull KR)	20

Goals

Diamond (Fulham)	136
Fitzsimons (Hunslet)	121
Crooks (Hull)	120
R. Beardmore (Castleford)	117
Hesford (Warrington)	113
Fenwick (Cardiff C.)	111
Jones (Swinton)	110
Whitfield (Wigan)	104
Kilner (Bramley)	104
Quinn (Featherstone R.)	98

Points

	Trs	Gls	Dr. gls	Pts
Diamond (Fulham)	12	136	—	308
R. Beardmore (Castleford)	14	117	—	276
Crooks (Hull)	11	117	3	270
Jones (Swinton)	11	110	—	253
Fitzsimons (Hunslet)	5	109	12	245

The publication of this book has been made possible through the generosity of Shopacheck Financial Services Ltd, 6 Wolfreton Drive, Springfield Way, Anlaby, Hull.